Windows 7

Vole Guides

Chris Kennedy

Questing Vole Press

Windows 7
by Chris Kennedy

Editor: Bill Gregory
Proofreader: Pat Kissell
Compositor: Birgitte Lund
Cover: Questing Vole Press

Contents

1

Windows Basics

Windows 7, the successor to Windows Vista, is the latest Microsoft operating system for computer users at home, work, and school. In creating Windows 7, Microsoft put special effort into fixing the (real or perceived) shortcomings of Vista and giving longtime Windows XP users a reason to upgrade.

Windows 7 is a small technological upgrade from Vista—it works with all Vista-compatible programs and hardware—but it performs better, feels snappier and more polished, and has much-improved networking and user-interface features.

Windows is complex software, but its user interface—the aspects of it that you see and hear and use to control Windows—is designed to let you wield a lot of power with a modest amount of learning. The secret is understanding the underlying consistency of the ways that Windows works. As you use Windows, techniques like switching programs, searching for files, resizing windows, drag-and-drop, and copy-and-paste will become familiar.

The Windows operating system controls:

The user interface
Windows manages the appearance, behavior, and interaction of the windows, buttons, icons, folders, cursors, menus, ribbons, pointers, and other visual elements on your screen, either directly or indirectly through another program.

Storage
Windows' file system allocates space for and gives access to files—programs and documents—stored on drives or in memory.

Other software

Windows is a launching platform for programs. Notepad, Excel, video games, and all Windows programs rely on the services and building blocks that Windows provides for basic operations such as drawing a user interface, saving files, and sharing hardware.

Peripheral devices

Windows controls or syncs with peripheral hardware such as your mouse, keyboard, trackpad, display, printer, scanner, external drives, speakers, headset, camera, ebook reader, smartphone, music player, and iPad.

Networks and security

Windows controls the interaction of a group of computers and peripheral devices connected by a communications link such as Ethernet or wireless. Windows also protects your system and data from harm or loss.

System resources

Windows handles the allocation and use of your computer's low-level hardware resources such as memory (RAM) and central processing unit (CPU) time.

Task scheduling

Windows acts like a traffic cop, setting priorities and allocating time slices to the processes running on your computer.

About This Book

This book is for you if you're new to Windows, you're upgrading from an earlier version of Windows, or you need a quick reference at hand. It's organized, linked, and cross-referenced to help you find things fast.

Conventions

A shorthand instruction to navigate to a nested folder or choose a command looks like this:

Choose Start > Control Panel > Appearance and Personalization > Folder Options > View tab > clear "Hide extensions for known file types" > OK.

Each name between the > symbols refers to an icon, folder, window, dialog box, menu, button, link, or control; just look on the screen for a matching label.

Keyboard shortcuts (page 42) are given in the form "Ctrl+Shift+N".

Default Settings

Windows' **defaults** are Microsoft-defined settings shipped with the product. In some cases, someone else—an administrator, your computer's manufacturer, or whoever set up your computer—will have changed some defaults, so your initial setup might look or behave a little differently than I describe.

Windows 7 Editions

The editions of Windows 7, from low end to high end, are

- Starter (minimal feature set)

- Home Basic

- Home Premium

- Professional

- Enterprise

- Ultimate (complete package)

Each edition builds on the one below it (meaning that the editions are true supersets in terms of features). Only Home Premium, Professional, and Ultimate are sold through retailers. Starter is sold only through computer makers (typically on netbooks). Home Basic is available only in emerging markets (Brazil, China, India, Mexico, and elsewhere). Enterprise, which is the same as Ultimate, is volume-licensed directly to big customers.

The core features in the different editions look and work alike, so most discussions apply to all editions equally. This book points out the differences among the editions where necessary. Microsoft compares the features of the different editions at "Compare Windows" (*windows.microsoft.com/en-US/windows7/ products/compare*). To find out which edition you're running, choose Start > Control Panel > System and Security > System. The edition is displayed near the top of the window. If you've installed a service pack (page 374), that update appears here too.

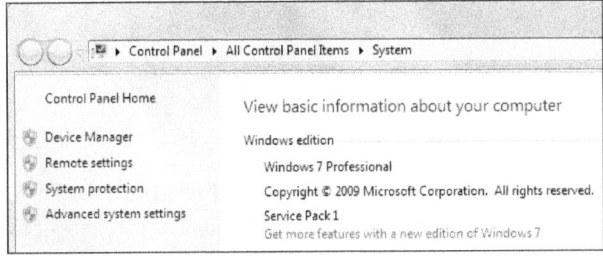

Also available are European "E" editions that are stripped of some features (to comply with European Union antitrust laws). All editions but Starter also come in 64-bit versions, which support up to 192 GB of memory (RAM).

Windows Anytime Upgrade

Windows Anytime Upgrade (WAU) lets you upgrade your copy of Windows to another edition. You can upgrade to anywhere higher on the editions ladder—from Starter to Home Premium or Ultimate, for example. You'll need an internet connection and a credit card. You don't need to download a code or insert your original Windows disc because upgrading simply "unlocks" the new edition's features.

To upgrade, choose Start > Control Panel > System and Security > System, click "Get more features with a new edition of Windows 7", and then follow the onscreen instructions. (This link won't appear if you can't upgrade or can't use WAU.) The upgrade won't change your programs, documents, or settings, but make a backup before upgrading.

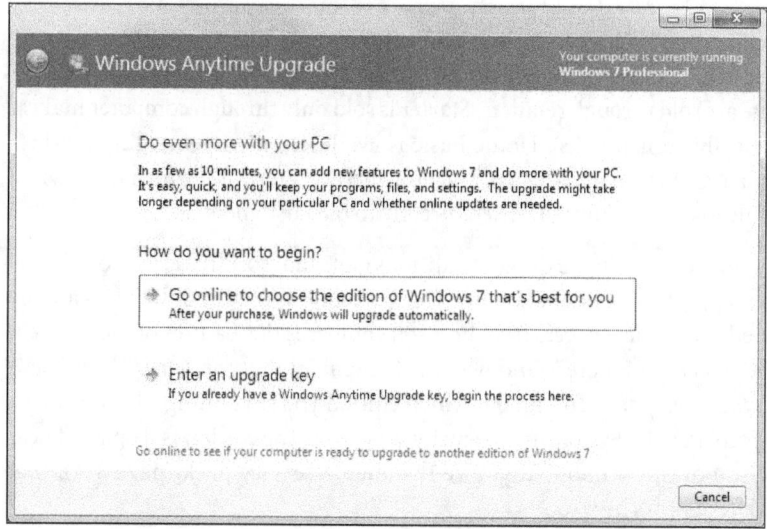

Windows, Cheap

A few ways to get discounted (or free) copies of Windows, in descending order of legality:

Get an upgrade

If you're not eligible to upgrade because you're a first-time Windows customer or your current Windows version doesn't qualify, it's cheaper to buy the Windows 7 *upgrade* version *and* get Windows XP or Vista from a friend, co-worker, computer swap meet, or *craigslist.org*. Plenty of free or cheap copies are around. If you have trouble with an already-used XP or Vista activation key, telephone a Microsoft activation representative and lie (they don't care). Install XP or Vista on your computer and then apply the Windows 7 upgrade. Don't throw out the XP/Vista disc; you may need it to reinstall Windows 7 someday.

Get an academic discount

Ask a discreet student or teacher to order a copy of Windows for you. Microsoft offers huge academic discounts (naturally, this violates the Windows license agreement if you're not a student or teacher yourself).

Pirate it

Download a free, pirated copy of Windows from a file-sharing network. Generally, a pirated copy is risky because Microsoft might detect it during an update (page 341). For details, see Chris Fehily's book *Cancel Cable: How Internet Pirates Get Free Stuff.* Popular file-sharing sites include The Pirate Bay (*thepiratebay.org*) and Torrentz (*torrentz.eu*).

Upgrading to Windows 7

If you're moving to Windows 7 from an earlier version of Windows, Microsoft gives you upgrade options that depend on the version you're currently running. A Windows 7 version upgrade is much cheaper than a full copy. You can upgrade from only Windows XP or Windows Vista; if you have an earlier version, you must buy a full copy of Windows 7. You have two ways to upgrade:

In-place upgrade

An **in-place upgrade** lets you install Windows 7 and keep your user accounts, programs, documents, and settings as they were in your previous version of Windows.

Clean (custom) install

A **clean install** (also called a **custom install**) overwrites your current copy of Windows with Windows 7, erasing everything. You can use Windows Easy Transfer (page 373) to reload your files and settings on your upgraded computer.

Windows XP users must always do a clean install. Windows Vista users can upgrade in-place to an equivalent or higher edition of Windows 7 (for example, you can upgrade in-place from Windows Vista Business to Windows 7

Professional or Ultimate, but not to Windows 7 Home). Microsoft publishes step-by-step instructions for upgrading:

- To upgrade from Windows Vista, go to *windows.microsoft.com/en-US/ windows7/help/upgrading-from-windows-vista-to-windows-7*

- To upgrade from Windows XP, go to *windows.microsoft.com/en-US/ windows7/help/upgrading-from-windows-xp-to-windows-7*

See also "Installing Windows" on page 367.

What's New

Microsoft lists Windows 7's new features at:

- "Explore Windows 7 features" at *windows.microsoft.com/en-US/windows7/ products/features*

Less-breathless write-ups include:

- Wikipedia's "Features new to Windows 7" at *en.wikipedia.org/wiki/ Features_new_to_Windows_7*

- Peter Bright's "Hasta la Vista, baby: Ars reviews Windows 7" at *arstechnica. com/microsoft/reviews/2009/10/windows-7-the-review.ars*

Windows 7's major new and updated features include the following.

New Features

- Aero Snap and Aero Shake window management (see "Windows" on page 54)

- Jump lists (see "Exploring the Start Menu" on page 82 and "Managing Windows by Using the Taskbar" on page 95)

- Aero Peek (see "Managing Windows by Using the Taskbar" on page 95)

- New Control Panel programs (see "Using Control Panel" on page 117)

- Content view of folder windows (see "Folder Views" on page 174)

- Federated search (see "Federated Search" on page 219)

- Libraries (see "Using Libraries" on page 224)

- Disk images/ISO files (see "Burning CDs and DVDs" on page 227)

- Windows logo-key shortcuts (see "Windows Logo Key Shortcuts" on page 232)

- Windows XP mode (see "Running Older Programs" on page 244)

- Internet games (see "Games" on page 264)

- Devices and Printers folder (see "Printing & Faxing" on page 271 and "Hardware & Drivers" on page 293)

- Homegroup networking (see "Homegroups" on page 322)

- BitLocker to Go (see "BitLocker Drive Encryption" on page 349)

- Troubleshooting tool (see "Solving Problems" on page 358)

Updated Features

- Windows Anytime Upgrade (see "Windows Anytime Upgrade" on page 4)

- User Account Control (see "User Account Control" on page 19)

- Ribbons (see "Ribbons" on page 50)

- Start menu, taskbar, and notification area (see "The Desktop" on page 81)

- Themes (see "Setting the Desktop Theme" on page 127)

- Fonts (see "Managing Fonts" on page 158)

- Windows Live Essentials (see "Installing Windows Live Essentials" on page 259)

- Network and Sharing Center (see "Managing a Network" on page 316)

- Action Center (see "Action Center" on page 337)

Removed Features

Features removed from Windows 7 include the classic (one-column) Start menu, sidebar, Quick Launch toolbar, Windows Ultimate Extras, Inkball, ClipBook Viewer, scrap files, Explorer bar, hardware profiles, HyperTerminal, offline browsing, PowerToys, and TweakUI.

User Accounts

Windows lets many people share the same computer without being able to see or change each other's files and settings. **User accounts** identify who has permission to log on a particular computer (or network).

To start a Windows session, you log on to your user account, which gives you personalized access to the system. You, like each user, have your own documents, files, folders, desktop, Start menu, taskbar, Control Panel settings, email accounts, internet favorites, browsing history, program settings, permissions, network connections, startup programs, and other odds and ends. Your private files, folders, and preferences are stored on the Windows drive in \Users*user_name*—your personal folder (page 167)—which lets Windows personalize your desktop each time that you log on.

Tip: This section covers mainly multiple-user setups. If you're the sole user on your computer, you can skip to "Logging On" on page 20 without loss of continuity. You can still refer to this section for account-related tasks such as changing your password or picture (page 11), or resetting a forgotten password (page 14).

Account Types

An **account type** defines a user's **privileges**—rights to perform specific tasks. Each user has an account type:

Administrator account

> An **administrator account** has sweeping systemwide rights to create, change, and delete user accounts and passwords; access all files (including other users' files); and install programs and hardware. Many of the settings described in this book require administrative privileges, which you should grant to few users besides yourself. Windows must have at least one Administrator account, and if you installed Windows or maintain it, this is your account type.

Standard account

> If you're not an administrator, you have an everyday **standard account**. You can change your own password, picture, desktop theme, and Start menu; change some Control Panel settings (you can't change the system time, for example); and access files in your personal folder (everyone else's files are off limits) and the Public folder (which Windows creates automatically under the Users folder as a shared location for all users).

It's good practice to assign standard accounts to young, naive, or guest users. Standard users can't install programs and so are less likely than administrators to infect your computer with malware (page 344).

Guest account

Windows also comes with a no-password **guest account** that has about the same privileges as a standard account. This account, intended for visitors, is turned off by default and should stay that way.

Workgroups and Domains

The type of network that you're on (if any) determines how you administer accounts:

Workgroup

A **workgroup** network (also called a **peer-to-peer** network) is a simple home or small-business network whose computers each maintain separate user accounts and security settings. These informal networks exist primarily to help users share printers, folders, files, and other resources among ten or fewer computers. User accounts don't float around the network; you need a separate account on each networked computer to access its files. All Windows editions support workgroups. To set up a workgroup, see "Setting Up a Network" on page 312.

Domain

A **domain** is a large, centrally administered, institutional network. Files can reside on local drives or on network servers that distribute files across the network. A domain can have thousands of users. Centralized user accounts let you log on to any computer that's joined to the domain. Setting up a workgroup is easy; setting up a domain isn't (typically, a full-time network administrator or IT department sets up and maintains a domain). Only high-end Windows editions support domains.

Creating User Accounts

The main tool for managing accounts is User Accounts in Control Panel. If you're an administrator (page 8), you can create, edit, and delete user accounts (your own and others'). If you're a standard user, you can change your own account's password and picture. On a new computer or during a clean installation (page 5), you create the first user account when you set up Windows (in some cases, your computer's manufacturer will have created a predefined account with a generic name—Owner or User, for example). If you upgraded in-place from an earlier version of Windows, your existing accounts migrated to the new installation and appear in the Welcome screen (page 21). If you're on a large network, ask your network administrator how to log on.

To open User Accounts:

- The fast way: click your account picture in the upper-right of the Start menu. The slow way: choose Start > Control Panel > User Accounts and Family Safety > User Accounts. (If you're a domain member, choose Start > Control Panel > User Accounts > User Accounts.)

    User Accounts opens to your account and shows links to account tasks.

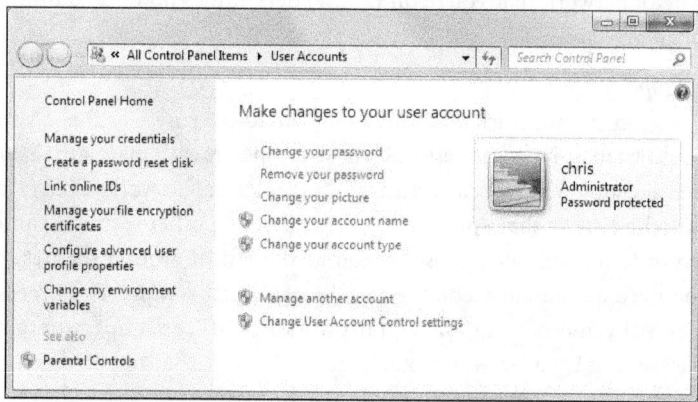

To create an account:

1   In User Accounts, click "Manage another account". A list of accounts appears in the Manage Accounts window.

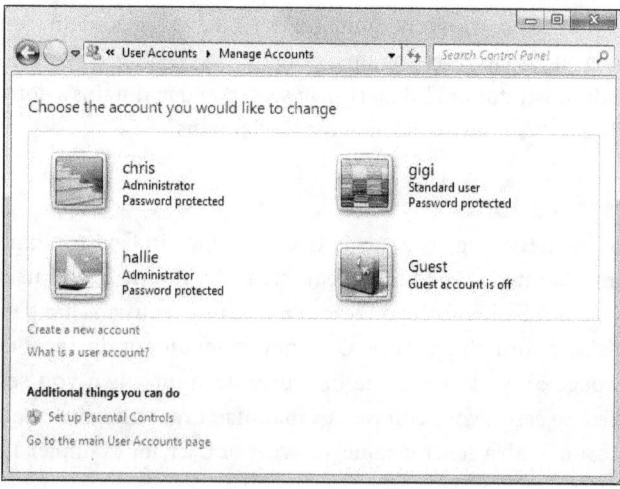

2   Click "Create a new account". Type a user name and then select an account type (page 8).

For easy typing in programs and command-line tools, don't use spaces in the user name. Capitalization doesn't matter, but favor only lowercase letters. Most punctuation is forbidden. Use a short name that will fit easily in messages and dialog boxes.

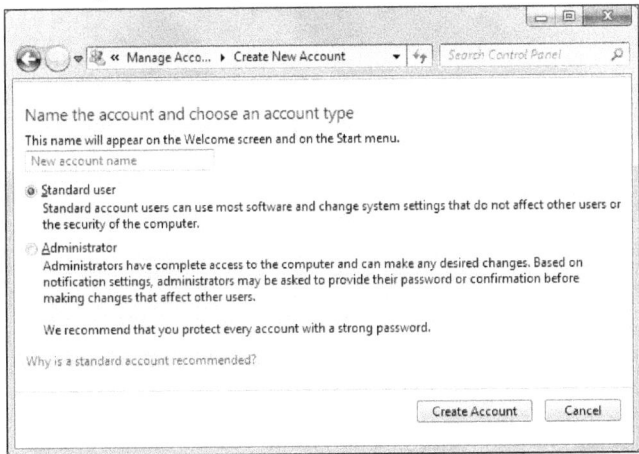

3   Click Create Account. The new account appears in the Manage Accounts window.

Note: To create an account if you're a domain member (page 9), in User Accounts, click "Manage user accounts", click Add, and then follow the onscreen instructions. The new account works only for the computer that you're using; it doesn't roam on the domain.

Editing User Accounts

After creating a user account, you edit it to set up its other information. You can change a user account's details, such as its password and picture, at any time after creating it.

To edit an account:

1   In User Accounts (page 9), click "Manage another account", and then click the account that you want to change.

Administrators have full access to all accounts. Standard users see about the same options, but if they don't have an administrator password, they can change only their account password and picture.

2   Choose among the following account settings.

Change the account name

Type a new user name, which will appear in the Welcome screen (page 21), Start menu, and User Accounts window.

Change the password

Type (and retype) a password (capitalization counts) and optional **password hint** to remind you of a forgotten password. If you provide a password hint, use one that's meaningful to only you, because everyone who uses your computer can see it on the Welcome screen.

Tip: To get password advice, click "How to create a strong password" or read Bruce Schneier's "Choosing Secure Passwords" (*schneier.com/blog/archives/2007/01/choosing_ secure.html*) or Randall T. Williams' "The passphrase FAQ" (*iusmentis.com/security/ passphrasefaq*).

Remove the password

If the account has a password, you can remove it. (In most situations, you should password-protect every account.)

Change the picture

Change the picture associated with the user in the Welcome screen (page 21), Start menu, and User Accounts window. (The picture doesn't appear if you're a domain member.) To use your own picture, automatically scaled to fit, click "Browse for more pictures".

Set up Parental Controls

Add Parental Controls restrictions (page 346) to a standard account.

Change the account type

Change the account type (page 8) from administrator to standard, or vice versa.

Delete the account

Delete the account (page 15) and, optionally, its files.

Manage another account

Choose another account to edit after you're finished with this one.

Note: To edit an account if you're a domain member (page 9), in User Accounts, click "Manage user accounts". On the Users tab, under "Users for this computer", click the user account name and then click Properties.

Resetting a Forgotten Password

If you're worried that you'll forget your password and draw a blank on your password hint, then create a **password reset disk** to recover it. You must create it now, before you actually need it. Keep the disk safe; anyone can use it to change your password. (An administrator can always reset your forgotten password, but a reset wipes your secondary passwords as a security measure.)

To create a password reset disk:

1 In User Accounts (page 9), click "Create a password reset disk" (on the left). The Forgotten Password wizard opens.

2 Follow the onscreen instructions.

You'll need a formatted floppy disk or USB flash drive. If you mistype a password in future logons, Windows displays a message that the password is wrong. Close the message and then click Reset Password. Insert your password reset disk and follow the steps in the Password Reset wizard. You don't need to make a new password reset disk after you're logged on; reuse the old one. You can have only one password reset disk for each account; if you make a new one, the old one becomes unusable.

Deleting User Accounts

An administrator (page 8) can delete any account that's not logged on. (To see who's logged on, press Ctrl+Shift+Esc to open Windows Task Manager and then click the Users tab.) You can't delete the account that you're logged on to or an only remaining administrator account. A deleted account is gone forever, along with its settings and secondary passwords. If you create a new account with the same name and password, Windows considers it to be a different account.

To delete an account:

1 In User Accounts (page 9), click "Manage another account", click the account that you want to delete, and then click "Delete the account"

2 Click Keep Files to save the user's desktop and personal files on your desktop in a folder named after the deleted user (documents and media files are saved; email and settings aren't saved). Or click Delete Files to erase the user's files. To make the deletion permanent, click Delete Account.

Tip: You can use Local Users and Groups (page 15) to disable an account temporarily rather than delete it.

Advanced User Account Tools

Windows includes other powerful (but hidden) tools for managing user accounts. Manage accounts only by using User Accounts (page 9) or these tools. Don't tinker with accounts directly in the \Users folder.

net user

    The fastest way to create (and delete) user accounts is via the *net user* command in Command Prompt (page 262). For details, read the Microsoft article "How to Use the Net User Command" at *support.microsoft.*

com/?kbid=251394 or type *net help user | more* at a command prompt (tap the spacebar to advance screens).

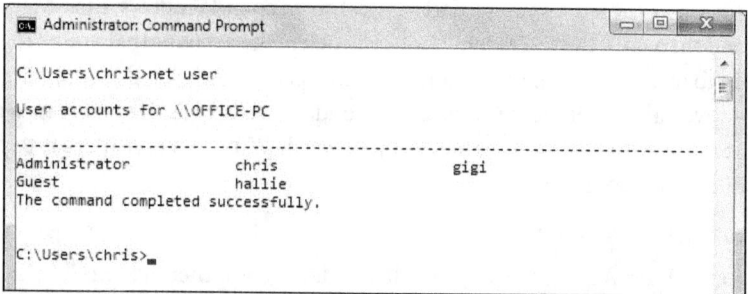

userpasswords2

Power users prefer the old-style User Accounts dialog box to manage accounts. To open it, press Windows logo key+R, type *control userpasswords2*, and then press Enter. This dialog box is more powerful and direct than Control Panel's User Accounts. You can create, edit, and delete accounts without slogging through a wizard. Click the Advanced tab for more options.

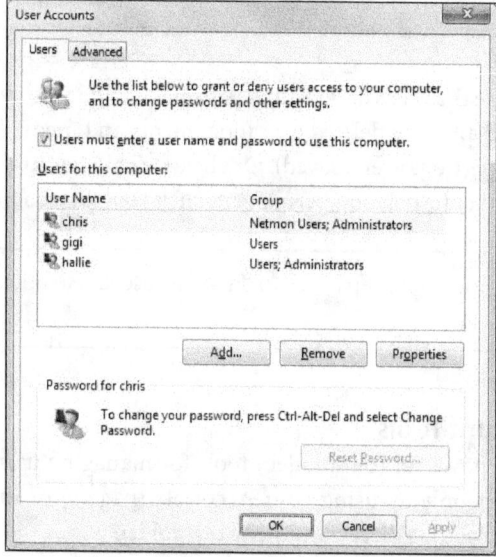

Local Users and Groups

For advanced user-management, use the Local Users and Groups console. To open it, press Windows logo key+R, type *lusrmgr.msc*, and then press Enter (alternatively, click the Advanced tab in userpasswords2 and then click the Advanced button). Despite its austere appearance, this tool offers power and flexibility. Double-click an account name to set advanced options, for example. You can also create and manage users and groups. **Groups** are named collections of users that transcend the administrator and standard account types (page 8) and give you great flexibility in fine-tuning file and folder permissions. It's also here that you can manage the built-in, no-password, hidden Administrator account that's used in emergencies (like recovering from a nasty crash).

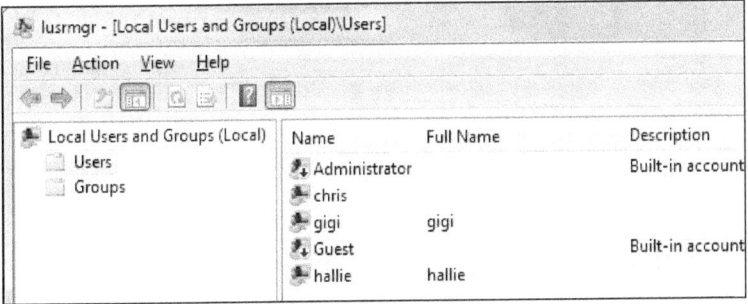

One thing Local Users and Groups lets you do that User Accounts doesn't is **disable** accounts temporarily, which may be preferable to deleting them (page 15) in some cases. A disabled account's files and settings aren't touched; they just become unavailable to the user. To disable an account, double-click the user in the Local Users and Groups list. In the Properties dialog box, on the General tab, select "Account is disabled". That user won't be able to log on until you enable the account again.

User Profiles

A **user profile** contains an account's personal settings that Windows uses to configure the desktop each time the user logs on. Each user's settings, network connections, and so on are saved in \Users*user_name*. Windows also has a default profile that defines settings for newly created accounts. (The default profile is a hidden folder in \Users.) To change this starting point, change the desktop, Start menu, taskbar, favorites, and theme of a normal account (your own, perhaps) to what you want the new default to be, and then complete the following steps.

To change the default user profile:

1   In Windows Explorer, choose Organize (on the toolbar) > "Folder and search options" > View tab > select "Show hidden files and folders" > OK.

2   Choose Start > Control Panel > System and Security > System > "Advanced
system settings" (on the left) > Settings (under User Profiles).

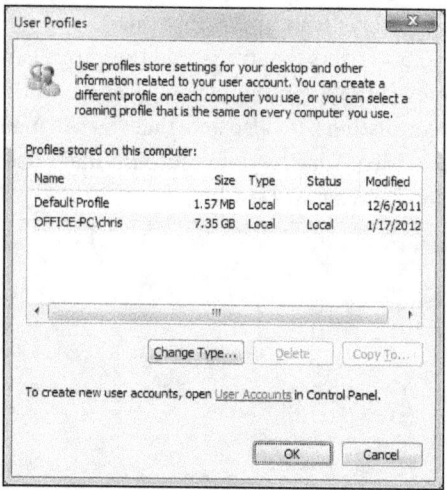

3   Select the account whose settings you want to copy and then click Copy
To. In the Copy To dialog box that opens, click Browse, and then navigate
to and select \Users\Default on the drive that contains Windows.

4   Click OK in each open dialog box. In Explorer, rehide hidden files.

Note: A roaming user profile, which your network administrator creates, is available
every time you log on to any computer on a network domain (page 9).

User Accounts and Security
A few tips for keeping your accounts and files safe:

*   If an administrator removes or changes the password of another user (of
    any account type), then the secondary passwords stored in that user's ac-
    count for websites, network files and folders, encrypted files, and so on,
    are lost, thus preventing a rogue administrator from, say, cleaning out a
    bank account courtesy of a password memorized by a browser.

*   To safely share files and folders with other users, see "Sharing Files" on
    page 320.

*   Consider using a standard account for everyday use and an administra-
    tor account for special occasions. You can browse the web, send email,

chat, use a word processor, and play games, all without an administrator account. When you try to do something that requires administrative privileges, a User Account Control dialog box (described below) opens to let you temporarily act as an administrator. To continue, type the password for one of the listed administrator accounts and then click Yes.

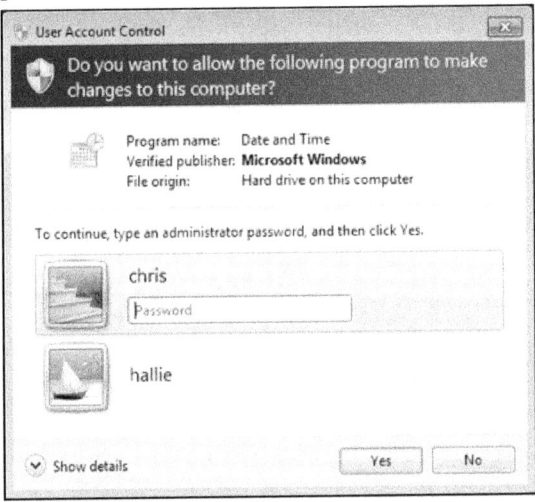

User Account Control

Microsoft's security-minded answer to years of viruses and spyware is User Account Control (UAC). If you've used Windows for even a little while, then you've seen a UAC dialog box.

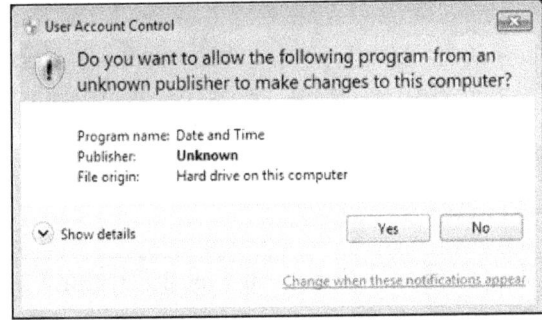

UAC helps stop unauthorized changes to your computer by asking you for permission or an administrator password (page 8) before you do something that affects your computer's operation or changes settings for other users. When the UAC prompt appears, the rest of the screen may darken until you consent to (or deny) the action. Windows marks administrator actions with a shield icon:

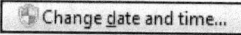

By verifying actions before they start, UAC can stop malware (page 344) from installing or making changes. You should set UAC's level of aggressiveness so that its interruptions aren't so frequent and irritating that over time, you robotically approve an actual threat when it appears.

To configure User Account Control:

1   Choose Start > Control Panel > User Accounts and Family Safety > User Accounts > "Change User Account Control settings".

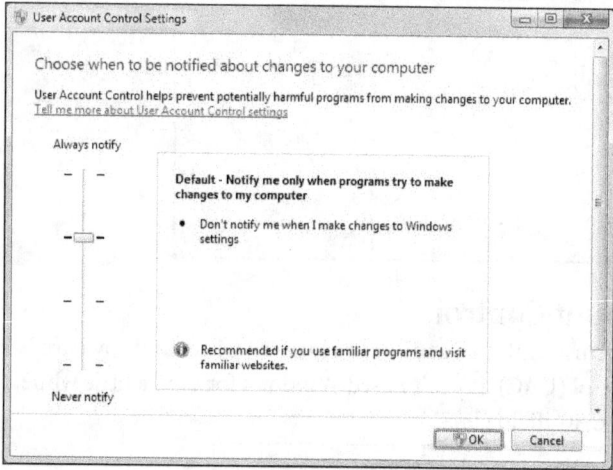

2   Drag the slider to set how often UAC notifies you. The least-secure setting turns off UAC, which, despite Microsoft's warnings, is a reasonable setting if you're naturally careful about where you browse and what you click. Click the "Tell me more" link for a detailed description of each setting.

Logging On

Logging on starts a session in Windows—the first thing you do after turning on your computer. After your computer powers up—or **boots**—you'll see the Welcome screen (described below), in which you enter your user name and (optional) password. Windows user accounts identify who has permission to use a particular computer (or network). User accounts are covered in detail earlier in this chapter (page 8), but for now you need to know only your user name and password, which depend on your installation:

- If your computer came with Windows 7 installed, either the Welcome screen will appear with a factory-installed account name or the computer will start in Windows Setup (page 367) the first time you turn it on. Follow the manufacturer's instructions.

- If you upgraded in-place (page 5) to Windows 7 from an earlier version of Windows, your existing accounts migrated to the new installation and appear on the Welcome screen.

- If you did a clean install (page 5) of Windows 7, you set up an account during installation. Use that user name and password.

- If you're on a large network (a domain, page 9) at work or school, ask your network administrator how to log on.

- If your computer has only one user account with no password, Windows bypasses the Welcome screen and boots to that account's desktop directly. (Windows comes with hidden Guest and Administrator accounts, but they don't apply here.)

The Welcome Screen

Your account identifies you uniquely so that Windows can load your personal settings and grant you certain permissions. In most situations, you use the Welcome screen to log on to Windows; it lists all the accounts on your computer. The bottom portion of the Welcome screen shows the edition of Windows that you're running and offers options for turning off your computer (page 30) and setting up your computer to accommodate disabled users (page 145).

To log on to Windows:

1   On the Welcome screen, click your user name or picture.

2   If your account is password-protected, type your password in the Password box and then press Enter or click the arrow. Your personalized Windows desktop appears. If you've set a password hint (page 11), it appears below the password box if you mistype your password. To cancel logon after you've started typing your password, press Esc.

Mistyped Passwords

Windows lets you mistype your password an unlimited number of times. The "try again" screen displays your password hint (if you've set one, page 11) and lets you use your password reset disk (if you've made one. page 14). Passwords are case-sensitive, so Windows warns you if the Caps Lock key is toggled on (its keyboard indicator is lit)—password characters appear as dots, so you may be typing uppercase letters without knowing it.

Secure Logons

For added security, force users to press Ctrl+Alt+Delete to log on. Secure logon halts any other programs running on your computer, preventing user-name and password theft by malware that mimics the logon screen.

To enable secure logon:

1 Choose Start, type *netplwiz* in the Search box, and then press Enter. (If you're a domain member, choose Start > Control Panel > User Accounts > Advanced Options.)

2 In the User Accounts dialog box, click the Advanced tab, select "Require users to press Ctrl+Alt+Delete", and then click OK. From now on, users are greeted with "Press CTRL + ALT + DELETE to log on".

Logging On Automatically

You can set up your computer to log on automatically at startup even if it has more than one account or if your account is password-protected. You might like automatic logon if you're the main user but sometimes others log on, or if you keep your own separate accounts for different tasks.

To log on automatically at startup:

1 Choose Start, type *netplwiz* in the Search box, and then press Enter. (If you're a domain member, choose Start > Control Panel > User Accounts > Advanced Options.)

2 In the User Accounts dialog box, on the Users tab, clear "Users must enter a user name and password to use this computer". (This checkbox won't appear if your computer doesn't support automatic logon or if your network administrator has disabled it.)

3 Click OK.

4 In the Automatically Log On dialog box, type the user name and password (twice) of the account that you want to log on to automatically

5 Click OK.

Now the system invisibly enters your user name and password at power-up. Anyone who turns on your computer can access the same files and resources that you do.

You can use the other accounts on the computer by using fast user switching (page 25) or by logging off and then logging on to another account.

Domain Logons

If you're a home or small-business user, you're probably using a stand-alone computer or one that's part of a small workgroup network (page 9), so you log on by using the Welcome screen. If you're on a large network at work or school, your machine is part of a centrally administered domain. You can log on to any computer in the domain without needing an account on that machine. Your network administrator or IT department will give you logon instructions, but here are a few basics:

- Professional, Enterprise, and Ultimate editions can join domains (Home and Starter editions can't).

- Secure logon (page 22) is usually enabled on domains; press Ctrl+Alt+Delete to display the logon screen.

- The domain logon screen, unlike the standard Welcome screen (page 21), doesn't list everyone's account (doing so would be insecure and impractical). Instead, you have a single place to enter your user name and password.

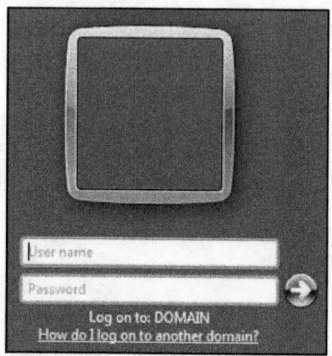

- By default, the logon screen shows the last account to log on and gives you the option to log on as a different user or to a different domain. Include the domain name with your user name: log on as *domain_name\user_name*. To log on to the local machine, type *.\user_name*, where *user_name* is a local (not domain) account.

- After logon, you can connect to the domain's shared network resources (printers, servers, and so on). Your computer might run an automated logon script to handle permissions, security, maintenance, updates, system scans, or whatever else your network administrator wants.

- To find the domain that you're on, choose Start > Control Panel > System and Security > System (or press Windows logo key+Break). If your computer is joined to a domain, under "Computer name, domain, and workgroup settings", you'll see the domain name; otherwise, you'll see a workgroup name.

- To join a domain, choose Start > Control Panel > System and Security > System (or press Windows logo key+Break). Under "Computer name, domain, and workgroup settings", click "Change settings". On the Computer Name tab, click Network ID to start the Join a Domain or Workgroup wizard and then follow the onscreen instructions. (Alternatively, click

Change instead of Network ID to set the domain quickly without using the wizard.)

- If your computer was a member of a workgroup before you joined a domain, it's removed from the workgroup.

Switching Users

Fast user switching lets more than one person log on at the same time. If you step away from your computer for a short time, you can leave your programs running and let someone else log on to, say, check email. When you log back on, Windows resumes your session where you left off.

Only one person at a time—the **active user**—can actually use the computer (type at the keyboard). People who are logged on but not active—**disconnected users**—can keep their programs running and files open in the background, invisible to the active user. To identify the active user quickly, click Start and then read the user name in the top-right section of the Start menu.

To switch users without logging off:

1 Press Ctrl+Alt+Delete and then click Switch User.

or

Press Windows logo key+L.

or

Choose Start, click the arrow next to the Power button, and then click "Switch user".

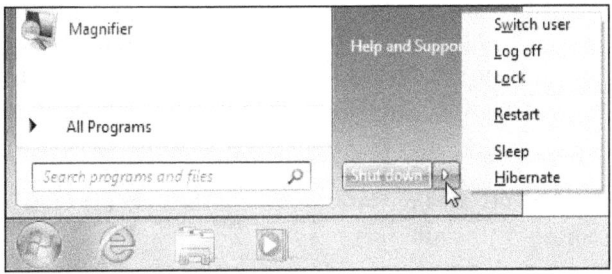

2 If secure logon (page 22) is enabled, press Ctrl+Alt+Delete.

3 In the Welcome screen (page 21), click another account name or picture and then log on normally.

Tip: Save all your work before switching—if another user shuts down the computer or logs you off, Windows won't save your open files automatically.

Other Logged-On Users

Task Manager's Users tab tells you who else is logged on via fast user switching.

To find out who else is logged on to your computer:

1   Right-click an empty area of the taskbar and then choose Start Task Manager (or press Ctrl+Shift+Esc).

2   Click the Users tab to view users and their status.

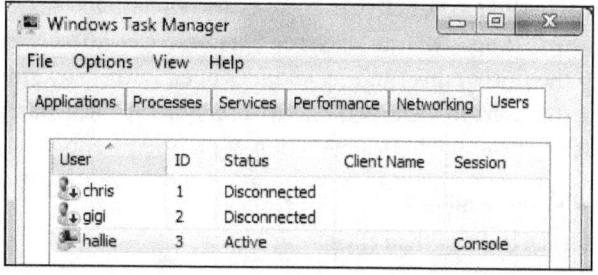

Tip: Fast way to switch users: right-click a user name in Task Manager's Users tab and then choose Connect or Disconnect from the shortcut menu.

Other Users' Running Programs

If your computer is running slowly, use Task Manager to see the programs that other logged-on users are running and how much memory they're chewing up. Task Manager lists filenames (*winword.exe*, for example) in the Image Name column and program names (*Microsoft Word*) in the Description column.

To find out which programs other users are running:

1   Right-click an empty area of the taskbar and then choose Start Task Manager (or press Ctrl+Shift+Esc).

2   Click the Processes tab and then select "Show processes from all users".

3   Click any column heading (Image Name, User Name, and so on) to sort by that column, or drag the headings to rearrange columns. A subtle color change and arrowhead in a column heading indicates a sorted column. Here, it's most useful to sort by User Name or by Memory.

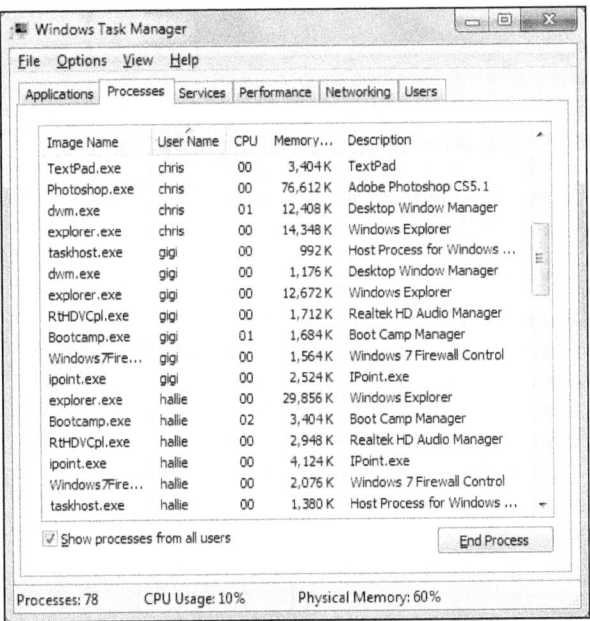

Tip: To disable fast user switching, choose Start, type *gpedit.msc* in the Search box, and then press Enter. In the Local Group Policy Editor, choose Local Computer Policy > Computer Configuration > Administrative Templates > System > Logon > enable "Hide entry points for Fast User Switching" > OK. (Local Group Policy Editor is available on only high-end Windows editions.)

Locking Your Computer

Without logging off, you can **lock** your computer—that is, set it so that the keyboard and mouse won't change anything—to protect your programs and personal information while you're away from your computer. Locking lets others know that you're using the computer and prevents everyone except you (or an administrator) from viewing your files or programs, though other users still can log on via fast user switching (page 25). A locked computer doesn't interfere with shared printers or other network resources, but is still subject to power-management settings (page 152).

To lock your computer:

• Choose Start, click the arrow next to the Power button, and then click Lock.

  or

Press Windows logo key+L.

or

Press Ctrl+Alt+Delete and then click "Lock this computer".

Windows displays a Locked screen with your user name until you return. Your programs continue to run while your computer is locked.

To unlock your computer:

- On the Locked screen, type your password in the Password box and then press Enter or click the arrow. If secure logon is enabled, press Ctrl+Alt+Delete to display the Locked screen.

Tip: You can set your screen saver (page 125) to lock your computer automatically after a set period of idle time.

Ctrl+Alt+Delete

The behavior of the well-known keyboard shortcut Ctrl+Alt+Delete (the "three-finger salute") has changed over the years. In Windows' infancy, it rebooted your machine (a common need). In Windows XP, it opened Task Manager or the Windows Security dialog box. Now it displays a screen of security-related options. You can still open Task Manager via the keyboard: press Ctrl+Shift+Esc.

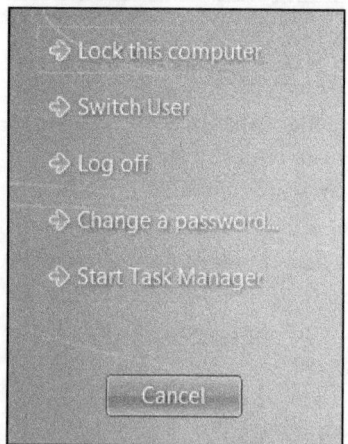

Logging Off

Logging off ends your session in Windows. When you log off, Windows closes all your open programs and files (each program prompts you to save any unsaved work), disconnects your network and online connections, and prevents others from using your user account to access your files or network. Your computer remains turned on and Windows shows the Welcome screen (page 21) or secure-logon screen (page 22) to let the next person log on.

To log off:

- Choose Start, click the arrow next to the Power button, and then click "Log off". Or press Ctrl+Alt+Delete and then click "Log off".

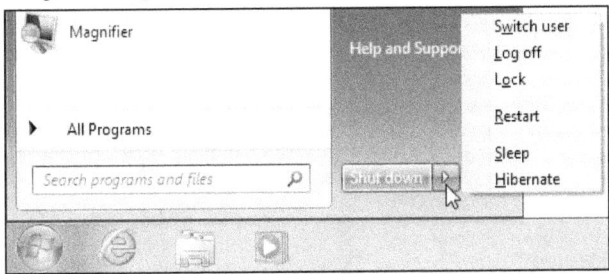

Logging Off via the Keyboard

You can use the keyboard to invoke any of the commands in the Power submenu. Tap the Windows logo key (or press Ctrl+Esc) to open the Start menu, press the right-arrow key twice to open the submenu, and then type the underlined letter of the command that you want: L for Log Off, U for Shut Down, and so on.

Actually, you can use the keyboard to choose any Start-menu command. After you open the Start menu, use the four arrow keys to move to the desired command and then press Enter. You can also press the first letter of a command to jump to it (provided that the cursor isn't in the Search box). If two or more commands have the same first letter, press that letter repeatedly.

Tip: To log off from a command prompt (page 262), type *shutdown -l.*

Logoff Troubleshooting

If there's a problem logging off (usually because you haven't saved your work in some program), Windows displays a screen listing the currently running programs and explaining the problem. Click Cancel to cancel the logoff, and then resolve the issue (by saving your work and exiting the program, for example). Alternatively, click "Force log off" to continue logging off—Windows forces the problem program to close and you might lose your work as a result.

Logging Off Other Users

If other users are logged on to your machine via fast user switching (page 25), you can use Task Manager to log them off. Beware: logging off other users kills their programs suddenly without saving their unsaved work.

To log off someone else:

1   Right-click an empty area of the taskbar and then choose Start Task Manager (or press Ctrl+Shift+Esc).

2   Click the Users tab to view logged-on users.

3   Select a user and then click Logoff (or right-click a user and then choose Log Off).

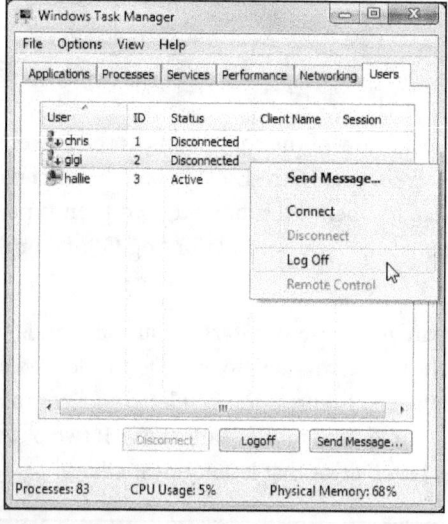

Turning Off Your Computer

Windows prepares itself for shutdown by saving session and system information and by disconnecting network and online connections. Windows still can recover if you lose power suddenly or yank your computer's plug from the wall, but you may get an "improper shutdown" message when you return (and your unsaved work will be lost). For peace of mind, always use one of the official Windows turn-off options.

By default, the Power button on the Start menu shuts down your computer. To change the Power button's default action, right-click the Start button and then choose Properties > Start Menu tab > "Power button action" menu.

To turn off your computer:

- Choose Start, click the Power button or click the arrow next to the Power button, and then choose one of the following options.

Shut down
   Ends your session and shuts down Windows so that you can turn off the power safely. Most computers turn off the power automatically; if yours doesn't, push the power button on the computer after the "It's safe" message appears. This option quits your programs, prompting you to save any unsaved work. After shutdown, it may take several minutes to start (boot) Windows, log on, and then start the programs that you were using. Use Shut Down when you're done for the day or when you need to muck around inside your computer.

Sleep
   Turns off the display, stops the hard disks and fan, and enters low-power-consumption mode. Windows saves your work automatically, so you don't have to save your files and exit programs before putting your computer to sleep. A light on your computer case may blink slowly or turn yellow while the computer sleeps. A sleeping computer springs to life quickly—with your desktop exactly as you left it—when you start working again. Use Sleep to stop using your computer for a short time and save power (especially useful for laptops).

Restart
   Ends your session, shuts down Windows, and starts Windows again automatically. This option quits your programs, prompting you to save any unsaved work. Use Restart if you've installed hardware or software that requires a restart, or if Windows is acting erratically or sluggishly.

Hibernate

Hibernate is an older turn-off option, supplanted by Sleep, that saves your session to a large file on your drive before powering down. Restarting the computer restores your desktop as you left it, faster than in a "cold" startup. Older computers may not support this option. Hibernate is disabled by default. To enable it, choose Start, type *cmd* in the Search box, and then press Ctrl+Shift+Enter. Type *powercfg -h* on, press Enter, type *exit*, and then press Enter again. Choose Start > Control Panel > System and Security > Power Options > "Change when the computer sleeps" (on the left) > "Change advanced power settings". Expand the Sleep options, set "Hibernate after", and then turn off "Allow hybrid sleep".

Waking a Sleeping Computer

A sleeping computer uses a tiny amount of power to maintain your work in memory. Sleeping laptops lose about 1 or 2 percent of battery power per hour. If a laptop has been sleeping for a few hours or its battery is low, Windows saves your work and turns off your computer, drawing no power. To learn about power options for laptops, see "Conserving Power" on page 152.

To wake a computer from sleep state:

* Press the power button on the computer's case, press a key on the keyboard, click the mouse, or (for a laptop computer) open the lid. The computer will usually wake within seconds.

Creating Turn-Off Shortcuts

To create a shortcut (page 110) that shuts down your computer, right-click an empty area on the desktop and then choose New > Shortcut. In the Create Shortcut wizard, type

```
shutdown.exe -s -t 0
```

in the Location box and then click Next. Type a name for the shortcut and then click Finish. The shortcut will appear on your desktop. Double-click it to shut down your computer. You can move, copy, delete, or rename it like you would any other shortcut.

The -t *n* option delays shutdown for *n* seconds. You can replace -s (shutdown) with -l (log off), -r (restart), or -h (hibernate). The shutdown.exe command is located in \Windows\System32. For more information, type shutdown /? at a command prompt (page 262).

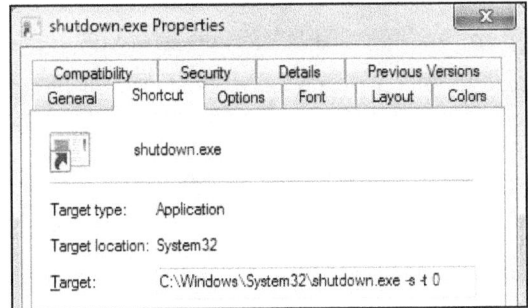

Shutting Down when Installing Hardware

You should follow the manufacturer's instructions when installing hardware on your computer, but here are a few general rules:

- Before you install hardware inside your computer (memory, drive, sound card, video card, and so on), shut down your computer and unplug it.

- Before you attach an older peripheral device (printer, display, external drive) that does not connect to a USB, SATA, or IEEE 1394 (FireWire) port, shut down your computer (no need to unplug it).

- When adding a USB, SATA, or IEEE 1394 device (most newer devices), you don't have to shut down.

Turn-Off Tips

- A shield on the Power button means that automatic updates (page 341) are ready to be installed on your computer. Clicking this button ends your session, installs the updates, and then shuts down your computer.

- If the desktop is active, you can press Alt+F4 to choose a turn-off option.

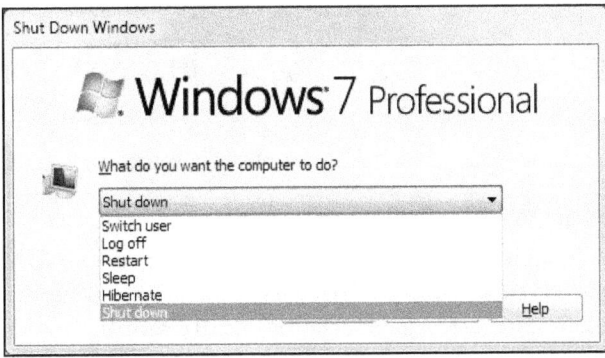

- The turn-off options are also available on the Welcome screen (page 21).

- For reasons of parts wearout, power consumption, power interruption, and heat stress, it's sensible to shut down your computer overnight. Even if you don't, you should always turn off your display when you're done.

- If your computer shuts down when you try to make it sleep, that's because your hardware doesn't support the sleep option (possibly because you have an old video card or outdated video driver) or an administrator has set the Power button to always shut down.

Using Getting Started

The **Getting Started** window helps you set up your computer for the first time. Common tasks include downloading essential programs from Microsoft, adding user accounts for other people, transferring files and settings from another computer, and personalizing Windows.

To open Getting Started, choose Start > All Programs > Accessories > Getting Started. Click a task, and a description and link appear in the top pane. Click the link to begin. Some Getting Started tasks depend on your Windows setup; for example, Add New Users won't appear if you're a domain member.

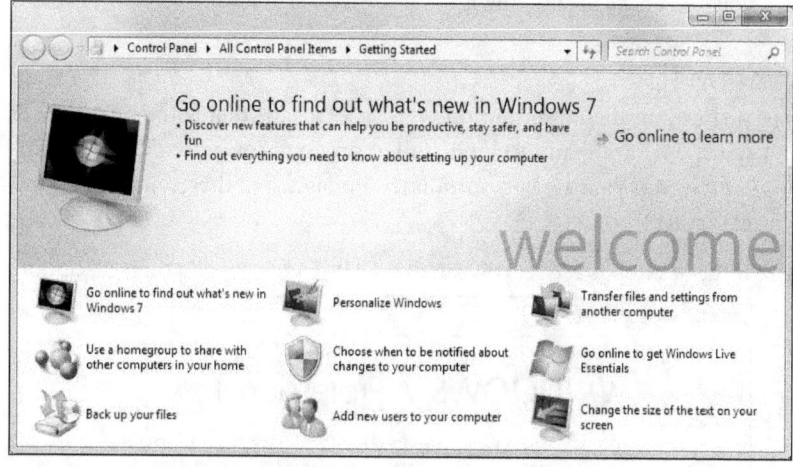

Exploring the Windows Workspace

You work with Windows through its **graphical user interface** (GUI, pronounced *gooey*), which offers pictures along with words to help you perform tasks. To make learning easier, Windows displays visual clues about how things work. Often, these clues are analogous to those you see in the real world. If a door has a flat plate rather than a handle to grasp, it's a clue to push that door, not pull it. The three-dimensional (3D) look of buttons on your screen implies that you're supposed to push them (click them). You'll recognize similar hints throughout the user interface.

The following figure shows the standard GUI elements that you'll find on the Windows desktop. Microsoft modeled Windows on a real-world office environment: you have a desktop, on which you work and use tools, and folders, in which you organize files. The desktop lets you move items and manage your tasks vaguely the same way that you would on a physical desktop.

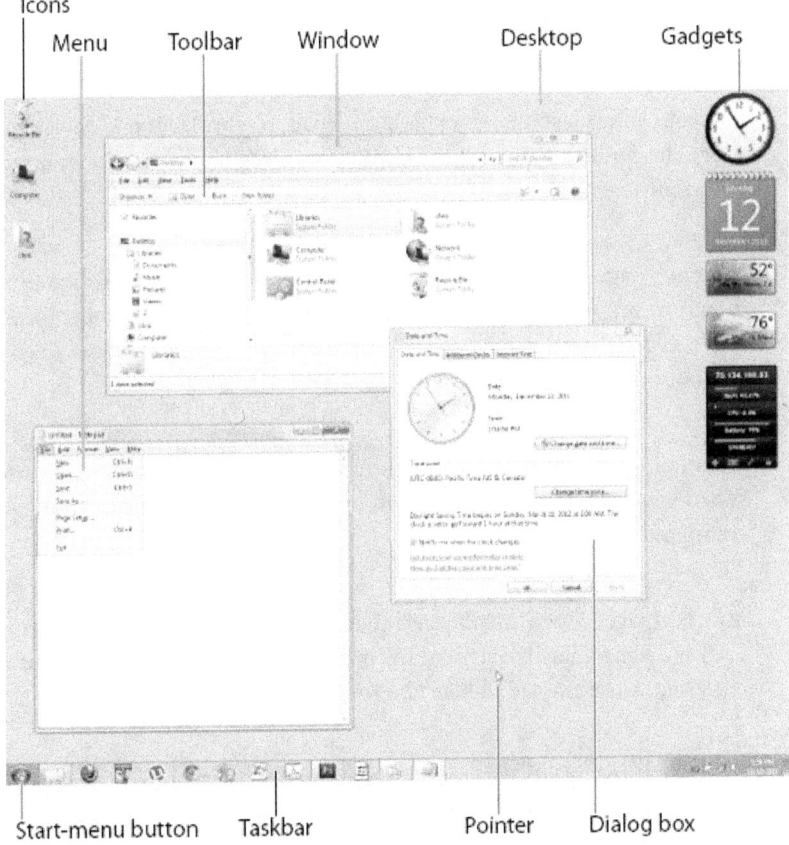

Icons
Menu   Toolbar   Window   Desktop   Gadgets

Start-menu button   Taskbar   Pointer   Dialog box

Desktop

    After you log on to Windows, the desktop—a work area that uses menus, icons, and windows to simulate the top of a desk—appears automatically.

Start menu

The Start menu (page 82) is the central menu that lets you access the most useful folders, programs, and commands on your computer.

Taskbar

The taskbar (page 94) lets you switch among open programs and documents. It also lets you launch programs and alerts you to certain events, such as appointment reminders or incoming email.

Gadgets

Gadgets (page 106) are single-purpose miniprograms that show live information (time, weather, headlines, and so on) and provide access to frequently used tools (calendar, CPU meter, clock, and so on).

Pointer

Use your mouse, stylus, trackball, trackpad, or similar input device to move the pointer (page 38) to select items, drag icons, or choose commands onscreen.

Menus

A menu (page 46) is a list of related commands. Most programs use menus to provide an easy-to-learn, easy-to-use alternative to memorizing instructions. In many popular Microsoft applications, ribbons (page 50) have supplanted menus.

Toolbars

A toolbar (page 50) is a row, column, or block of buttons or icons. When you click one of these buttons or icons, the program carries out a command or task.

Icons

An icon (page 51) is a small image that represents an item to be opened, such as a file, folder, drive, program, or the Recycle Bin. An icon's picture is a visual cue designed to help you recall what the icon represents.

Windows

A window (page 54) is a rectangular portion of your screen where a program runs. You can open many windows at the same time. Each window can be independently resized, moved, or closed; maximized to occupy the entire screen; or minimized to a button on the taskbar.

Dialog boxes

A special type of window called a dialog box (page 62) contains text boxes, buttons, tabs, scrolling lists, drop-down lists, and other controls that let you set preferences or run commands. Some dialog boxes—such as Open, Save, and Print—are similar in every Windows program. Others, such as Properties dialog boxes (page 65), depend on the program or context.

The Mouse

The mouse is one of two primary input devices in Windows (the other is the keyboard, page 42). Moving the mouse on your physical desk controls the motion of the pointer on your screen. By moving the pointer over an icon or control and then clicking, you can select an item, open or move a file, run a program, or throw something away, for example.

A mouse has a left and a right button. You'll use the left button for most actions, but frequent use of the right button, which displays a shortcut menu (page 48), is a key to working quickly. Advanced mice have extra buttons for other functions. In addition to (or instead of) a mouse, you may have a trackpad (used on laptops), pointing stick (tiny joystick), trackball, or stylus (used on pen-input devices and older tablet computers).

Mouse Gestures

Clicking and dragging

To **point**, move the tip of the **pointer** over the target item to which you want to point (one tiny pixel is the pointer's hot spot, which you use to point precisely). To **click**, point to an item and then press and then release the left mouse button without moving the mouse. To **double-click**, point to an item and then click the left mouse button twice quickly without moving the mouse (if you click too slowly, Windows interprets it as two single clicks). To **right-click**, point to an item and then click the right mouse button without moving the mouse. (To "right-click" with a one-button mouse, hold down the Ctrl key and then click normally.) To **drag**, point to an item, press-and-hold the left mouse button while you move the pointer to a new location, and then release the button (press Esc during a drag to cancel the drag). The normal pointer ⌖ may change depending on what you're dragging or pointing to. A **right-drag** is the same as a drag except holding down the *right* mouse button.

Scrolling

If your mouse has a wheel, trackball, or multitouch surface, you can use it to scroll documents, webpages, and more. On some mice, you can press the scroll wheel as a third button.

Modifiers

Modifier keys (page 42) work with the mouse gestures. To **Ctrl+click**, hold down Ctrl, and then click before releasing the key. To **Ctrl+drag**, hold down Ctrl, and then drag and drop before releasing the key. To **Ctrl+scroll**, hold down Ctrl while spinning the mouse wheel. Clicks, drags, and scrolls can be similarly modified by using the Shift or Alt keys.

Insertion point

In text documents, don't confuse the **insertion point** (also called the **cursor**), a steadily blinking vertical bar |, with the pointer, a nonblinking I-beam I. The insertion point indicates where text or graphics will be inserted when you type or paste. To move the insertion point, click the pointer (I-beam) at a new insertion point or use the arrow keys.

Mouse Pointers

The pointer's shape changes depending on what it's pointing to.

Pointer	Description
⌖	The normal pointer. Click the area or item that you want to work with.
⌖?	Appears when you click the question mark (?) in the top-right corner of a dialog box. Click any dialog-box item to get "What's This?" help.
⌖○	Windows is doing something in the background—opening or saving a temporary file, for example. You can keep doing your own work, but response time may be longer than usual.
○	Windows is busy with a task and will ignore you until it finishes. Typically, this pointer will appear in only one program window at a time; if it appears everywhere, your computer is indeed busy.
↕ ⇔ ⬉	Appears when you point to a window's border (side or corner). Drag the border to resize the window. See also "Windows" on page 54.

Pointer	Description
🖑	Appears when you point to a word or image linked to a help page, command, or website. Click the link to jump to a related destination or display pop-up information.
⊘	The action that you're trying to perform is forbidden, or the item that you're pointing to is unavailable.
I	The I-beam or I-bar appears where you can select or edit text. Click to set the insertion point, or click and drag to select (highlight) text.
+	Helps you move an item precisely. This pointer often appears in drawing programs.
✥	Appears when you choose Move or Size from a window's control menu. When it does, use the arrow keys to move or resize the window and then press Enter, or press Esc to cancel. See also "Windows" on page 54.

Configuring the Mouse

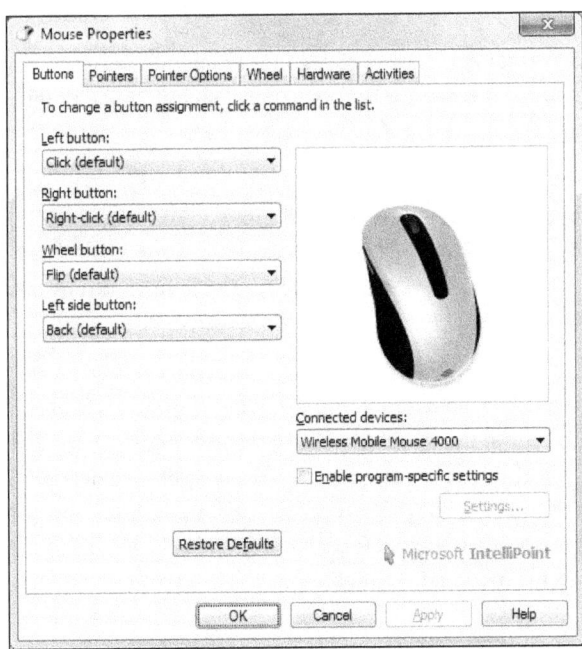

Use the Mouse utility in Control Panel to control settings such as button configuration, double-click speed, pointers, responsiveness, and wheel behavior.

To configure the mouse:

1   Choose Start > Control Panel, type *mouse* in the Search Control Panel box, and then select Mouse in the results list.

or

Choose Start > Control Panel, switch to icon view, and then click Mouse.

2   Update the settings on the following tabs (some tabs and settings vary by mouse).

Buttons/Activities tab

To swap the left and right mouse-button functions, select "Switch primary and secondary buttons", or choose mouse-button assignments from the drop-down lists. If Windows often interprets your double clicks as two single clicks, drag the "Double-click speed" slider toward Slow. To make dragging easier, select "Turn on ClickLock"; then you can select text or drag icons without holding down the mouse button continuously (useful for trackpad users).

Pointers tab

Select predefined pointer schemes (which range from cute to practical), create your own pointer schemes, or browse to select an individual pointer (rather than an entire scheme).

Pointer Options tab

Adjust the pointer's speed to have it respond more quickly or slowly to mouse movements. If the pointer distracts you while you type, select "Hide pointer while typing". If you need to keep track of the pointer as it moves, select "Display pointer trails" (useful for laptop screens).

Wheel tab

If your mouse has a wheel, adjust its scroll behavior. A mouse wheel can stand in for scrollbars; roll the wheel to scroll up or down a list, document, or webpage. The wheel on some mice can tilt left or right for horizontal scrolling. If your mouse has no wheel, these settings are ignored. If your default pointing device is a trackpad (on a laptop), the Wheel tab may be replaced with a tab for trackpad settings.

Hardware tab

This tab lists the pointing devices attached to your computer. To see a device's properties (drivers, status, and other details), select it in the Devices list and then click Properties.

Tip: To drag an icon with ClickLock turned on, point to the icon, press the left mouse button for the ClickLock interval, release the button, drag the icon to a destination, and then press the button again for the ClickLock interval.

Alternative Mouse Behavior

Windows' alternative mouse setting invokes a weblike interface, letting you open icons by single-clicking—instead of double-clicking, which can be awkward for beginners. (Right-clicking and dragging remain unchanged.)

To open items with a single click:

1   Choose Start > Control Panel > Appearance and Personalization > Folder Options > General tab.

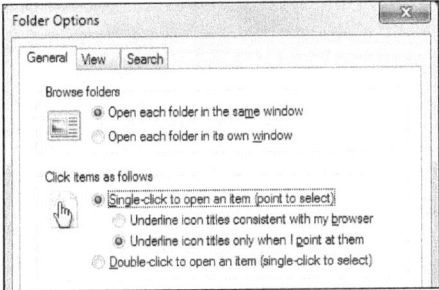

2   Under "Click items as follows", select "Single-click to open an item (point to select)".

3   Choose an option for underlining icon titles: permanent (like links on a webpage) or temporary (only when you point to icons).

4   Click OK (or Apply).

The instructions in this book assume that you use the default mouse behavior, but if you choose the alternative:

•   There's no more double-clicking. To open an icon, click it. To select an icon, move the pointer over it; don't click.

•   To select multiple icons, hold down the Ctrl or Shift key while moving the pointer over each desired icon; again, don't click. Ctrl selects individual icons; Shift selects a range of adjacent icons.

•   To rename an icon, point to it, press F2, type the name, and then press Enter. Or right-click it, choose Rename, type the name, and then press Enter.

Mouse Tips

- Drag an icon or selection with the right mouse button pressed to display a shortcut menu (page 48) when you reach the new location.

- Press Esc during a drag to cancel it.

- Drag in a folder window or on the desktop to draw a rectangular marquee around icons. Releasing the mouse button selects the enclosed icons.

- Fancy mice from Microsoft, Logitech, Kensington, and other manufacturers come with their own driver software. Installing these drivers adds new options and can change some default mouse settings. A cordless mouse may add a tab that indicates remaining battery life, for example. Some drivers add their own Control Panel programs or Start-menu items.

- To configure an alternative pointing device such as a trackpad or pen-input tablet, look for a Control Panel program or Start-menu item devoted to that device.

- To set up a Bluetooth mouse, see "Bluetooth Devices" on page 300.

- To adjust the mouse for mobility impairments, see "Accommodating Disabled Users" on page 145.

- To see a mouse's properties, choose Start > Devices and Printers (or Start > Control Panel > Hardware and Sound > Devices and Printers), and then double-click the mouse's icon. Like all peripherals, mice have properties and drivers that you may want to inspect or update from time to time. See also "Managing Device Drivers" on page 302.

The Keyboard

The keyboard isn't just for typing text. Experienced Windows users use keystrokes instead of the mouse to issue commands. You can also configure the keyboard to suit your typing style.

Keyboard Shortcuts

Keyboard shortcuts save you from moving your hand from keyboard to mouse repeatedly. Windows provides hundreds of keyboard shortcuts that replicate almost every common mouse maneuver. You can use keyboard shortcuts to open, close, and navigate the Start menu, desktop, menus, ribbons, windows, dialog boxes, programs, documents, and webpages. Using a keyboard shortcut is usually faster than using the mouse to do the same thing. In addition to keys for letters, numbers, punctuation, and common symbols, your keyboard has other types of keys:

Modifier keys

Modifier keys alter the meaning of the other key(s) being pressed. They sit in the bottom corners of the keyboard's main section. Press these keys—**Shift**, **Ctrl** (for Control), or **Alt** (for Alternate)—together with other keys to change the action. For example, the C key pressed by itself types a lowercase *c*; pressed along with the Shift key, it types an uppercase C; and pressed along with the Ctrl key, it issues the Copy command. In this book, modifier keys are joined to other keys with a plus sign. Ctrl+C, for example, means "Press the Ctrl key, hold it down while you press the C key, and then release both keys". A three-key combination such as Ctrl+Shift+N means "Hold down the first two keys while you press the third one, and then release all three". The modifiers are always listed first.

Alt behaves a little differently from Shift and Ctrl. Shift or Ctrl does nothing when pressed by itself, but Alt pressed by itself activates the menu bar (page 46) or ribbon (page 50). If you tap Alt accidentally, tap Alt again to get back to normal.

Windows-specific keys

Most PC keyboards have extra Windows-specific keys on either side of the spacebar. Press the **Windows logo key** 🏁 alone to open the Start menu or press it in combination with other keys for other actions (see "Windows Logo Key Shortcuts" on page 232). Pressing the **Application key** 🗐 displays the shortcut menu (page 48) for the selected item (the same as right-clicking).

Function keys

Function keys are the keys along the keyboard's top or left side labeled F1, F2, and so on. Their functions depend on the program that you're using.

Navigation keys

The **navigation keys** move things around and scroll windows. The four **arrow keys** scroll in that direction, move the insertion point (page 37) or selected item(s), or select the adjacent item. **Home** and **End** jump to the start or end of whatever is active: a webpage or document, a list of files in Windows Explorer, the frames of a movie, a series of photos, a line of text, the cells of a table row, and so on. **Page Up** and **Page Down** scroll up or down one page or windowful.

Return and Enter

The **Return key** and the **Enter key** usually do the same thing (typically, inserting a paragraph break or confirming a dialog box).

Backspace and Delete

The **Backspace key** deletes the character or selection *before* the insertion point (page 37). The **Delete key** deletes *after* the insertion point. If an object or a block of text is selected, pressing Backspace or Delete deletes the selection.

Tab

The **Tab key** advances to the next tab stop in a line of text or moves through dialog-box and webpage fields. Shift+Tab jumps backward. Its behavior depends on the context and active program.

Esc (Escape)

The **Escape key**, in the keyboard's upper-left corner, means "Never mind" or "Stop". Press it to close dialog boxes, cancel commands, interrupt long processes, close menus, change modes, or dismiss message boxes. Sometimes Escape does nothing. Its behavior depends on the context and active program.

Eject

Press-and-hold the **Eject key** (if your keyboard has one) to eject a CD or DVD.

Tip: For a list of keyboard shortcuts, choose Start > Help and Support, and then search for keyboard shortcuts. Some keyboard shortcuts are consistent across most programs (F1 for help and Ctrl+C to copy, for example), but programs also define custom shortcuts. Also, some keyboard shortcuts won't work if Sticky Keys is turned on in Ease of Access Center (page 145).

Modifying Mouse Gestures

Modifier keys also work with mouse clicks and drags. To **Shift+click**, for example, hold down Shift and then click before releasing the key. To **Shift+drag**, hold down Shift and then drag and drop before releasing the key. Windows also recognizes **Ctrl+click**, **Alt+click**, **Ctrl+drag**, and **Alt+drag**, which are frequently used in Windows Explorer for file operations.

Configuring the Keyboard

A standard keyboard should work after you plug it in, with no adjustments in software. You can use the Keyboard utility in Control Panel to change settings after installation.

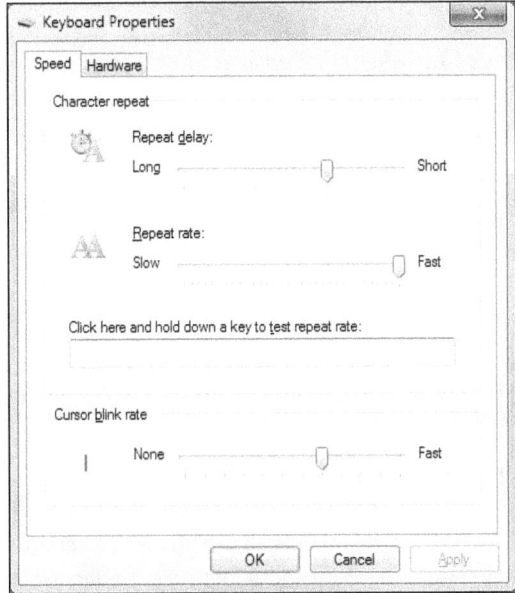

To configure the keyboard:

1   Choose Start > Control Panel, type *keyboard* in the Search Control Panel box, and then select Keyboard in the results list.

    or

    Choose Start > Control Panel, switch to icon view, and then click Keyboard.

2   On the Speed tab, update the following settings.

Repeat delay
Controls the amount of time that elapses before a character begins to repeat when you hold down a key.

Repeat rate
Adjusts how quickly a character repeats when you hold down a key.

Cursor blink rate
Controls the blink rate of the text cursor (insertion point). To stop the cursor from blinking, set the blink rate to None.

Note: The Hardware tab of the Keyboard Properties dialog box lists the keyboards attached to your computer.

Keyboard Tips

- Fancy keyboards from Microsoft, Logitech, Kensington, and other manufacturers come with their own driver software. Installing these drivers adds new options and can change some default keyboard settings. A cordless keyboard may add a tab that indicates remaining battery life, for example. Some drivers add their own Control Panel programs or Start-menu items.

- To set up a Bluetooth keyboard, see "Bluetooth Devices" on page 300.

- To choose an international keyboard layout, see "Localizing Your System" on page 142.

- To adjust the keyboard for mobility impairments, see "Accommodating Disabled Users" on page 145.

- To see a keyboard's properties, choose Start > Devices and Printers (or Start > Control Panel > Hardware and Sound > Devices and Printers), and then double-click the keyboard's icon. Like all peripherals, keyboards have properties and drivers that you may want to inspect or update from time to time. See also "Managing Device Drivers" on page 302.

Menus

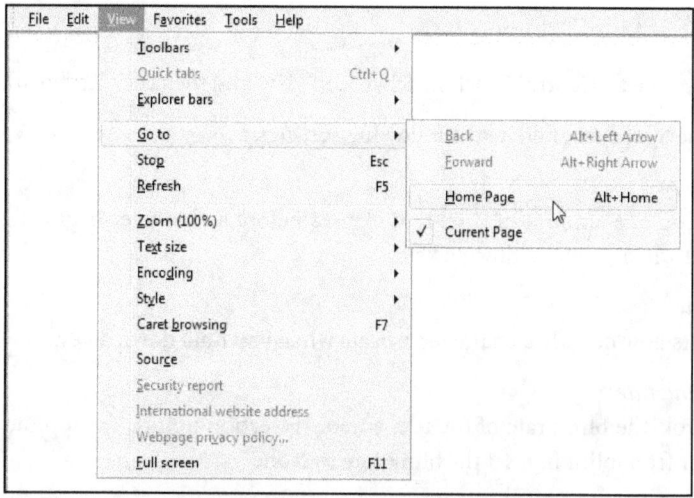

A **menu bar** runs along the top of most program windows (if the menu bar isn't visible, tap the Alt key). The pull-down **menus** in the bar list commands in groups. A command with a ▶ next to it has additional choices listed in a **submenu**. A **checked command** ✓ represents an on/off option or mutually exclusive choice. An **inactive command** is dimmed if it's unavailable in the current context (the Copy command is unavailable if nothing is selected, for example) or you lack the administrative privileges (page 8) to invoke that command.

Tip: A program that has a ribbon (page 50) has no menu bar.

To choose a menu command, click the menu name, point to the desired menu command, and then click to choose the command. Most commands take effect as soon as you choose them. A command followed by an **ellipsis** (...) opens a dialog box because it needs more information to complete (the Find command, for example, has an ellipsis because it needs to know what to find). Some commands, such as Properties and Help > About, show a dialog box but have no ellipsis because no more information is needed to run that command.

Some menus are consistent across programs. The File menu almost always has the commands New, Open, Save, Save As, Print, and Exit; the Edit menu has the commands Undo, Cut, Copy, and Paste.

Tip: If you're a Mac user, note that OS X has only one menu bar that runs along the top of the desktop screen (and changes with the active program), whereas Windows places a separate menu bar in each window.

Menu Keyboarding

Experienced users prefer to use keyboard shortcuts (page 42) instead of the mouse to choose menu commands. Programs often provide a keyboard shortcut for a frequently used command, which appears to the right of the command on its menu line. To choose Copy, for example, press Ctrl+C.

If no shortcut key is listed for a command, you can still use the keyboard to choose it: hold down the Alt key, press the underlined letter in the menu name, and then release both keys (in some programs, the underlines or menu bar won't appear until you tap Alt). On the keyboard, press the underlined letter of a menu command. If a submenu appears, press the underlined letter of a submenu command. If two or more menu commands have the same under-lined letter, press the letter repeatedly until you select the right command, and then press Enter. (To close a menu without choosing a command, press Esc twice or click outside the menu.)

Another way to use the keyboard: press F10 or Alt (by itself) to activate the menu bar, use the arrow keys to navigate to a command, and then press Enter.

Tip: To always display underlines in dialog boxes and other windows, choose Start > Control Panel > Ease of Access > Ease of Access Center > "Make the keyboard easier to use" > select "Underline keyboard shortcuts and access keys".

Shortcut Menus

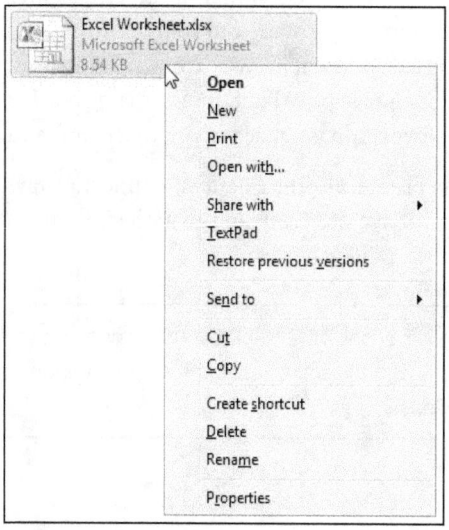

A **shortcut menu** (also called a **right-click menu** or **context menu**) is a context-sensitive menu that appears when you right-click an item or selection. Shortcut menus offer common commands quickly and Windows provides them for almost everything: icons, files, folders, drives, devices, Start-menu items, and so on. Commands apply to only the item (or group of items) to which you point. Shortcut menus are among the most useful features in Windows. Try right-clicking any item to see whether a shortcut menu pops up. If multiple icons are selected, right-click any one of them to open the shortcut menu for the group. Programs have custom shortcut menus: right-click a link in

Internet Explorer or Firefox, selected text in Notepad or Microsoft Word, or a photo in Photo Gallery or Adobe Photoshop. Right-click a window's title bar or Shift+right-click a taskbar button to open the control menu (sizing menu) for that window.

You can also choose a shortcut-menu command by using the keyboard: select (highlight) an item, press the Application key ▤ (or press Shift+F10), and then press the underlined letter of a menu command (or use the arrow keys to navigate to a command and then press Enter). Some shortcut menus have a default command in boldface; you can press Enter to choose this command.

To close a shortcut menu without choosing a command, press Esc or left-click off the menu. (Right-clicking off the menu only makes the menu jump to the pointer.)

Editing Shortcut Menus

Utilities, shareware, and other programs often add their own entries to shortcut menus with or without your permission. If a shortcut menu gets too crowded, you usually can remove items via the programs' Options or Preferences dialog boxes; look for options labeled *context menu* or *Explorer integration*. WinZip, for example, adds commands (such as Add to Zip) to Windows Explorer's shortcut menus. WinZip's Option > Configuration > Explorer Enhancements tab lets you show or hide these commands.

If no context-menu option is available, you can edit the registry (page 357). Many context-menu commands are in *HKEY_CLASSES_ROOT\Directory\ shell* and *HKEY_CLASSES_ROOT\Folder\shell*. Double-click shell to reveal the keys corresponding to each menu command. (You won't see and can't remove Windows' built-in commands.) Delete the keys that you don't want.

In some cases, the keys are hidden elsewhere in *HKEY_CLASSES_ROOT*, and you'll have to hunt for the program's key (sometimes tricky—*Adobe.Acrobat. ContextMenu*, for example) or choose Edit > Find to find the menu-item text (*Scan for Viruses* or whatever). For instructions, see the software publisher's website or search the web by using the terms *context menu, registry*, and the name of the program. Sometimes no keys are available, and you must live with the custom menu item. In Registry Editor, choose File > Export to back up the registry before you edit it.

Menu Buttons

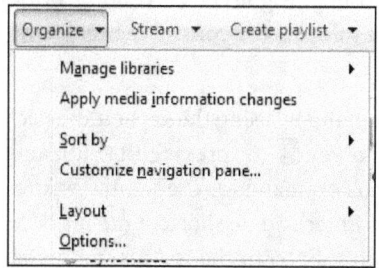

A **menu button** looks like an ordinary button except that it has a menu drop-down arrow ▼ within it. In some cases, clicking the button reveals a menu. In others, hovering the pointer "splits" the button into two parts: a larger part that runs the main command and a smaller one (with the drop-down arrow) that shows a small menu of related commands and options. Some panes have buttons and links that display menus within the pane.

Ribbons

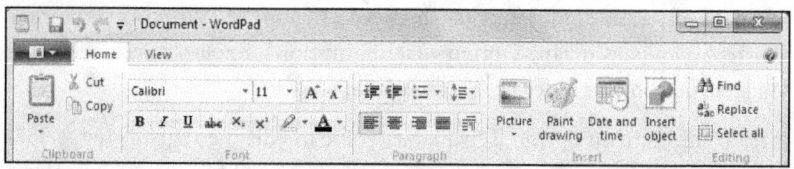

Ribbons replace traditional menus and toolbars, making it easier to find commands that previously were buried in the interface. A ribbon is organized as a set of tabs that exposes many more commands than the older system of menus, toolbars, task panes, and dialog boxes. A few Windows programs and most of the applications in Microsoft Office 2007 and later have ribbons.

To choose a ribbon command by using the keyboard, tap the Alt key and then press the letter or number keys that appear on the ribbon, or use the arrow and Tab keys to navigate.

Toolbars

A **toolbar** is a row, column, or block of buttons with icons that you click to perform some action, choose a tool, or change a setting. Toolbar buttons often duplicate common menu commands, but they're more convenient because they're always visible—generally at one edge of the work area. Hover the pointer over a button for a pop-up help tag (called a **tooltip**).

Programs typically have several toolbars, each responsible for a group of tasks. In a word processor, for example, there's one toolbar for formatting text and paragraphs, and there's another for performing file operations. Toolbars can appear and disappear automatically, depending on what you're doing in the program.

A toolbar button with a small triangular arrow pointing right ▶ or down ▼ is a menu button: click the arrow to reveal a small, self-contained menu. Some toolbars have toggle buttons that push in (turn on) with one click and pop out (turn off) with the next. They can set global options or conditions that apply to only the current selection.

Often, you can customize toolbars, create new ones, and move them around onscreen to suit your preferences. Experiment. Right-click a toolbar to see whether a shortcut menu appears. Click-and-hold an empty area of a toolbar (usually its left side), and then try dragging to dock it at an edge of the window or just let it float in the middle.

Icons

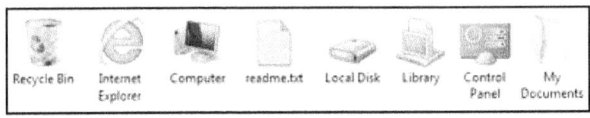

An **icon** is a small picture that represents an item you can manipulate. Windows uses icons on the desktop and in folders to represent folders, files, drives, documents, programs, searches, the Recycle Bin, and hardware devices. An icon's image depends on what it represents. System objects such as Computer, Control Panel, and the Recycle Bin have default images. All documents of the same type—text (.txt) files, for example—have the same icon. Program (.exe) files such as Internet Explorer have icons that the software publisher built into the program.

You select (highlight) an icon or group of icons to perform an action. Click to select; right-click to open a shortcut menu (page 48); drag to move or copy; or double-click to open.

What happens when you open an icon depends on the icon's type:

- A folder, drive, network server, removable-storage, or portable-device icon opens in a Windows Explorer window (page 170).

- A document, picture, video, or music icon opens in its associated program, launching that program if it's not already open.

- A program icon launches the program.

- A saved search icon (page 223) searches your computer and lists all files that match what you're looking for.

- A library icon (page 224) shows the aggregated contents of its locations.

- The Recycle Bin icon (page 203) shows the items to be deleted when you empty it.

Tip: In Windows Explorer it's easiest to work with multiple icons in Details, List, or Content view, in which all icons appear in columns. Click ▦ ▾ on the toolbar to change the view. To sort icons in Details view, click the column headings (Name, Date modified, Type, Size, and so on).

Selecting Icons

You have various ways to select single or multiple icons by using the mouse or keyboard.

To select an icon: Do one of the following: Click it. • Press the arrow keys until the icon is selected. • Press the first letter of the icon's name; if two or more icons have the same initial letter, press that letter repeatedly until you select the right icon. (To configure Windows to select an icon just by pointing at it, see "Alternative Mouse Behavior" on page 41.)

To select multiple icons: Do one of the following: Ctrl+click each icon to select it. • Starting from an empty area, drag a selection rectangle diagonally around the icons. • Click the first icon that you want to select, and then Shift+click the last icon (all icons in between are selected automatically).

To extend a previous selection: Normally, selecting icons deselects any previously selected icons. To keep these icons selected, press Ctrl or Shift when you make a new selection.

To select all icons in a window: Do one of the following: Choose Organize > Select All (on the toolbar). • Choose Edit > Select All (on the menu bar). • Press Ctrl+A.

To select almost all icons in a window: Press Ctrl+A and then Ctrl+click each icon that you *don't* want.

To reverse which icons are selected and which are not: Choose Edit > Invert Selection (or tap Alt, E, I).

To deselect icons: To deselect all icons, click anywhere in the window or desktop other than a selected icon. To deselect a specific icon in a multiple selection, Ctrl+click it.

To select or deselect icons by using checkboxes: Choose Start > Control Panel > Appearance and Personalization > Folder Options > View tab > select "Use check boxes to select items". Checkboxes appear when you hover the pointer over an icon. To select all the icons, select the box in the Name column heading (in Details view).

Moving Icons

To move an icon, drag it to a new position in the window or on the desktop. You can move multiple icons at the same time by dragging any icon in a multiple selection. You can't drag icons to new positions within a sorted folder window. See also "Moving and Copying Files and Folders" on page 198.

Opening Icons

To open an icon, double-click it (or select it and then press Enter). To open multiple icons of the same type at the same time, select the icons and then press Enter (or right-click one of the selected icons and then choose Open). To open a document or picture with something besides its associated (default) program, right-click its icon and then choose Open With. (To configure Windows to open an icon with a single click, see "Alternative Mouse Behavior" on page 41.) See also "Launching Programs" on page 242 and "Opening Documents" on page 252.

Windows

The Windows interface takes its trademark name from the rectangles on your screen—the **windows**—in which you work. Windows lets you work multiple overlapping windows so that you can, say, alternate working with a word processor, email program, and web browser. Each window has its own boundaries and can present different views of its contents.

In a window for an application (such as Internet Explorer, Word, or Photoshop), you identify the window by its **title bar**, which lists the name of the program and the current document.

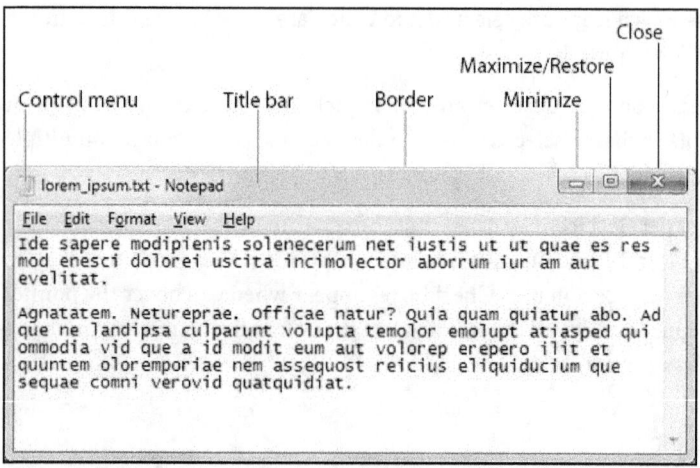

In a folder (page 170) or library (page 224) window (such as Documents or Control Panel), the title bar is blank, and the **address bar** displays the current location as a series of links separated by arrows. The control menu is still there, invisible, in the top-left corner.

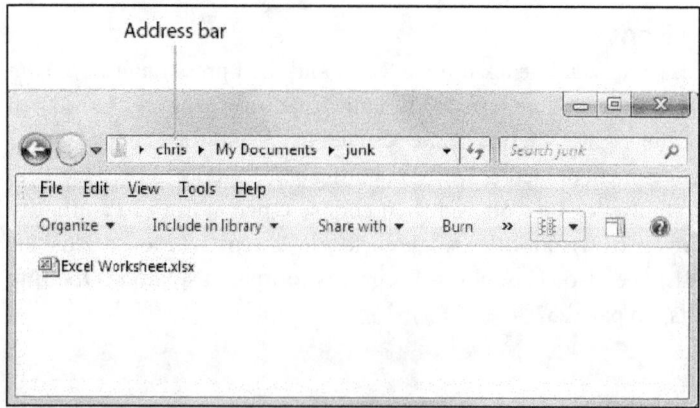

Note: Windows don't *have* to be rectangular. Gadgets (page 106) come in many shapes, and some applications (Windows Media Player, for example) let you apply odd-shaped "skins".

Activating Windows

When multiple windows are open, only one is active at any time. The **active window** is the one that receives your keystrokes (text entry, navigational movements, or commands). You can identify the active window by its darker title bar, borders, and shadow. The edges of inactive windows have a washed-out color. An inactive window can be hidden behind other windows and remains inactive until you bring it to the foreground.

To activate a window:

• Click anywhere on the window (but don't click a button or menu lest you activate it accidentally).

or

Point to the taskbar button of the window's parent application and then click the thumbnail image of the window when it appears above the button. If only one window is open, you can click the taskbar button itself. The pop-up list of thumbnails shows live images of a program's open windows. Point to a thumbnail to peek at its full-size version on the desktop. If you've changed the taskbar's default behavior, each open window will have its own taskbar button.

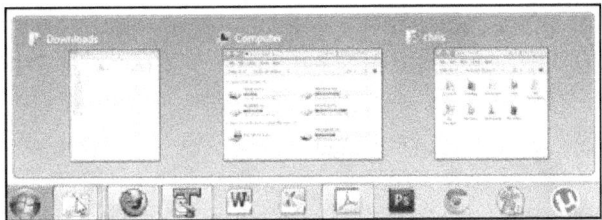

or

Hold down Alt, press Esc repeatedly until the desired window appears, and then release both keys.

or

Hold down Alt, press Tab repeatedly until the desired window icon is highlighted in the pop-up selection bar, and then release both keys. (This common technique is called **Alt-tabbing**.)

or

Hold down the Windows logo key, press Tab repeatedly until the desired program window appears, and then release both keys.

or

To cycle through the windows (or tabs) of a particular application, Ctrl+click its taskbar icon.

Programs whose windows are inactive can still carry out tasks—called **background tasks**—such as downloading files or printing documents. *Inactive* means that *you* are ignoring the window, but Windows still gives it the resources to do its job.

Generally, the active window is in front of all other windows. But some windows, such as Task Manager and Help, can be set to stay on top—in the foreground—even when inactive.

See also "Managing Windows by Using the Taskbar" on page 95 and "Switching Programs" on page 246.

Resizing Windows

To change the size of a window, you can:

- **Maximize** a window to the size of your whole screen. A maximized window reduces the need for scrolling but hides other windows. When a window is maximized, its Maximize button changes to the Restore button.

- **Minimize** it to a button on the taskbar (page 94). A minimized window reduces screen clutter and reveals other windows hidden behind it. Depending on your taskbar settings, a minimized window has its own labeled button or, by default, is combined with other windows of the same type in a single program button.

- **Restore** it to a free-floating rectangle on your desktop. You can resize or move a restored window to work with multiple windows conveniently. When a window is restored, its Restore button changes to the Maximize button.

- **Vertically maximize** a window from top to bottom only (its width stays the same). A vertically maximized window is useful for reading email or webpages on a high-resolution or widescreen display when your eye can't track a line of text all the way across the screen.

- **Dock** a window to occupy the left or right half of the screen. Tiling two windows to fill the left and right halves of the screen makes side-by-side operations easier. You can drag-and-drop between the windows, for example, or compare two documents.

Note: Some utility programs, such as Calculator, can't be maximized or resized.

To resize a window:

- Drag any window border (side or corner). The pointer changes to a double-headed arrow when it's moved over a border.

  or

  Activate the window, press Alt+spacebar, press S, use the arrow keys to resize the window, and then press Enter. (Hold down Ctrl to make the arrow keys resize in fine increments.)

  or

  To resize a window to fill half the screen, drag its title bar to the screen's left or right edge until you see the resize animation. Keyboard shortcut: Windows logo key+left (or right) arrow.

To maximize a window:

- If the window is minimized, Shift+right-click its taskbar button and then choose Maximize from the window's control menu. (If no window is open, the program's shortcut menu opens instead.) You can also right-click a graphic thumbnail in a taskbar pop-up list to open a window's control menu.

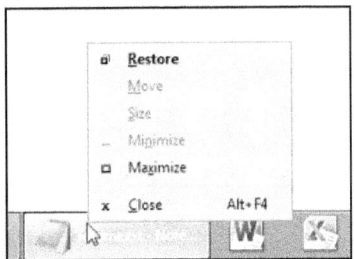

or

If the window is restored, click its Maximize button or double-click its title bar.

or

If the window is restored, activate it, press Alt+spacebar, and then press X.

or

Drag its title bar to the screen's top edge until you see the maximize animation. Keyboard shortcut: Windows logo key+up arrow.

or

To maximize a window vertically, move the pointer over the window's top (or bottom) edge; when it becomes a double-headed arrow, drag up (or down) to the screen's edge until you see the maximize animation. Keyboard shortcut: Shift+Windows logo key+up (or down) arrow.

To minimize a window:

- Click its Minimize button. Keyboard shortcut: Windows logo key+down arrow (you may have to tap the down arrow twice).

or

Activate the window, press Alt+spacebar, and then press N.

or

To minimize all windows, click the Show Desktop button ▌ at the right edge of the taskbar. Click it again to restore the windows. Keyboard shortcut: Windows logo key+D.

or

To peek briefly at the desktop without minimizing windows, point to (don't click) the Show Desktop button ▌ at the right edge of the taskbar. Keyboard shortcut: Windows logo key+spacebar (press and hold).

or

To minimize all windows but one, click and hold a window's title bar, and then shake the mouse left and right a few times. Shake it again to restore the minimized windows. Keyboard shortcut: Windows logo key+Home.

To restore a window:

- Shift+right-click its taskbar button and then choose Restore.

  or

  If the window is maximized, click its Restore button or double-click its title bar.

  or

  If the window is maximized, press Alt+spacebar and then press R.

  or

  Drag its title bar away from the edge of the screen until the window autorestores. Keyboard shortcut: Windows logo key+any arrow key.

Tip: To prevent windows from resizing when they're dragged, choose Start > Control Panel > Ease of Access > Ease of Access Center > "Make the mouse easier to use" > select "Prevent windows from being automatically arranged when moved to the edge of the screen". This setting lets you move a window so that it lies almost completely off any screen edge.

Moving Windows

You can move windows by using the mouse or keyboard.

To move a window:

- Drag its title bar.

  or

  Activate the window, press Alt+spacebar, press M, use the arrow keys to move the window, and then press Enter. (Hold down Ctrl to make the arrow keys move in fine increments.)

  or

  If you have multiple displays, press Shift+Windows logo key+left (or right) arrow to move the active window from screen to screen. (To move a maximized window, drag it down by its title bar, move it over to another screen, and then snap it to the top, all in one motion.)

Tip: The title bar provides convenient ways to move or resize a window: drag it within the desktop to move the window, drag it to or away from a screen edge to autoresize the window, double-click it to alternate between restored and maximized states, or right-click it (or left-click near the left corner) to show the control menu.

Closing Windows

When you close a document window, you're prompted to save any unsaved work.

To close a window:

* Click its Close button [X].

    or

    Point to (don't click) the taskbar button of the window's parent application, move the pointer over the thumbnail image of the window when it appears above the button, and then click the thumbnail's Close button [X]. (The Close button doesn't appear until you hover the pointer over a thumbnail.)

    or

    Right-click its taskbar button and then choose Close Window or Close All Windows.

    or

    Shift+right-click its taskbar button and then choose Close or Close All Windows.

    or

    Right-click its title bar and then choose Close from the control menu.

    or

    Double-click the icon or an empty area at the left edge of the title bar.

    or

    Activate the window and then press Alt+F4 (to close the program) or Ctrl+F4 (to close the active document but leave the program running).

    or

    Activate the window, press Alt+spacebar, and then press C.

or

Choose File > Close (or tap Alt, F, C) to close the file or File > Exit (Alt, F, X) to quit the application, whichever is appropriate. (This distinction between Close and Exit isn't consistent across programs.)

Tip: The desktop itself is a window open under all other windows; you "close" it by logging off or shutting down. Pressing Alt+F4 when the desktop is active displays the Shut Down Windows dialog box.

Scrolling

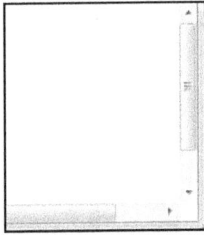

A window that's too small to show all its contents displays scrollbars. A **scrollbar** is a vertical or horizontal bar at the side or bottom of a window used to slide that window's contents around. Drag the **scroll box** to move to an arbitrary location, or click an empty area in the scrollbar **shaft** (the long, narrow background in which the scroll box travels) to jump by one windowful at a time (like pressing Page Up or Page Down). Click the **scroll arrows** at the ends of scrollbars to move contents incrementally (like pressing an arrow key or spinning the mouse wheel). The size of a scroll box is proportional to the fraction of the window contents displayed, so the scroll box indicates visually how much you *can't* see, as well as showing you where you are.

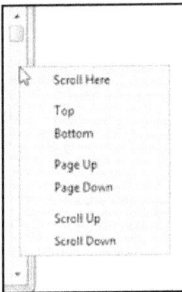

You can right-click anywhere on a scrollbar to show a navigation shortcut menu that makes it easy to jump long distances.

In many programs you can press Ctrl+Home and Ctrl+End to go to a document's beginning or end. Holding down the mouse button on a scroll arrow or shaft autorepeats the scrolling behavior. (If you lean on the shaft for more than a few seconds, Windows can lose track of video memory, and the window contents will appear distorted or sliced up before Windows recovers.)

Many programs scroll automatically in common situations. Dragging or extending a selection of text or graphics near a window's edge autoscrolls in the direction of the drag, often at a speed proportional to how far past the edge you drag. Tabbing to a text box or typing in a partially hidden text box autoscrolls a form to reveal the whole box. Using Find, Go To, or a similar command autoscrolls to show the matching selection or new cursor location.

Tip: You can use the Scroll Lock key for keyboard scrolling. When Scroll Lock is toggled on (its keyboard indicator is lit) and you press a navigation key, some programs scroll the view without affecting the cursor or selection.

Dialog Boxes & Controls

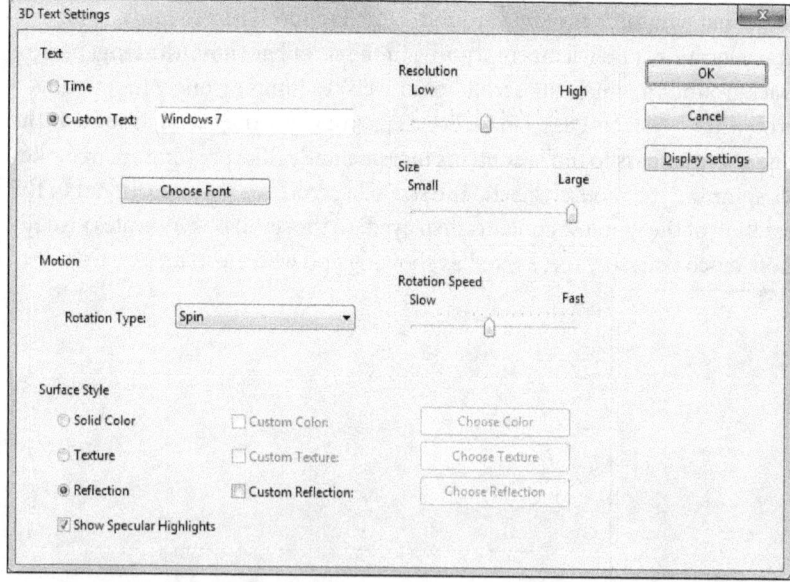

A **dialog box** is a small temporary window that a program opens to respond to a command or event. **Controls** let you enter new content or view or change existing settings. The common controls in dialog boxes and other parts of the user interface include:

- *Radio buttons* ⊙◯ choose one of several mutually exclusive options.

- *Checkboxes* ☑☐ turn options on or off.

- *Drop-down lists* [Spin ▾] select one option from a list.

- *Sliders* ◌ set a value in a restricted range.

- *Buttons* [OK] are labeled by actions (pressing Enter "clicks" the button with the thicker border or shadow).

- Clicking a command or button that has an *ellipsis* (…) [Settings…] makes a dialog box appear.

- *Text boxes* [Text] contain typed or pasted (input) text. When you edit text, you can't use a menu or ribbon to Cut, Copy, Paste, Undo, and Select All but you can use keyboard shortcuts (Ctrl+X, Ctrl+C, Ctrl+V, Ctrl+Z, and Ctrl+A, respectively) or right-click to use a shortcut menu.

- *Tabs* [Date and Time][Additional Clocks][Internet Time] show individual pages within a dialog box.

When a control is dimmed, it's unavailable in the current context or you lack the administrative privileges to use it. Some open dialog boxes (called **modal windows**) won't let you keep working in their program until you close them. You still can use other programs, though.

OK, Cancel, and Apply Buttons

Most dialog boxes have an OK button and a Cancel button, and many have an Apply button too. Clicking **OK** saves your changes and closes the dialog box (often equivalent to pressing Enter). Clicking **Cancel** discards your changes and closes the dialog box (equivalent to pressing Esc). Clicking **Apply** saves your changes and leaves the dialog box open for more changes (handy if you want to try out a change with the chance to change it right back).

The Apply button's behavior has a slight wrinkle: if you click Apply and then click Cancel, changes made before you click Apply are saved, but changes made after you click Apply are lost—usually, that is. Some programs behave differently.

Dialog-Box Keyboard Shortcuts

You can use keyboard shortcuts (page 42) to navigate dialog boxes quickly.

To	Press
Select the next tab	Ctrl+Tab
Select the previous tab	Ctrl+Shift+Tab
Select the next option	Tab
Select the previous option	Shift+Tab
Select the corresponding option or click the corresponding button	Alt+underlined letter
Click a button, toggle a checkbox, or choose an option button (if that option is active)	Spacebar
Select an item in an option-button group or list, or move a slider	Arrow keys
Display Help	F1
Display drop-down list items	F4
Click the selected button (with the dotted outline) or the default button (with the thicker border or shadow)	Enter
Click the Cancel button	Esc

Specialized Dialog Boxes

- The standard Open (page 252) and Save (page 250) dialog boxes (for opening and saving files) are resizable, to let you vary the number of files that they display. Most other dialog boxes aren't resizable.

- Windows uses a **message box** to notify you of events or ask for a decision. Message boxes bring your program to a halt. You must respond before the program can do anything further.

- A **wizard** is a series of interactive dialog boxes that steps you through a complex task. The purpose of each wizard page is stated at the top. Many pages have links that you can click for help. The Back button is in the top-left corner.

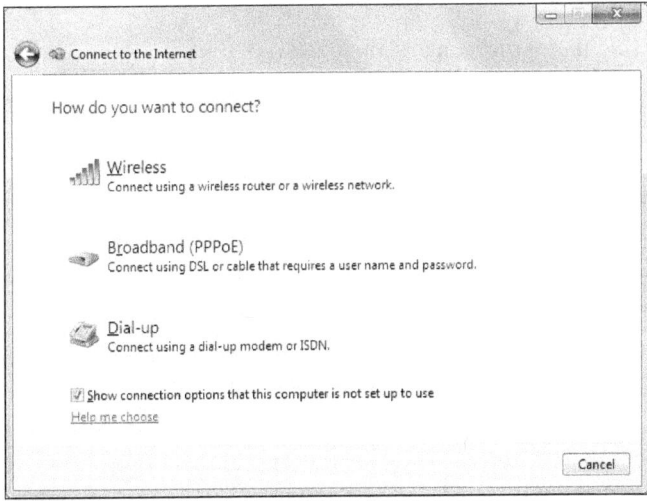

Properties

Almost every item (icon) has a **Properties** dialog box full of information, called **metadata**, about its contents and settings. The attributes shown are appropriate for the item selected. The Properties dialog box for a drive shows capacity statistics, for example; for a file or folder, it shows creation and modification dates.

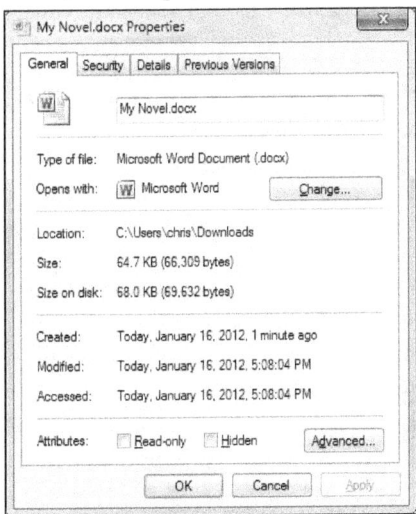

To show an item's properties:

- Right-click the item and then choose Properties. (The Properties command is usually at the bottom of the shortcut menu.)

  or

  Select (highlight) the item and then press Alt+Enter.

  or

  Hold down Alt and then double-click the item.

Windows lets you change some properties; you can rename the file or compress the hard drive, for example. Many properties are **read-only**, however, meaning that Windows sets them and you can't change them. You can inspect—but not change—a hard drive's capacity or a file's creation date, for example.

A read-only property usually is shown as black text on a plain background; a modifiable (read–write) property is set in a text box, checkbox, drop-down list, or similar control. If it's not obvious whether you can change a property, try to click it or tab to it. You can copy the text of some read-only properties by dragging across the text to select it and pressing Ctrl+C. Paste it somewhere with Ctrl+V.

Properties Tips

- To see a few basic properties without opening the Properties dialog box, point to (don't click) an icon to display a pop-up info window, or open the Details pane in any folder window (Organize > Layout > "Details pane") and then click an icon.

- To open Computer properties quickly, right-click Computer on the Start menu and then choose Properties. The terser classic System Properties dialog box appears when you click "Advanced system settings" in Computer properties.

- To change the picture of a folder or shortcut icon, open its Properties dialog box, click the Customize tab (for a folder) or the Shortcut tab (for a shortcut), and then click Change Icon. Choose a new picture from the list or click Browse to hunt for more. You can find icons embedded in program (.exe) and .dll files, download them from the internet, or create them yourself with freeware or shareware (search the web for *create icons*). When you're done, click OK in each open dialog box. (This trick doesn't work for document or system-folder icons.)

- Some dialog boxes have a button labeled Restore, Restore Defaults, Defaults, or Reset. Clicking this button changes your current settings back to Windows' factory-installed settings. Be careful, because you (or the programs that you've installed) probably have made more changes than you remember—or even know about.

- Some programs let you add file properties such as comments and custom name-value attributes. In a Microsoft Office document, for example, choose File tab > Info > Properties > Advanced Properties > Custom tab. See also "Tagging Files" on page 183.

- To see how much drive space a group of files or folders occupies, select the files' or folders' icons (page 52) and then display the properties for the selected group.

Transferring Content

Windows gives you a few ways to move data around: copy webpage text to an email message, put photos in a word-processing document, embed charts and graphics in reports and slides, move paragraphs around in a text file, export spreadsheet rows to a database, and so on.

Cut, Copy, and Paste

Cut, copy, and paste are used to organize documents, folders, and drives. **Cut-and-paste** removes (cuts) content and places it on the clipboard so that it can be moved (pasted) elsewhere. Cutting deletes the content from its original location. **Copy-and-paste** copies content to the clipboard so that it can be duplicated (pasted) elsewhere. Copying leaves the original content intact (nothing visible happens when you copy).

The **clipboard** is the invisible area of memory where Windows stores cut or copied content, where it remains until it's overwritten when you cut or copy something else. This scheme lets you paste the same thing multiple times in different places. You can transfer content from one program to another provided that the second program can read content generated by the first. A little experimenting shows that you often can combine dissimilar content; you can paste text from Notepad into Photoshop, for example. You can't paste something that you've **deleted** or **cleared** (as opposed to cut), because Windows doesn't place the deleted item on the clipboard.

The Cut, Copy, and Paste commands are in a program's Edit menu or Home tab, but each program may handle these operations differently. In Windows Explorer, for example, you can copy files and folders from one drive or folder to another. In Word, you can copy or move text or graphics to another part of a document or to a different document. In a browser, you can only copy material from webpages, not cut it. If nothing is selected, the Cut and Copy commands are unavailable (dimmed).

Edit	Format	View	Help
Undo			Ctrl+Z
Cut			Ctrl+X
Copy			Ctrl+C
Paste			Ctrl+V

To cut: Select (highlight) the content to remove, and then choose Edit > Cut (Ctrl+X), or right-click the selection and then choose Cut.

To copy: Select (highlight) the content to copy, and then choose Edit > Copy (Ctrl+C), or right-click the selection and then choose Copy.

To paste: Click the mouse (or move the cursor to) where you want the content to appear, and then choose Edit > Paste (Ctrl+V), or right-click and then choose Paste.

To undo a cut or paste: Immediately choose Edit > Undo (Ctrl+Z).

You might lose formatting (font size, style, color, typeface, and so on) when you paste text from one program to another, for the following reasons:

- The source program doesn't support formatting. Copying text from text editors (Notepad, for example) or early versions of web browsers won't pick up formatting along with the text.

- The target program doesn't support formatting. Text editors and email messages set to Plain Text (rather than HTML) won't show formatting of pasted text.

- You didn't pick up the formatting when you copied the text. In Microsoft Word and other word processors, an invisible symbol (¶) at the end of each paragraph contains that paragraph's formatting information. You must copy the symbol along with the text to carry the formatting; otherwise, the pasted text will take on the formatting of the target. To view invisible symbols in Word, press Ctrl+Shift+* (asterisk).

Many programs have an Edit > Paste Special command that pastes, links, or embeds the clipboard contents in a document in the format you specify. The Paste Special command in Word, for example, lets you strip all formatting from pasted text, for example.

Drag-and-Drop

WordPad, Windows Mail, Microsoft Office, and many other programs let you drag-and-drop as a faster alternative to cut-and-paste: click-and-hold in the middle of some highlighted content, and then drag it elsewhere within the same document or to a different window or program. (This technique doesn't involve the clipboard and won't change its contents.) You can press the Ctrl key as you drag to copy, rather than move, the content. When you drag highlighted content near the window's edge, the document autoscrolls until you move away from the edge.

Intermediate Formats

Another way to exchange data between programs is to save it in a format that both the source and target programs can read and write. To read a list of addresses into a mailing-list program from a spreadsheet or database, for example, save the addresses in a CSV-format file (a text file of comma-separated values), and then open it in the mailing-list program. The source program's Save dialog box lists the format types that you can save. The target program usually autoconverts the CSV file when you open it with File > Open, but you may have to step through a wizard to organize the incoming data. Image-editing programs such as Photoshop and Microsoft Paint can exchange files in JPEG, GIF, TIFF, PNG and other popular graphic formats.

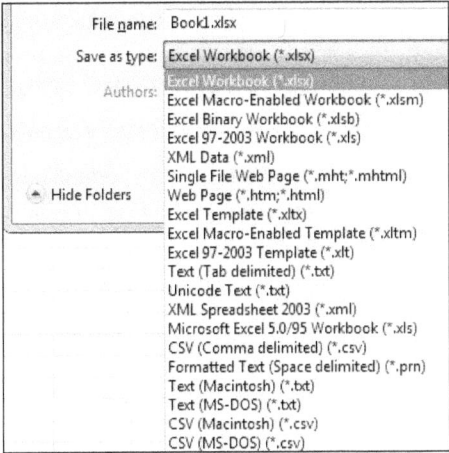

Import/Export

Use import and export tools to transfer large amounts of data or data in incompatible formats. Most address-book, browser, email, office-suite, and database programs have Import and Export commands, typically in the File menu. The commands vary by program (they're not part of Windows), so read the documentation for both the source and target programs. Import/export operations can be routine—most database and accounting programs can skip the CSV step and export to the native Excel format directly, for example—but they're superlative when no standard exchange-format exists. If you want to try new email and browser programs, then import/export is the only practical way to transfer all your addresses, messages, bookmarks, cookies, and other content. Choosing File > Import in Mozilla Firefox, for example, lets you import browser settings and bookmarks from Internet Explorer.

OLE

OLE (pronounced *oh-lay*), for **Object Linking and Embedding**, lets you insert self-updating content from a source document in one program into a target document running in another. If you insert an Excel spreadsheet as a linked object into a Word document, for example, any changes that you make to the spreadsheet separately in Excel appear in the Word document automatically. To insert an OLE object, choose Insert > Object in a program that supports OLE (Word, Excel, or PowerPoint, for example). In the Object dialog box, you can insert a new object or an existing file. Select "Link to file" if you want the data to self-update when the source file is edited. The Result box explains the inserted object's behavior.

You can cut, copy, and paste OLE objects. To delete one, click it and then press Delete. To edit an OLE object, double-click it. If it's linked to a document, the document opens in its own window. If it's not linked, the source program's menus appear in place of the current program's menus; click off the object or press Esc when you're done editing, and the original menus reappear.

After editing a linked object, you may have to "encourage" it to update itself. Select it, and then use the program's Update command (the F9 key in Microsoft Office programs).

Getting Help

Windows **Help and Support** (Help for short) lets you access standard documentation, tutorials, troubleshooting guides, and Windows Help websites. To open Help and Support, choose Start > Help and Support (or press Windows logo key+F1). If the desktop is active, press F1. You navigate Help and Support by using weblike buttons, icons, links, and searches. The Help toolbar always is visible at the top of the window. Hover the pointer over a toolbar button for a pop-up tip.

To search for help topics, type or paste a search phrase (one or more keywords) in the Search box and then press Enter or click the magnifying glass. If your search phrase contains multiple words, Help searches for topics that contain all the words. A search for *keyboard shortcuts*, for example, yields pages that contain *keyboard* and *shortcuts*, though not necessarily adjacent in the text.

To find an exact phrase, enclose it in quotes (*"keyboard shortcuts"*). Searches include common synonyms: the search phrases *erase file* and *delete file* and *remove file*, for example, all return similar results (the official term is *delete*). Help handles some misspelled keywords, and ignores noise words like *a*, *the*, *of*, *from*, and so on. Search terms aren't case sensitive.

Tip: Search for *troubleshoot* to see a list of topics that help you identify and resolve hardware, software, and networking problems.

Help Keyboard Shortcuts

You can use keyboard shortcuts (page 42) to navigate Help quickly.

To	Press
Show the customer support page	Alt+A
Show the table of contents	Alt+C
Show the Connection Settings menu	Alt+N
Show the Options menu	Alt+O or F10
Move back to the previously viewed topic	Alt+left arrow
Move forward to the next previously viewed topic	Alt+right arrow
Show the home page	Alt+Home
Go to the beginning of the current topic	Home
Go to the end of the current topic	End
Select all the text of the current topic	Ctrl+A
Copy the selected text of the current topic	Ctrl+C
Search the current topic	Ctrl+F
Print the current topic	Ctrl+P
Move to the Search box	F3

Getting Help from the Web

You can get Windows help from several websites:

Windows Online Help and Support
An online version of Help and Support, plus instructional videos, articles, and other odds and ends. Go to *windowshelp.microsoft.com*.

Microsoft Support
A collection of solutions to common problems, how-to topics, troubleshooting steps, and the latest downloads. Go to *support.microsoft.com*.

Microsoft Answers
Lets you ask questions and search for answers to previously asked questions. Go to *answers.microsoft.com*.

Microsoft Knowledge Base
A huge searchable database of articles with detailed solutions to specific problems and computer errors. Go to *support.microsoft.com/kb/242450*.

Microsoft TechNet
A resource for technical professionals. Go to *technet.microsoft.com* and then click the link for your version of Windows.

Google
A general search engine that often indexes Windows pages, articles, and help topics better than Microsoft does. Go to *google.com*.

Tip: Click the Ask button on the Help and Support toolbar to see which support options apply to your computer.

Remote Assistance

Remote Assistance lets you invite a friend or technical helper—anyone you trust who's running Windows XP or later, or Windows Server 2003 or later—to help you by connecting to your computer over the internet or a network. That person can swap messages with you, view your screen, or (with your permission) use his mouse and keyboard to control your computer. All sessions are encrypted and password protected. Remote Assistance relieves novices of having to explain problems in jargon they haven't learned, and lets helpers cut the chatter and work on the novice's machine directly. Helpers can even install software, update hardware drivers, and edit the registry.

Like all remote-control technologies, Remote Assistance has security implications beyond the ordinary issues of strong passwords and firewalls. When you invite someone to take control of your computer, you must balance your trust with others' inclinations toward malice. That person is free not only to fix your problem, but also to, say, erase your hard drive or steal your files. You can view everything he's doing onscreen, and if you don't like what you see, press Esc or click Cancel to break the connection immediately. Still, damage done in a moment can take ages to undo. Even if that person can't control your computer, you could follow his bad advice and delete critical files or turn off security features yourself. Furthermore, you may not be able to confirm the identity of the other person.

Before starting a Remote Assistance session, set invitation and time limits. Choose Start > Control Panel > System and Security > System > "Remote settings" (on the left) > Remote tab. If necessary, select "Allow Remote Assistance connections to this computer". Click Advanced and then set the remote-control and invitations options.

In a Remote Assistance session, the two connected parties—the novice and the helper—must be on the same local area network (LAN) or have active internet connections, and not be blocked by a firewall (page 339). The order of events in a Remote Assistance session is:

1 The novice sends the helper an invitation via email.

2 The helper accepts the invitation. The helper can use (and reuse) the invitation until it expires.

3 Remote Assistance opens a window that shows the novice's desktop to the helper.

4 The helper views the novice's desktop and exchanges messages with the novice or, with permission, takes control of the novice's computer.

5 Either party disconnects to end the session.

To get help via Remote Assistance:

1 Choose Start > All Programs > Maintenance > Windows Remote Assistance. The Windows Remote Assistance wizard starts.

2 Click "Invite someone you trust to help you". (Note that you can detour here if you want to give help rather than get it.)

3 If you use an email program (such as Windows Live Mail), click "Use e-mail to send an invitation".

or

To send the invitation as an attachment via web-based email (such as Yahoo or Gmail), click "Save this invitation as a file".

or

If both you and the helper are using Windows 7 and are connected to the internet, click "Use Easy Connect".

4 Set a folder location if you're saving the invitation as a file, and then click Next. (The invitation file has the filename extension .MsRcIncident.)

5 Give the onscreen password to the helper in person, on the phone, via email, or via instant messaging.

If your email program is set up, Remote Assistance launches it and creates a message with boilerplate text telling the helper how to respond to your invitation; you can add some personal text if you like.

6 Type the helper's email address in the To box and then send the message.

or

If you're using web-based email, attach the invitation file that you created earlier to a message and then send it to the helper. (Instead of emailing it, you can transfer this file over a network, on a USB flash drive, or via instant messaging.) After you send the invitation, the Windows Remote Assistance window will appear. It will notify you when the helper accepts your invitation.

or

If you're using Easy Connect, follow the onscreen instructions; there's no need to send an invitation.

7 Approve the invitation to start the session. If you let the helper use his mouse and keyboard to control your desktop, you'll see ghostly pointer movements, self-typing text, and self-opening windows as he fixes your problem.

8 To end the session (which either you or the helper can do at any time), click Cancel, click Stop Sharing, or press Esc.

Tip: If you select "Allow *helper* to respond to User Account Control prompts" when the helper asks to control your desktop, he can run administrator-level programs without your participation. You can allow him to run these programs only if you can run them yourself, so you'll be asked for consent or credentials before giving him these abilities. He can't see your desktop while you provide them.

Getting System Information

The **System** window displays helpful information about your Windows edition, hardware (processor and memory), network settings, and activation status. You'll need some of this information when you request help from Microsoft or others. To open System, choose Start > Control Panel > System and Security > System (or press Windows logo key+Break).

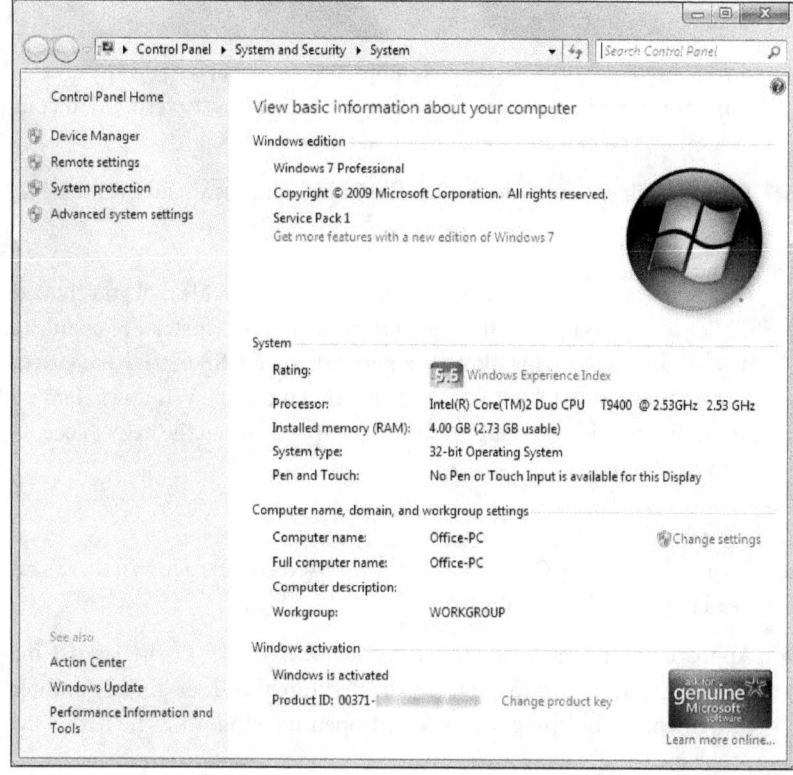

Windows Experience Index

In System, you can click "Windows Experience Index" to get your computer's **base score**: Microsoft's numeric rating of your computer's capabilities. A computer's base score is determined by the lowest subscore; it's not an average. Click "What do these numbers mean?" for an explanation.

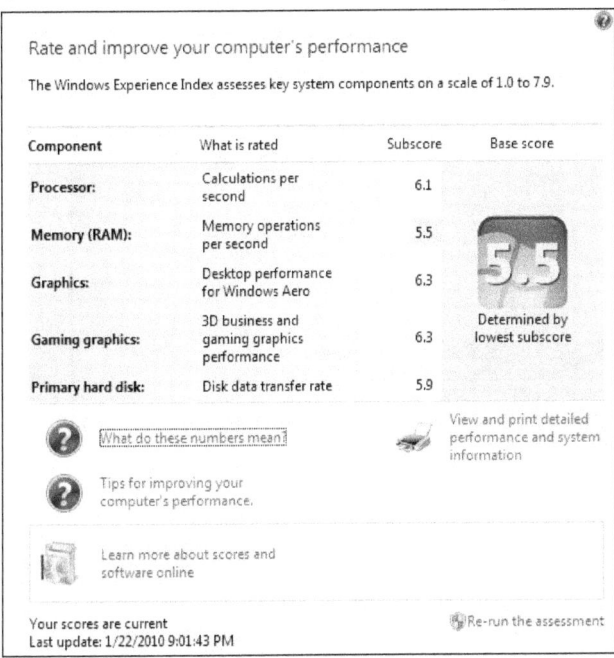

You can also get system information in text format: choose Start > All Programs > Accessories > Command Prompt (page 262), type *systeminfo* at the prompt, and then press Enter. To redirect the output to a text file in the current directory, type *systeminfo > info.txt*. (The *systeminfo* command works in high-end Windows editions.)

System Information

The System window provides basic information, but for real troubleshooting use the **System Information** program, which compiles and reports information about your computer's hardware, drivers, system resources, and internet settings. This overview saves you from visiting scores of Control Panel dialog boxes to see how your computer is configured. To open System Information, choose Start > All Programs > Accessories > System Tools > System Information.

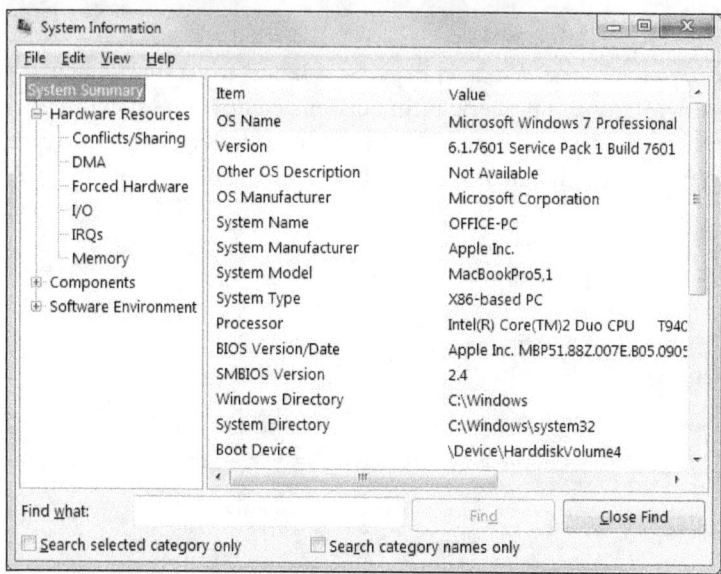

Use the Explorer-like tree to display information in the various categories:

Hardware Resources
Displays hardware settings, such as IRQs (interrupt requests) and memory addresses. The Conflicts/Sharing view identifies devices that are sharing resources or are in conflict.

Components
Displays Windows configuration information for device drivers, as well as networking and multimedia software.

Software Environment
Displays a snapshot of the software loaded into computer memory. Use this information to see whether a process is still running or to check version information.

To find system data, type search text in the Find box at the bottom of the window, select the desired search-option checkboxes, and then click Find. To get system information for a different computer on your network, choose View > Remote Computer (Ctrl+R). To save system data in a System Information file—which you can archive or email to a techie to open in his copy of System Information—choose File > Save. To save system data in a text file, choose File > Export. In general, you shouldn't print hardcopy system information: choosing File > Print produces a 50-page printout. Instead, export the data to a text file and then print the desired sections in Notepad.

Options

Many applications have an Options (or Preferences) dialog box that sets pro-gramwide options. Options is one of the first places to look at when you're new to a program. In general, any changes that you make to options apply to only your user account.

Open or activate a program and look for a menu, toolbar, or ribbon command named Options or Preferences. You'll often find this command in the Tools or Edit menu. In Microsoft Office, it's on the File tab.

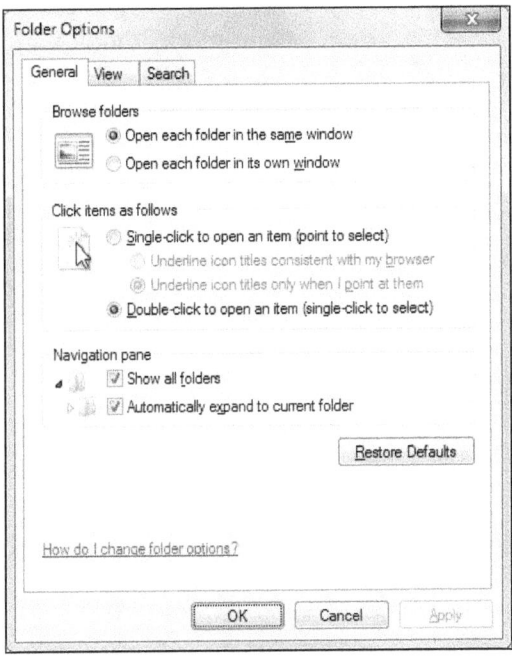

2

The Desktop

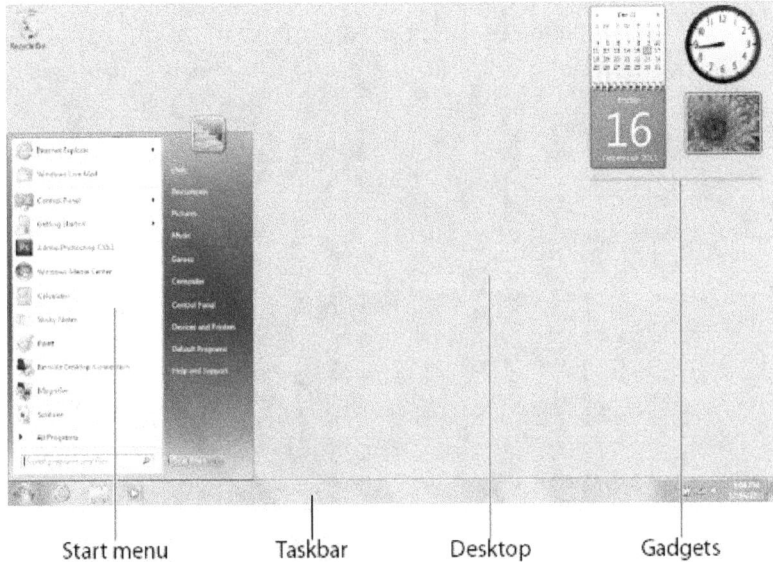

| Start menu | Taskbar | Desktop | Gadgets |

After you log on (page 20), Windows displays the **desktop**, which is the backdrop of your working environment and lets you organize your computer's resources. This chapter covers the main desktop-management tools. The **Start menu** is the central location that lists the most useful folders, programs, and commands. The **taskbar** tells you what programs are running on your computer and lets you launch, activate, or close them. **Gadgets** are handy mini-programs that reside on the desktop.

The other parts of the desktop, covered elsewhere, are Windows Explorer (page 170) and the Recycle Bin (page 203). You can also use various Control Panel tools to personalize your desktop (page 117).

Exploring the Start Menu

The Start menu lets you:

- Start programs

- Open commonly used folders

- Search for files, folders, and programs

- Get help

- Adjust computer settings

- Switch users, lock your computer, log off, or turn off your computer

To open the Start menu:

- Click the Start button (at the left end of the taskbar).

    or

    Press Ctrl+Esc.

    or

    Tap the Windows logo key.

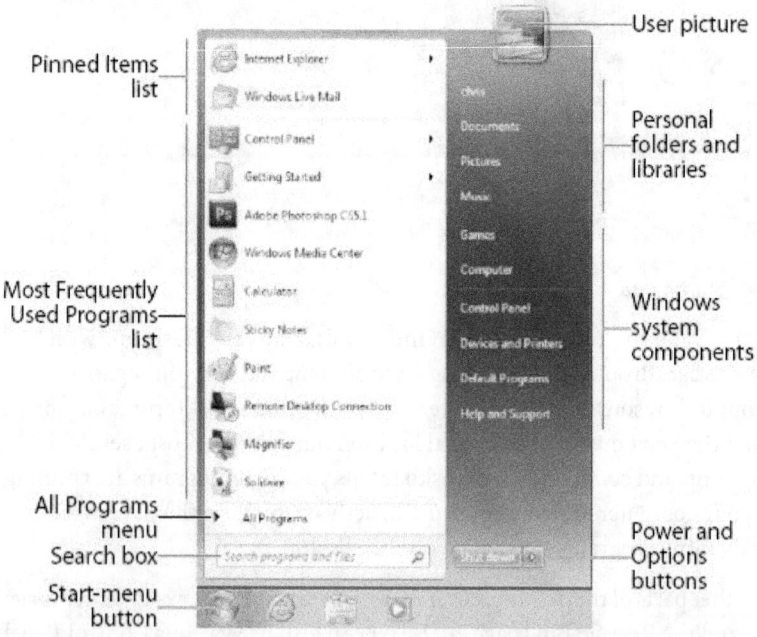

Pinned Items list

User picture

Personal folders and libraries

Most Frequently Used Programs list

Windows system components

All Programs menu

Search box

Start-menu button

Power and Options buttons

Hover the pointer over a Start-menu item for a pop-up tip. If these tips distract you, you can turn them off: choose Start > Control Panel > Appearance and Personalization > Folder Options > View tab > clear "Show pop-up description for folder and desktop items".

To close the Start menu without choosing a command, tap the Windows logo key, press Esc, or click anywhere off the menu (on the desktop or in a program, for example).

The left side of the Start menu lists programs and has a Search box:

Pinned Items list
> Items in the top section of this column remain there, always available to open. You can select programs to appear here and rearrange them. See "Adding Items to the Start Menu" on page 85.

Most Frequently Used Programs list
> Windows maintains this list by appending programs as you use them. Each added program replaces one that you haven't used recently. You can delete items from this list and set the number of items displayed, but you can't rearrange or add them manually. A right-pointing triangle ▶ next to a program name denotes a **jump list** (a program-specific pop-up menu). To open a jump list, click the triangle, point to the program name, or press the right-arrow key.

All Programs menu
> Displays a master list of all the programs installed on your computer. Click or point to All Programs to expand the menu. Click Back (at the bottom of the list) to collapse it. Use the menu's scrollbar or your mouse's scroll wheel to move up and down the list. See also "Launching Programs" on page 242.

Search box
> This feature finds files, folders, and programs (including Control Panel programs) on your computer. Type search text in the Search box. As you type, items that match your text appear instantly in the menu. Search looks at your personal folder, offline files, email, contacts, calendar events, internet favorites, and browsing history, basing its search on filenames, program titles (*excel*, for example), text in documents, tags, and other file properties. Click an item in the results list to open it, or press Esc to cancel the search. For details, see "Searching for Files and Folders" on page 211.

The right side of the Start menu has links to personal folders and Windows system components:

User picture

Shows your account picture (page 8). This picture initially shows your user-account picture and changes to the icon of whatever you're pointing to on the right side of the menu. If you click the picture, the User Accounts tool opens to let you make changes to your account.

Personal folder

Opens your personal folder (page 167). This link shows the user name of the currently logged-on user—you, usually. Personal folders are stored in \Users\user_name.

Documents, Pictures, and Music

Opens libraries (page 224) that show specific subfolders in your personal folder (page 167) and the Public folder (page 320).

Games

Lets you play games.

Computer

Opens a window that lets you access drives, cameras, and other hardware connected to your computer. See "Exploring Your Computer" on page 163.

Control Panel

Opens Control Panel, which lets you configure and manage your system. See "Using Control Panel" on page 117.

Devices and Printers

Opens a window that lets you view, use, and troubleshoot all the printers, cameras, drives, mice, and other devices connected to your computer (page 293).

Default Programs

Shows the Default Programs window, which lets you choose the programs that Windows uses by default for web browsing, email, documents, pictures, and more. You can also associate file types with programs (page 254), change AutoPlay settings, and set program access.

Help and Support

Gets Windows help (page 71).

Power and Options

Provides options for switching users (page 25), locking your computer (page 27), logging off (page 29), and turning off your computer (page 30).

Using the Start Menu

Start-menu commands are a click away. If you don't like the Start menu's default layout, you can change it. Changes that you make apply only to you, the logged-on user.

To choose a Start-menu item:

- Click the item.

  or

  Use the arrow keys to navigate to the item and then press Enter.

  or

  Press any arrow key once to move out of the Search box, press the key of the item's first letter, and then press Enter. If two or more items have the same first letter, press that letter repeatedly until the desired item is highlighted and then press Enter.

  or

  If an item has a right-pointing triangle ▶ next to its name, click the triangle, point to the name, or press the right-arrow key to open the item's jump list or submenu.

Tip: If you open the All Programs menu, you can close it again by clicking Back at the bottom of the menu.

Adding Items to the Start Menu

Icons in the Start menu are **shortcuts**—links to computer or network items such as programs, files, folders, drives, webpages, printers, connected hardware, and other computers. You can add items to the Start menu by dragging and dropping or by pinning. You can also remove or reorder items.

Changing or deleting a shortcut has no effect on the item that it's linked to. Removing a shortcut won't uninstall a program, delete a file or folder, or erase a drive, for example.

To pin an item to the Start menu:

1   Locate the item (icon) that you want to display.

2   Drag the item to the Start button. You can pin a program, folder, file, or drive to the Start menu by dropping it on the Start button. The Start menu pops open if you pause on the Start button while dragging, letting you drop the item in the desired position.

or

Right-click the icon and then choose Pin to Start Menu. You can right-click a program in the Start menu, in Windows Explorer, in Computer, or on the desktop. For documents, pictures, folders, and drives, use drag-and-drop.

If you don't know the item's location, press Windows logo key+F (or press F3 while the Start menu is visible), use the Search box to find it, and then drag it from the results list to the Start button. If you're looking for a program (rather than a document, folder, or drive), type the program name in the Start menu's Search box, right-click it in the results list, and then choose Pin to Start Menu.

If you can't drag icons onto the Start menu, or if right-clicking the menu has no effect, turn on Start-menu dragging and dropping: right-click the Start button and then choose Properties > Customize > select "Enable context menus and dragging and dropping".

Tip: Hold down Shift when you right-click a file in a folder window, and "Pin to Start Menu" will appear in the shortcut menu.

To move a pinned item:

- Drag the item to a new position. A horizontal black line shows where the item will land when it's dropped.

To remove a pinned item:

- Right-click the item and then choose "Remove from this list". This technique works in both the Pinned Items and Most Frequently Used Programs lists. In the Pinned Items list, you can also choose "Unpin from Start Menu".

Using the All Programs Menu

The All Programs menu appears when you click or point to All Programs in the Start menu. It superimposes itself over the left side of the Start menu and displays all the programs that you, Windows Setup, the computer manufacturer, or your administrator have installed on your computer. Program installers add their own icons to the All Programs menu, but you can add, delete, or reorder them manually. The menu accepts not only program icons, but also document, folder, and drive icons.

By default, Windows keeps the All Programs menu sorted automatically—files alphabetically at top, followed by folders alphabetically. If you want to add an item to a specific place without having it jump to its sorted position, or if you want to move an item within the menu, turn off autosorting.

See also "Launching Programs" on page 242.

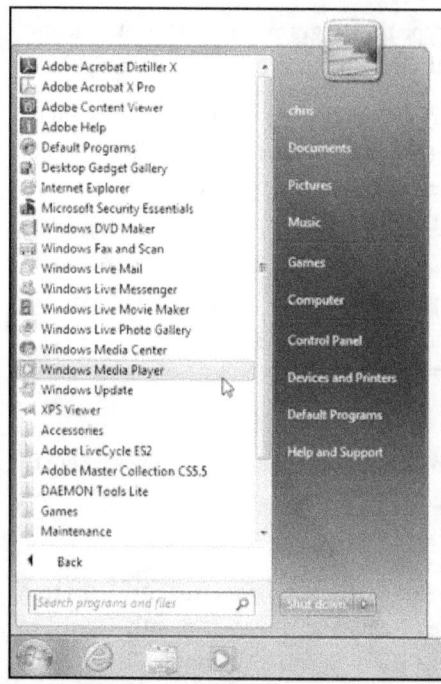

To turn off All Programs autosorting:

• Right-click the Start button and then choose Properties > Customize > clear "Sort All Programs menu by name".

To add an item to the All Programs menu:

1 Locate the item (icon) that you want to add.

2 Drag the icon over the Start button and then pause until the Start menu opens.

3 Continue to drag and then pause over All Programs until the menu opens.

4 Drag the icon to the place in the All Programs menu where you want it to appear. You can drag near the menu's top or bottom edge to autoscroll up or down, or pause over a folder to open it. A black horizontal line shows where the icon will appear when you drop it.

5 Hold down the Alt key.

Holding down Alt guarantees that Windows will create a link (shortcut) in the All Programs menu rather than moving or copying the item to the All Programs folder.

6 Drop the icon on the All Programs menu and then release Alt. If All Programs autosorting is turned off, the item stays where you drop it; otherwise, it jumps to its proper position in the sort order.

Instead of dragging, you can right-drag (that is, hold down the right mouse as you drag). When you drop the icon, a shortcut menu appears to let you create the link (you don't have to hold down Alt).

Adding a folder to the All Programs menu creates a subfolder that lists its contents. The default name for an item's shortcut ends with "- Shortcut" (*Downloads - Shortcut*, for example). To change the name, right-click the item and then choose Rename.

To delete an item from the All Programs menu:

- Right-click the item and then choose Delete. If your desktop is clear, you can drag an item off the menu and drop it into the Recycle Bin to delete it.

To move an item in the All Programs menu:

- Drag the item to a new position. (All Programs autosorting must be turned off.)

To sort the All Programs menu alphabetically:

- Right-click any menu item and then choose Sort by Name. (This command isn't available if autosorting is turned on.) Windows sorts files in alphabetical order at the top, followed by folders in alphabetical order. You can also use this command to sort any subfolder individually within the All Programs menu.

Managing All Programs Items with Folders

To keep your All Programs menu from growing too long, you can consolidate menu items into submenus. You add submenus by creating folders. A menu item with a folder icon spawns a submenu when you click it.

Every item that appears in the Start menu is contained in one of two folders: a folder that applies only to you, the logged-on user (which only you can access); and a folder that applies to all users (which everyone who has a user account can access).

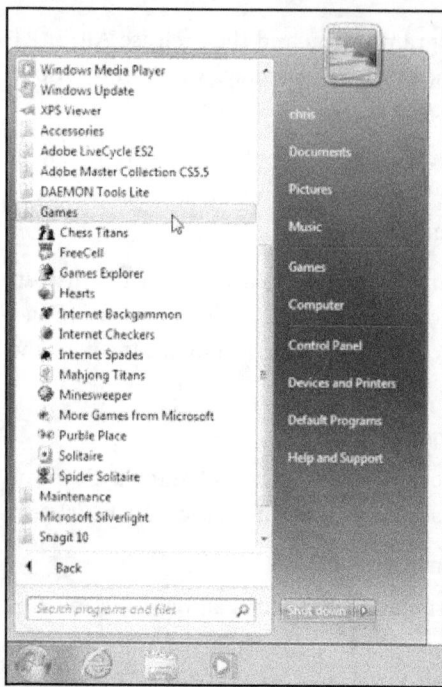

To add or delete All Programs items:

1   Open the Start menu and then right-click All Programs.

2   To add or delete items for only you, choose Open.

    or

    To add or delete items for everyone with a user account, choose Open
    All Users.

3   To add (or delete) menu items, drag icons into (or delete icons from) the
    Start Menu folder, the Programs folder, or any folder nested in the Start
    Menu or Programs folders.

    The Start Menu folder and its subfolders determine what appears in the
    All Programs menu. Click the right-pointing triangle ▶ next to a folder
    (or double-click the folder icon itself) to reveal its nested folders.

    Icons placed inside the Start Menu folder or the Programs folder appear
    in the All Programs menu. Subfolders inside the Programs folder appear
    as submenus.

To add an All Programs submenu:

1 Open the Start menu and then right-click All Programs.

2 To add a submenu for only you, choose Open.

or

To add a submenu for everyone with a user account, choose Open All Users.

3 Click "New folder" (on the toolbar).

or

Press Ctrl+Shift+N.

or

Right-click an empty area in the right pane and then choose New > Folder.

or

Right-click the Start Menu folder or one of its subfolders in the Navigation pane (on the left) and then choose New > Folder. (If the pane is hidden, choose Organize > Layout > "Navigation pane".)

4 Type the name of the folder and then press Enter.

You create an empty folder, which is an empty submenu.

5 To make items appear in the new submenu, drop shortcuts (page 110) into the new folder and then close the Explorer window.

6 Choose Start > All Programs to see the new submenu. The new folder appears as a submenu in the All Programs menu. If All Programs autosorting is turned off, you can drag the folder up or down the menu to reposition it.

Tip: To create a nested submenu, create a new folder inside the first folder that you added.

Customizing the Start Menu

The Start menu's Windows components and default behavior are easy to change. You can, for example, change the name of your Documents library, decide which icons the menu displays, and highlight recently installed programs.

To rename a Start-menu item:

1   Right-click a menu item and then choose Rename. If the Rename command doesn't appear in the shortcut menu, you can't rename that item.

2   Type or paste a new name or edit the existing one, and then press Enter. The keyboard shortcuts for Cut, Copy, Paste, Undo, and Select All (Ctrl+X, Ctrl+C, Ctrl+V, Ctrl+Z, and Ctrl+A, respectively) work when you're editing the name. To cancel renaming an item, press Esc while editing.

Don't rename the Startup folder. If you do, Windows won't launch programs automatically when the computer starts. See "Launching Programs Automatically" on page 243.

To customize the Start menu:

1   Right-click the Start button and then choose Properties.

   or

   Choose Start > Control Panel > Appearance and Personalization > Taskbar and Start Menu > Start Menu tab.

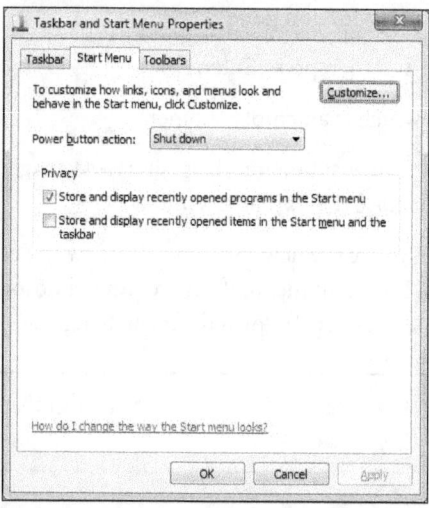

2   Choose a default action for the Power button.

3   In the Privacy section, clear one or both checkboxes if you don't want someone else to know what you've been running or working on.

   The top checkbox applies to the Most Frequently Used Programs list (in the left column) and the Run command history (if it's displayed). The bottom checkbox applies to the Recent Items submenu (in the right column of the Start menu) and to taskbar jump lists. Selecting these boxes again makes Windows repopulate the lists over time.

4   Click Customize to open the Customize Start Menu dialog box.

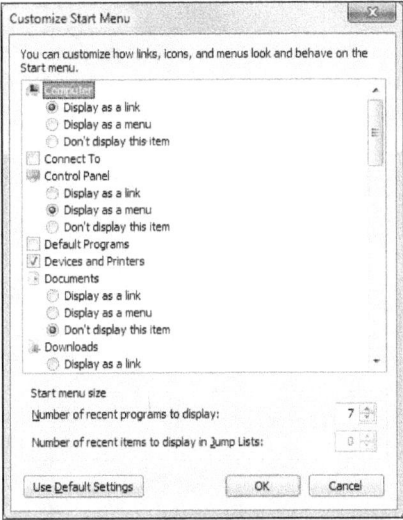

5   Choose the desired options.

The Customize Start Menu dialog box affects what you see in the menu's left column, where programs are listed, and the right column, where your personal folders and the Windows system components are listed. "Display as a menu" makes Start-menu folders expand as submenus; "Display as a link" makes them open as windows.

6   For "Start menu size", type or select the number of recently opened items to display in the menu's left column and in jump lists.

Displaying more items gives you quicker access but takes up more vertical space.

7   If you want to revert to the Start menu's original factory settings, click Use Default Settings.

8   Click OK in each open dialog box.

You can still open a folder even if you've chosen "Display as a menu": right-click it in the Start menu and then choose Open.

To clear the Recent Items list, right-click Recent Items in the Start menu and then choose "Clear Recent Items list". To clear an individual item in the list, right-click it in the Recent Items submenu and then choose Delete. Clearing recent items from the list doesn't delete the originals from your computer.

Exploring the Taskbar

The taskbar provides quick access to programs and the status of background processes. It appears at the bottom of your screen by default and is divided into segments with distinct functions.

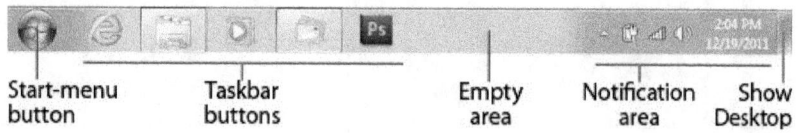

Start-menu button   Taskbar buttons   Empty area   Notification area   Show Desktop

Start-menu button
> Click this button to open the Start menu.

Taskbar buttons
> Buttons on the taskbar show pinned programs, open programs, and open windows. You can use these buttons to open, resize, switch among, or close programs.

Empty area
> The taskbar has its own shortcut menu, which you reach by right-clicking an empty area. If your taskbar is crowded, right-click just to the left or right of the Start-button "orb", where there's always an unoccupied sliver.

Notification area
> This area displays the clock and shows the status of programs and activities.

Show Desktop button
> Click this button to minimize all windows. Click it again to restore them. Point at it to peek briefly at the desktop—typically, to see gadgets (page 106)—without resizing any windows.

Tip: Point (without clicking) to a taskbar icon to show a pop-up tooltip (if the program is closed) or thumbnail views of its windows (if the program is open).

Managing Windows by Using the Taskbar

Use the taskbar to:

Determine which programs are running

Shortcuts to **pinned** programs appear in the taskbar whether or not the programs are running. An unpinned program's icon appears only after you launch the program and disappears after you quit it. Borders around the icons indicate the status of the programs and their windows.

The default taskbar comes with a few pinned programs (the Internet Explorer, Windows Explorer, and Windows Media Player icons next to the Start button). You can pin other programs by dragging icons to the taskbar. A single border indicates a running program with zero or one open windows. A multiple border indicates two or more open windows. No border indicates that a program is pinned but not running. Pointing to a taskbar button highlights it in the dominant color of its icon. The brightest icon in the taskbar indicates the active (frontmost) program. A blinking taskbar icon means that a program is trying to get your attention.

View or activate open windows

Point to an active program's bordered taskbar icon to see graphic thumbnails of that program's open windows. For example, point to Internet Explorer to see open webpages (tabs and windows), Windows Explorer to see open folder windows, or an application to see its open documents.

Each thumbnail shows a live image of the window's contents. Hover the pointer over a thumbnail to preview the full-size window without activating it. (Other windows on the desktop become transparent while you preview.) Click a thumbnail to activate that window. If a program has only one open window, click the program's taskbar icon to activate that window (or minimize it, if it's already active). Pointing to the unbordered icon of a closed program displays a pop-up tip showing the program name.

Close or resize windows

To close a window, point to its thumbnail and then click its Close button ⊠. The Close button doesn't appear until you hover the pointer over the thumbnail. Alternatively, right-click the taskbar icon of the window's parent program and then choose Close Window (or Close All Windows). To resize a window, right-click its thumbnail to open its control menu.

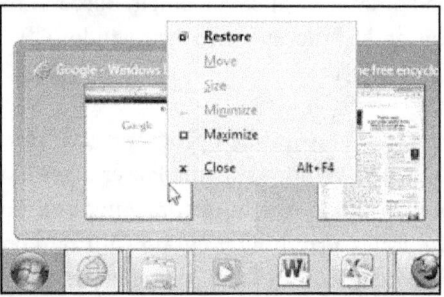

Open windows

Right-click a taskbar icon to open its jump list and then choose a window in the list. A **jump list** is a program-specific menu that provides quick access to common tasks, recently opened windows, and pinned windows. Jump lists vary by program. Depending on the application, a jump list lists webpages, folders, documents, pictures, videos, or songs. You can think of a jump list as a program's own miniature Start menu. See also "Using Jump Lists" on page 98.

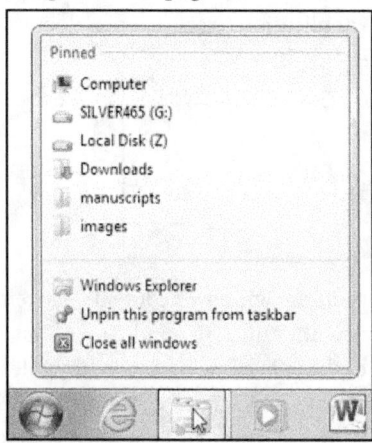

Launch or quit programs

To launch a program, click its taskbar icon. Alternatively, right-click its taskbar icon and then choose the program's name from the jump list. To quit a program, right-click its taskbar icon and then choose Close Window (or Close All Windows). You may have to do this twice: once to close the program's window(s) and again to close the program itself.

Tile windows

If you're working with multiple windows that overlap or hide one another, you can arrange them neatly on your desktop. To arrange all windows, right-click an empty area of the taskbar and then choose a Cascade or Show command. To arrange only the windows of a specific program, Shift+right-click the program's taskbar icon and then choose a Cascade or Show command. The taskbar's shortcut menu applies to all desktop windows. A program's shortcut menu applies to only that program's windows. The Cascade and Show commands resize only unminimized windows. Before choosing a command, minimize all windows that you *don't* want to be resized.

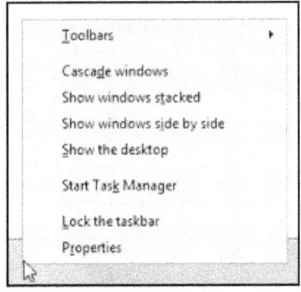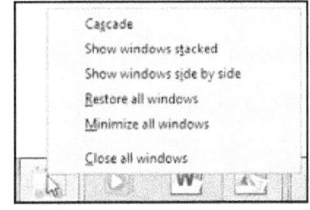

View live thumbnails

Thumbnails show static images for documents and pictures or playing images for videos, movies, and animations. Windows Media Player even includes playback controls on the thumbnail. If you're installing a program or downloading a big file, you can check its progress by looking at its thumbnail's live progress bar.

Clear or peek at the desktop

To minimize all windows, click the Show Desktop button ▯ at the right edge of the taskbar or press Windows logo key+D. Repeat the action to restore the windows. Alternatively, choose "Show the desktop" (or "Show open windows") from the taskbar shortcut menu. To peek briefly at the desktop without resizing windows, point to Show Desktop ▯ or press and hold Windows logo key+spacebar. Peeking at the desktop turns all windows transparent for as long as you point to the Show Desktop button. Peeking is most useful for taking a quick look at your desktop gadgets (page 106).

Using Jump Lists

Pointing to a file or folder in a jump list reveals a pushpin 📌, which you can click to pin and unpin the item in the list. A pinned item stays on the jump list until you unpin it. An unpinned item stays on the list until it's replaced by a more-recently opened item.

Another way to open a jump list: click and hold an icon on the taskbar, and then slide the pointer up the icon without releasing the mouse button. (This gesture is actually designed for touchscreen users.)

Jump lists appear in the Start menu too. If an item in the menu's left column has a right-pointing triangle ▶ next to its name, click the triangle, point to the name, or press the right-arrow key to open that item's jump list.

To prevent all jump lists from showing recently opened (unpinned) items, right-click the Start button and then choose Properties. On the Start Menu tab, clear the "Store and display" checkboxes.

Microsoft adds a few default tasks to every program's jump list, but third-party developers can customize their programs' jump lists as they please.

Taskbar Tips

- To cycle through a program's open windows or tabs, Ctrl+click its (multiple-bordered) taskbar icon.

- To open the shortcut menu of a program that's not running, Shift+right-click its (unbordered) taskbar icon.

- To start a new instance of a program (even if it's already running), Shift+click its taskbar icon (or middle-click if you have an extra mouse button). To start a new instance with administrator privileges (page 8), Ctrl+Shift+click instead.

- To press taskbar buttons by using the keyboard: Press Windows logo key+T to activate the taskbar. Next, use the arrow keys or press Windows logo key+T repeatedly to highlight the desired taskbar item, and then press the spacebar to activate it or Shift+F10 to open its shortcut menu.

- Press Windows logo key+*number* key (1, 2, ..., 0) to open the corresponding pinned icon on the taskbar.

- To disable desktop peeking, right-click an empty area of the taskbar and then choose Properties. On the Taskbar tab, clear "Use Aero Peek to preview the desktop".

- If a program is busy, clicking its taskbar icon or thumbnail may not activate it.

- To switch windows without using the taskbar, press Alt+Tab, or see "Switching Programs" on page 246.

Customizing the Taskbar

You can change the taskbar's default behavior; change its location on the screen; pin, unpin, or rearrange its icons; and resize it.

To customize the taskbar:

1   Right-click an empty area of the taskbar and then choose Properties.

    or

    Choose Start > Control Panel > Appearance and Personalization > Taskbar and Start Menu > Taskbar tab.

2   To keep the taskbar at its current size and position, select "Lock the task-bar"; clear it if you want to resize or move the taskbar or any of its toolbars or icons. (To toggle the taskbar lock quickly, right-click an empty area of the taskbar and then choose "Lock the taskbar".)

3   To hide the taskbar when you're not using it, select "Auto-hide the taskbar". The taskbar disappears until you point to the edge of the screen where it's located (or press the Windows logo key or Ctrl+Esc).

4   If you're working with a small screen or want to devote more pixels to your windows, select "Use small icons".

5   Choose the taskbar's screen location. Open windows self-adjust to accommodate a new location. (To move the taskbar quickly, unlock it, point to an empty area of the taskbar, and then drag to any screen edge.)

6   Set the button appearance and behavior in the "Taskbar buttons" drop-down list. The default setting is "Always combine, hide labels". The other settings label taskbar buttons with filenames and give each open window its own button, reminiscent of the taskbar in earlier Windows versions.

7   Click OK (or Apply).

Tip: Try moving the taskbar to the screen's left edge. It may feel awkward at first, but it reduces the amount of mousing needed for routine tasks, shows the day (not just the date and time), and displays more icons in the notification area.

To pin an item to the taskbar:

- Right-click an item in the Start menu and then choose "Pin to Taskbar", or drag the item from the Start menu to the taskbar. Right-clicking to pin is fast, but dragging directly to the taskbar is more versatile. You can pin from anywhere within the Start menu: left column, right column, All Programs menu, jump lists, and submenus. You can even drag items from a Search results list to the taskbar.

  or

  If a program is running, right-click its taskbar icon and then choose "Pin this program to taskbar". A program's jump list toggles to let you pin or unpin the program.

  or

  Drag a file or folder icon from the desktop or a folder window to the taskbar. This action pins the parent program to the taskbar (if it's not already pinned) and pins the dragged item to that program's jump list. When you drag a file to an empty area of the taskbar, a pop-up message indicates the file's default program. To pin the file to a different (nondefault) program's jump list, drag the file directly onto that program's icon. If you've created an HTML (webpage) file, for example, you can drag it first to Internet Explorer (for viewing) and then to Notepad (for editing) to pin it to both programs' jump lists.

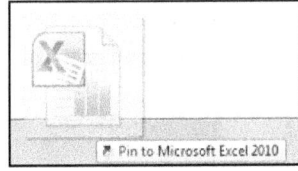

  or

  Right-click a program icon (.exe file) and then choose "Pin to Taskbar", or drag it to the taskbar.

Tip: If the taskbar can't hold an item, a circled slash ⃠ appears near the pointer when you drag onto the taskbar.

To unpin a taskbar item:

- Right-click its taskbar icon and then choose "Unpin this program from taskbar".

To rearrange taskbar items:

- Drag icons within the taskbar to reorder them. (To cancel in mid-drag, press Esc.)

To resize the taskbar:

- If the taskbar is locked, unlock it (right-click an empty area of the taskbar and then clear "Lock the taskbar"). Point to the inside edge of the taskbar (the pointer becomes a double-headed arrow), and then drag toward the desktop for a larger taskbar or toward the screen edge for a smaller one. Taskbars at the screen's top or bottom resize in button-height increments. Taskbars to the left or right resize without constraints. If you make a horizontal taskbar more than a row deep, truncated buttons and toolbars will expand to fill the space (handy if you've set the taskbar buttons to not combine).

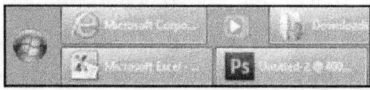

Using the Notification Area

The **notification area**, formerly called the **system tray**, lives at the right end of the taskbar, holding the clock and small icons that monitor activities on your computer or network. Notification-area icons give the status of background programs, tasks, and services. The number of available icons grows as you install more programs.

Windows and other programs use icons here to let you know things—that you've received new email, for example. Some icons display a warning badge or pop-up message to get your attention, whereas others appear silently for the duration of an event (such as printing a document). Point to or click an icon to find out what it represents. These icons have no standard controls. Some, you click; others, you double- or right-click; and some ignore clicks. For example, point to the clock to show the day and date, or click it to show a calendar and an analog clock. Or click the Network icon (or) to see your computer's network or internet connection status.

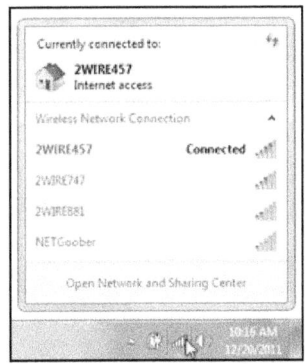

To "click" notification-area icons by using the keyboard, press Windows logo key+B to activate the first icon, use the arrow keys to highlight the desired icon, and then press the spacebar to "click" (or press Tab to move to the other parts of the taskbar).

Occasionally, an icon in the notification area will display a pop-up message (called a **notification**) to tell you about something. For example, you may see an "installed successfully" message after connecting a new hardware device to your computer. You can click the × in the notification to dismiss it, or do nothing, and the notification will fade away on its own after a few seconds.

In earlier versions of Windows, third-party programs often abused the notification area by displaying clingy icons that were more junk advertising than valid status messages. Now you have complete control. You can choose which icons appear in the notification area and whether their notifications are displayed. The Show Hidden Icons button ▣ indicates hidden icons or notifications. Click the button to reveal the icons and then point to an icon to see its notification. To show, hide, or reorder icons quickly, drag them between or within the hidden-icons window and the notification area. (Fast way to hide a notification-area icon: drag it to ▣). You control Windows system icons as well as the icons of third-party programs.

To customize the notification area:

1   Right-click an empty area of the taskbar and then choose Properties > Taskbar tab.

    or

    Choose Start > Control Panel > Appearance and Personalization > Taskbar and Start Menu > Taskbar tab.

2   In the Notification Area section, click Customize.

3   In the Notification Area Icons window, select which icons and notifications appear on the taskbar. You can specify the behavior of notification icons displayed currently as well as in the past.

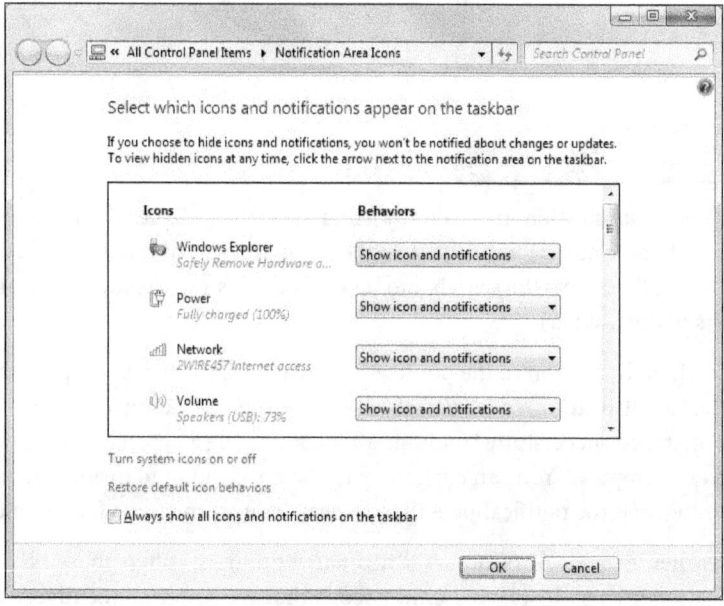

4   Click "Turn system icons on or off" (near the bottom of the window).

5   In the System Icons window, select which system icons and notifications appear on the taskbar. You can click "Restore default icon behaviors" to revert to the icons' standard behavior. To return to the Notification Area Icons window, click "Customize notification icons".

6   Click OK in each open dialog box.

Adding Toolbars to the Taskbar

Specialized toolbars are available on the taskbar:

Address
   A text box that accepts any address on the web, on your network, or on your computer. Type or paste a web address (URL) to launch or activate Internet Explorer (or your default browser), a program name to launch the program, a document name and path (page 179) to open the document

in its associated program (launching the program if necessary), or a folder name to open it in Windows Explorer.

The Address toolbar autocompletes—that is, proposes matching entries that you've typed before. You can keep typing, or you can use arrow keys to select a match and then press Enter. If you type something that Windows doesn't understand, Windows searches and either finds what you want or displays a not-found message.

Desktop
Links to all desktop shortcuts, so that you don't have to minimize all windows to reach them.

Links
Links to Internet Explorer's Favorites folder. You can drag file, folder, drive, program, and webpage (URL) shortcuts onto this toolbar. Right-click links to delete or rename them, or drag to reorder them.

Tablet PC Input Panel
Lets you enter text by using a stylus (Tablet PCs only).

To show or hide taskbar toolbars, the taskbar must be unlocked: right-click an empty area of the taskbar. If "Lock the taskbar" is selected, then clear it.

To show or hide taskbar toolbars:

- Right-click an empty area on the taskbar, point to Toolbars, and then select a name in the submenu to toggle that toolbar. You can show or hide each toolbar independently of the others.

To resize a toolbar:

- Drag the vertical rib at its left end.

To create a custom toolbar:

- Right-click an empty area of the taskbar, choose Toolbars > New Toolbar, navigate to a folder whose contents you want to make into a toolbar, and then click Select Folder. Sadly, this toolbar vanishes when you close it or log off; you repeat the New Toolbar process to get it back.

To customize a taskbar toolbar:

- Right-click an empty area of the toolbar and then choose one of the following commands at the top of the shortcut menu:

View

Shows large (double-size) or small (default) toolbar icons.

Open Folder

Opens the folder that the toolbar represents. Adding, changing, and deleting shortcuts in the folder is easier than manipulating the toolbar's small icons.

Show Text

Displays a text label next to each toolbar icon, which takes a lot of space. This feature is on by default for Links and user-created toolbars.

Show title

Shows the toolbar name—generally a waste of space except as an extra empty area for right-clicking.

Close toolbar

Closes the toolbar.

Tip: Toolbars occupy a lot of taskbar space. Click the chevron button ⟫ that appears at a toolbar's right edge to display a menu of items or commands that won't fit on the taskbar.

Using Gadgets

Gadgets are single-purpose mini-programs that reside on the desktop, behind all other programs unless you set them to float on top. Windows comes with a small collection of gadgets, and you can get more online. Windows' starter gadgets include a puzzle, calendar, slideshow viewer, clock, stock ticker, CPU meter, headline feed, currency converter, weather display, and Windows Media Center player.

You can customize individual gadgets to organize the information that you want to access quickly. You can also drag gadgets around your desktop and view them quickly even when they're hidden behind other windows.

You need an internet connection for continuously updating "live" gadgets like news feeds and stock tickers. An always-on connection like DSL or cable works best, but a dial-up modem works too, in a creaky sort of way. Some live gadgets display a staleness timestamp (*2 hours ago*, for example) when they're offline.

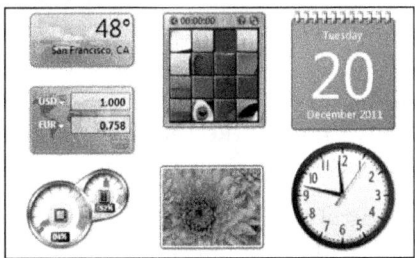

To add a gadget:

1   Right-click an empty area on the desktop and then choose Gadgets.

    or

    Choose Start > Control Panel > Appearance and Personalization > Desktop Gadgets.

    or

    Choose Start, type *gadgets* in the Search box, and then select Desktop Gadgets in the results list.

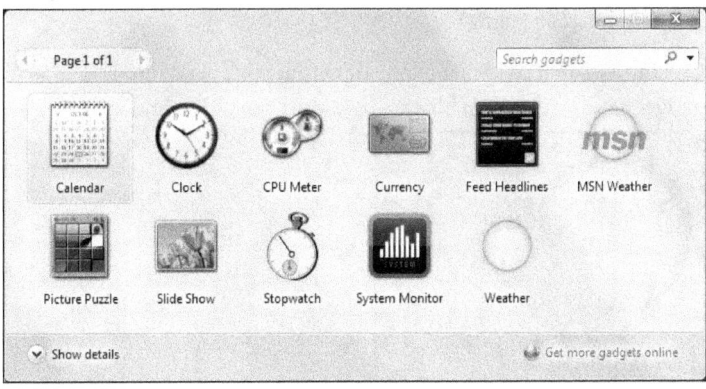

2   Double-click a gadget to add it.

    or

    Right-click a gadget and then choose Add.

    or

    Drag a gadget to the desktop.

To download and install more gadgets, in the Gadget Gallery, click "Get more gadgets online" to open the Microsoft Gadgets website.

If you have a lot of gadgets installed, click the arrows in the top-left corner of the Gadget Gallery to page through them, or type a gadget name in the Search box in the top-right corner. You can narrow the search further by clicking the down-arrow to the right of the Search box. Choosing "Recently installed gadgets", for example, narrows the search to gadgets installed in the past 30 days.

You can add multiple instances of a particular gadget and customize each one. For example, you can add clocks set to different time zones or weather trackers for different cities.

To uninstall a gadget:

- Right-click it in the Gadget Gallery and then choose Uninstall.

To close a gadget:

- Click the Close button that appears when you hover your pointer over the gadget.

  or

  Right-click the gadget and then choose "Close gadget". (Each gadget has its own shortcut menu.)

  Closing a gadget purges it of any data that you typed into it. The Weather gadget loses your town, Stocks loses your portfolio, and so on.

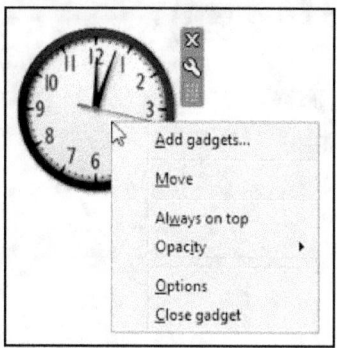

To view desktop gadgets:

- To minimize all windows but the gadgets, click the Show Desktop button at the right edge of the taskbar, or press Windows logo key+D. Repeat the action to restore the windows.

or

To peek briefly at the gadgets without resizing windows, point to Show Desktop ▌ or press and hold Windows logo key+spacebar. The nongadget windows turn transparent while you peek.

or

To bring all gadgets temporarily to the front of other windows, press Windows logo key+G.

If desktop peeking doesn't work, right-click an empty area of the taskbar and then choose Properties. On the Taskbar tab, select "Use Aero Peek to preview the desktop".

To show or hide all gadgets:

• Right-click an empty area on the desktop and then choose View > "Show desktop gadgets".

You can reposition gadgets by dragging them around on the desktop. If there's no suitable dragging place on the gadget itself, drag the gridded square that appears when you hover your pointer over the gadget. To make a gadget always float on top of other windows, right-click it and then choose "Always on top". Hiding all gadgets saves power and memory by unloading the *sidebar.exe* background process, which all gadgets run in.

To customize an individual gadget:

• Right-click the gadget and then choose Options.

or

Click the Options (wrench) button that appears when you hover your pointer over the gadget.

If a gadget is distracting, you can dim it by displaying its shortcut menu and lowering its opacity. The gadget returns to full brightness temporarily when you hover your pointer over it.

Some gadgets—such as Weather and Calendar—run in compact and expanded sizes. Click the Size button that appears when you hover your pointer over the gadget.

Managing Shortcuts

You can create, edit, and delete shortcuts in the Start menu (page 85) and taskbar (page 99). Shortcuts can also appear on the desktop and in folders. A **shortcut** is a link to a program, file, folder, drive, printer or other device, web address (URL), or system folder (such as Computer). When you double-click a shortcut, its linked file or location opens. You can create and modify a shortcut for any item and store it anywhere; it's a tiny file.

Windows offers two types of shortcut files: Windows shortcuts (.lnk files) to items on your computer or network, and internet shortcuts (.url files) to webpages. A shortcut shares the icon of the original but adds a small boxed arrow in one corner.

You can distinguish a shortcut from the original file to which it's linked by the small curved arrow. This makes it easy to identify the shortcut so that you don't mistakenly delete the original when you meant to delete the shortcut.

You can make several shortcuts to the same object and store them in different places. You can also make shortcuts to network-accessible items, not just items on your local computer. Don't confuse a shortcut *icon*, which is a placeholder for an object, with a shortcut (right-click) *menu* or a keyboard *shortcut*, which is a command keystroke.

To create a shortcut:

1 Locate the item (icon) that you want to create a shortcut to.

2 Right-drag (page 37) the icon to a destination (typically, the desktop or a folder) and then choose "Create shortcuts here".

   or

   Right-click the icon and then choose Send To > "Desktop (create shortcut)".

   or

   Right-click the icon, choose Copy, right-click where you want the shortcut to appear, and then choose "Paste shortcut".

   or

Right-click the icon and then choose "Create shortcut". This method creates a shortcut in the same location as the original. You can move the shortcut anywhere.

or

Right-click an empty area of the desktop or a folder window and then choose New > Shortcut. The Create Shortcut wizard opens. Follow the onscreen instructions.

or

Alt+drag the icon to a destination.

or

Ctrl+Shift+drag the icon to a destination.

or

In a folder window, drag the small icon from the left edge of the address bar (page 177).

To create a shortcut to a webpage:

1   In your web browser, go to the page that you want to create a shortcut to.

2   Drag the small icon from the left edge of the address bar to the desktop or a folder window. Before you drag, move or resize your browser window so you can see the shortcut's destination.

If you create a shortcut and its icon doesn't have a small curved arrow, it's not a shortcut; you've moved or copied the original. Press Ctrl+Z to undo your action and then try again. If you create a shortcut to a shortcut, the new shortcut points to the original target. If you double-click a shortcut and the Problem with Shortcut dialog box appears, then the original file has been moved or deleted (you can delete the shortcut or restore the original file from the Recycle Bin).

If you want to create a shortcut to a program, the easiest way is to right-click the program on the left side of the Start menu (or in the All Programs submenu) or a Search results list and then choose Send To > "Desktop (create shortcut)". If you can't find a program in the Start menu, look for it—specifically, for its .exe file (Word's executable file is *winword.exe*, for example)—in a folder nested in the \Program Files folder or, for the small utility programs that come with Windows, in the \Windows or \Windows\System32 folder.

To display system-folder shortcuts on the desktop:

1   Right-click an empty area of the desktop and then choose Personalize.

    or

    Choose Start > Control Panel > Appearance and Personalization > Personalization.

2   Click "Change desktop icons" (on the left).

3   In the "Desktop icons" section, select the checkboxes for the shortcuts that you want on the desktop, and then click OK (or Apply).

    The Desktop Icon Settings dialog box also lets you change the system icons. Select the icon and then click Change Icon to choose a new icon. (To restore the original icon, select the icon and then click Restore Default.)

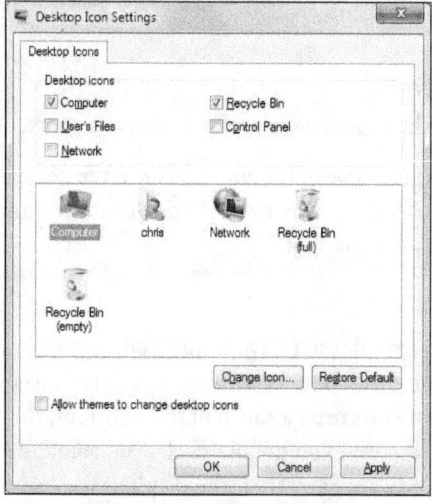

To rename a shortcut:

1   Right-click the shortcut and then choose Rename.

    or

    Select (highlight) the shortcut and then press F2.

    or

    Click the shortcut's title (not its icon) twice slowly; don't double-click.

2 Retype or edit the name and then press Enter. You can use the Cut, Copy, Paste, Undo, and Select All keyboard shortcuts (Ctrl+X, Ctrl+C, Ctrl+V, Ctrl+Z, and Ctrl+A, respectively) while editing.

To cancel renaming a shortcut, press Esc while editing. Shortcut names can include letters, numbers, spaces, and some punctuation marks but not these characters: \ / : * ? " > < |. You can also rename a shortcut in the General tab of the shortcut's Properties dialog box.

To delete a shortcut:

- Right-click the shortcut and then choose Delete.

    or

    Select (highlight) a shortcut or multiple shortcuts and then press Delete.

To recover (undelete) a shortcut from the Recycle Bin, see "Deleting Files and Folders" on page 203.

To view or change a shortcut's properties:

- Right-click the shortcut and then choose Properties.

    or

    Select (highlight) the shortcut and then press Alt+Enter.

The Properties dialog box for Windows shortcuts (to documents and programs) has a Shortcut tab, whereas the Properties dialog boxes for internet shortcuts (URLs) have a Web Document tab.

An internet shortcut's Web Document tab shows the number of times that you've visited the page. The Run Maximized setting is useful for programs that "forget" to run in full-screen mode when you start them from the shortcut. If you use Run Minimized for Startup-folder icons, programs will start automatically as taskbar buttons, and your logon desktop won't be cluttered with windows. You can update the target (path) of the object that a shortcut points to, but usually it's easier to create a new shortcut.

Information in a shortcut's Properties dialog box depends on what the shortcut represents. Some common properties are:

Target
> The name of the item that the shortcut points to. A shortcut to a file needs the full path (page 179)to its location (unless the file is in a Windows system folder).

Start in
> The folder in which the program looks for files to open or save, by default.

Shortcut key
> The keyboard shortcut with which to open (or switch to) the program. Press any key to make Ctrl+Alt+*key* appear here. You can assign Ctrl+Alt+E to Windows Explorer, for example, to open it without hunting for its shortcut. A shortcut key requires at least two of Ctrl, Shift, and Alt but can't use Esc, Enter, Tab, spacebar, Delete, Backspace, or Print-Screen. Shortcut keys work for desktop and Start-menu shortcuts. Pick shortcuts that don't conflict with program-defined or other shortcut keys.

Run
> Tells the program to open in a normal (restored), minimized, or maximized window.

Comment
> Provides the descriptive text (tooltip) that appears when your pointer hovers over the shortcut.

Open File Location
> Opens the folder containing the target file that the shortcut points to. The file will be selected in the folder window that appears.

Change Icon
> Allows you to change the default icon of a shortcut, which is the same as that of the target. Changing a shortcut's icon doesn't change its target's icon.

URL
Displays the target web address (URL) of an internet shortcut.

Details tab
Displays more properties and their associated values.

Organizing Desktop Icons

Over time, shortcuts tend to accumulate on your desktop. Microsoft's productivity elves have provided cleanup tools.

To arrange desktop shortcuts:

- Right-click an empty area of the desktop, point to View, and then choose one of the following commands from the submenu:

Large icons, Medium icons, or Small icons
Changes the size of all the icons on the desktop. The default is Medium.

Auto arrange icons
Places icons in neat columns, starting on the screen's left edge. Clear this option to drag icons anywhere on your desktop. This option won't work if your desktop is full.

Align icons to grid
Turns on an invisible grid that makes icons snap into equally spaced alignment when you move them. Clear this option to turn off the grid (useful only if "Auto arrange icons" is turned off).

Show desktop icons
Clear this option to hide all desktop icons; select it to show them.

Show desktop gadgets
Clear this option to hide all gadgets (page 106); select it to show them.

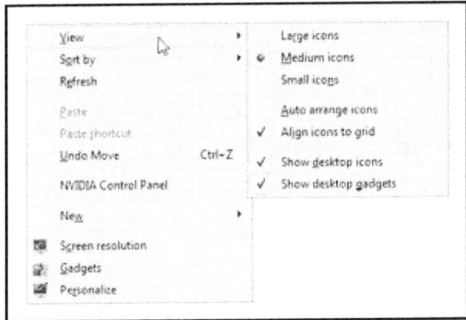

To sort desktop shortcuts:

- Right-click an empty area of the desktop, point to "Sort by", and then choose one of the following commands from the submenu:

Name
> Sorts alphabetically by name.

Size
> Sorts by file size, with the smallest first. If the shortcut points to a program, the size refers to the size of the shortcut file.

Item type
> Sorts by file type, which keeps files with the same filename extension together (.docx for Microsoft Word files or .exe for programs, for example).

Date modified
> Sorts by the date when the shortcut (not the linked original) was last modified, with the most recent first.

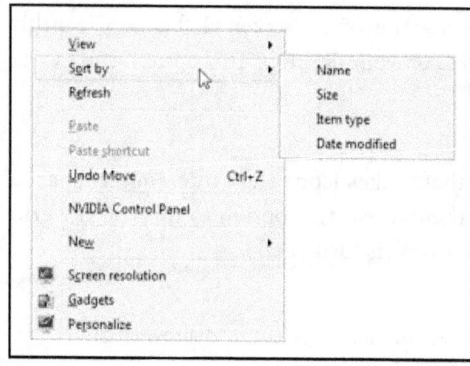

Tip: If your icons look grainy or badly drawn, right-click an empty area of the desktop and then choose Refresh to redisplay the icons.

---

3   Personalizing Windows

You can change Windows' factory settings to suit your own preferences and abilities. The hundreds of customizable settings range from superficial to meaningful. Changes to graphics, colors, and animation are usually cosmetic, whereas some other settings—the language used or features for disabled users—change the way that you work with Windows.

Using Control Panel

Control Panel is the central container of tools for changing personal and systemwide settings. Windows veterans are familiar with **icon view**, which consolidates all tools in one window.

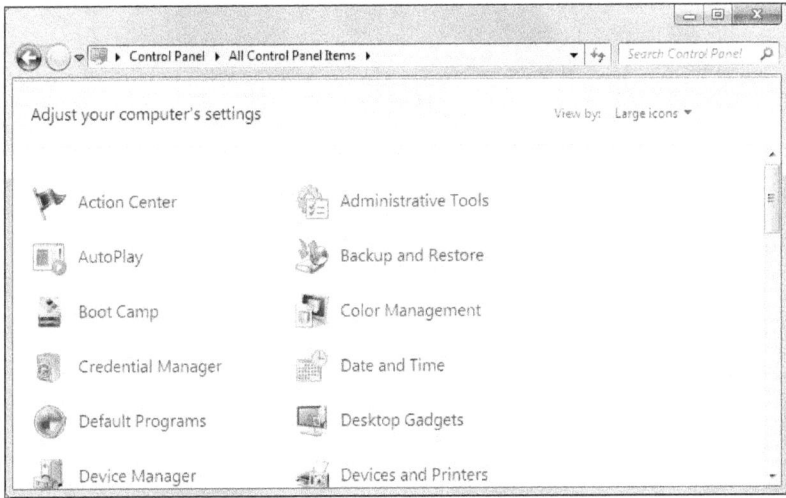

Control Panel defaults to **category view**, which groups tools into functional categories, saving you from having to memorize the icon names and functions. In either view, you can hover your pointer over a category heading or icon to see a pop-up description of it.

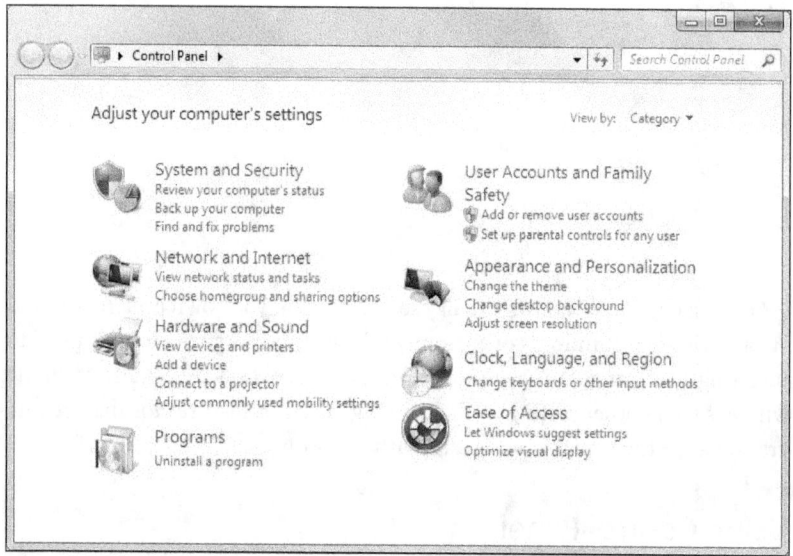

To open Control Panel:

- Choose Start > Control Panel.

    or

    Choose Start, type *control panel* in the Search box, and then press Enter.

    or

    Press Windows logo key+R, type *control*, and then press Enter.

To open an item in category view:

- Click a category heading or icon to display a list of related tasks and Control Panel tools.

    or

    Click a task link under a category heading to go right to that task.

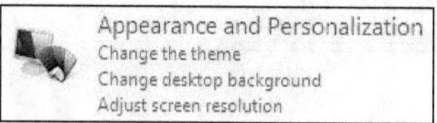

To open an item in icon view:

• Click the item.

   or

   Use the arrow keys to navigate to the desired item, and then press Enter.

   or

   Press the key of the item's first letter, and then press Enter. If multiple items have the same first letter, press that letter repeatedly until the desired item is highlighted, and then press Enter.

To search for a Control Panel item:

• In the top-right corner of Control Panel, type search text (one or more keywords) in the Search box. Control Panel lists the matching tasks as you type. Click any link in the results list. Search works the same way in category or icon view.

   Control Panel understands synonyms. If you search for wallpaper, for example, you'll see "Change desktop background" (the precise term) in the results. You can also search Control Panel from the Start menu's Search box. See also "Searching for Files and Folders" on page 211.

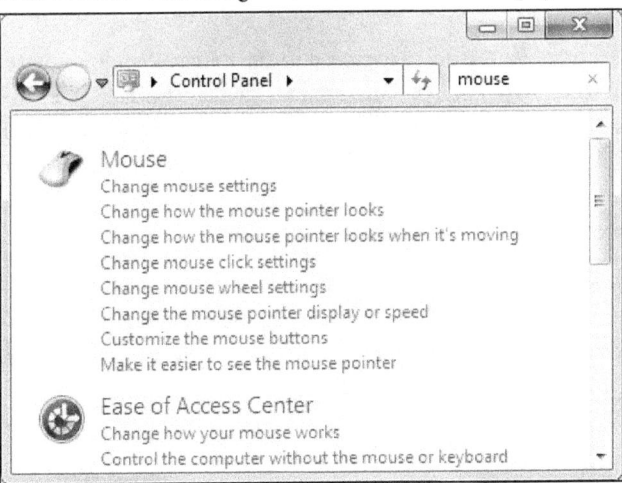

To switch Control Panel views:

1 Open Control Panel.

2 Choose a view from the "View by" dropdown list (in the upper-right).

Control Panel Tips

- When you're browsing a category, the left pane includes a link to take you to the Control Panel Home page, links for each category, and links for related tasks.

- Unlike the Search box in the Start menu (which searches your whole computer, in addition to Control Panel), the Control Panel Search box finds only tasks related to Control Panel. Some example searches to try: *screen resolution, add a printer,* and *connect internet.*

- If you're using a laptop computer, you have an additional Control Panel category—Mobile PC—that desktop users don't have.

- Some icons appear in more than one category. You can find Power Options, for example, in both the Hardware and Sound category and the System and Security category.

- If you can't find the item that you want in category view, switch to icon view.

- In either view, you can drag an item to the desktop, taskbar, or Start menu to create a shortcut (page 110).

CPL Files

The files for Control Panel tools are stored in the folder \Windows\System32, and they have the extension .cpl. To see them, navigate to that folder in Windows Explorer and then sort the files by Type (or search for *cpl*). The Time and Date applet, for example, is *timedate.cpl,* and Programs and Features is *appwiz.cpl.* For details, read the Wikipedia article "List of Control Panel applets" at *en.wikipedia.org/wiki/Control_panel_applets.*

You can bypass Control Panel by creating direct shortcuts (page 110) to .cpl files or by typing *control cpl_file* in the Run dialog box (replace *cpl_file* with the actual filename). To open Action Center, for example, press Windows logo key+R, type control *wscui.cpl,* and then press Enter.

Setting the Window Color

You can fine-tune the color and style of the frames of your windows.

To set the window color:

1   Choose Start > Control Panel > Appearance and Personalization > Personalization > Window Color. Or right-click an empty area of the desktop and then choose Personalize > Window Color.

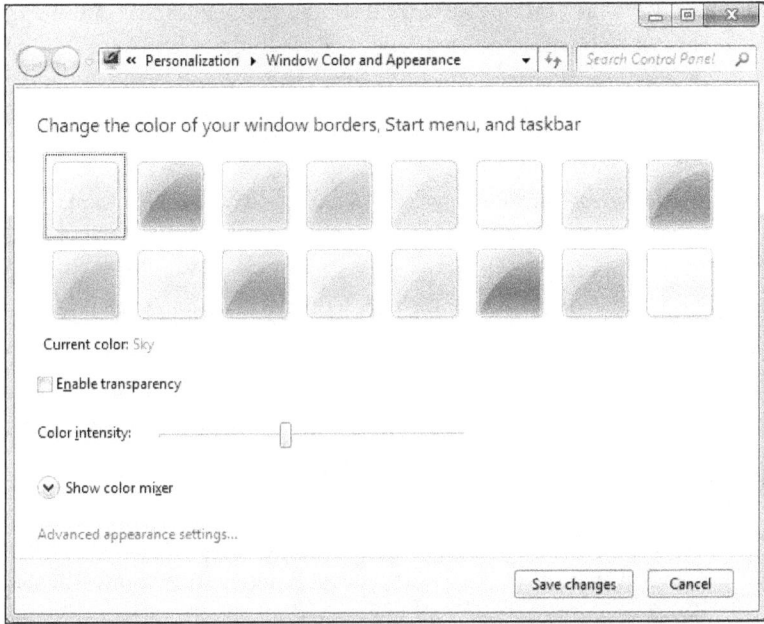

2   Click a color in the list or click "Show color mixer" to create your own color. Drag the "Color intensity" slider to dilute or deepen the chosen color. The color and transparency of window borders and title bars change dynamically as you adjust the controls.

3   Select "Enable transparency" if you want to see through the edges of windows; clear it for opaque edges (which use less power).

4   Click "Save changes".

Turning Off Aero

Windows picks an interface for you based on your computer's memory, display hardware, and video card, but you can change it manually. The following interfaces are available:

Aero

> The top-tier display, with advanced visual effects like transparent-glass windows and Start menu; realtime thumbnails on taskbar buttons and in the Alt+Tab window switcher; Flip 3D (Windows logo key+Tab); subtle animations; dynamic reflections; drop shadows; and color gradients. This interface is available in the higher-end Windows editions and only with suitable display hardware.

> Without Aero you lose only flash, not function, so you may want to change to a less-fancy interface if it makes your computer's response snappier. If your computer lacks the horsepower to run Aero, Windows won't let you switch to it. See also "Setting the Desktop Theme" on page 127.

Basic

> Like Aero but without transparency, live thumbnails, Flip 3D, and other gee-whizzery. It has the same hardware requirements as Aero. If you're using a laptop, use Basic to save battery power.

Classic

> Mimics the look of Windows 98/2000, with minimal hardware requirements. It changes only appearance, not functionality; you still get Search boxes, column controls, and so on.

High Contrast

> For people with vision problems. See also "Accommodating Disabled Users" on page 145.

To set the interface:

1   Choose Start > Control Panel > Appearance and Personalization > Personalization.

2   Select an interface in the theme list. The themes are grouped in Aero and non-Aero categories. (See also "Setting the Desktop Theme" on page 127.)

3   Click OK in each open dialog box.

Setting the Desktop Background

You can change the image, or **wallpaper**, that appears under the icons on your desktop. You can use your own pictures in addition to the ones that Windows or your computer manufacturer provides. Windows can show a static background image or cycle through a multiple-image slideshow. By default, Windows looks for background pictures in your personal Pictures folder (\Users*user_name*\Pictures), the shared Pictures folder (\Users\Public\ Pictures), and \Windows\Web\Wallpaper.

To set the desktop background:

1   Choose Start > Control Panel > Appearance and Personalization > Personalization > Desktop Background. Or right-click an empty area of the desktop and then choose Personalize > Desktop Background.

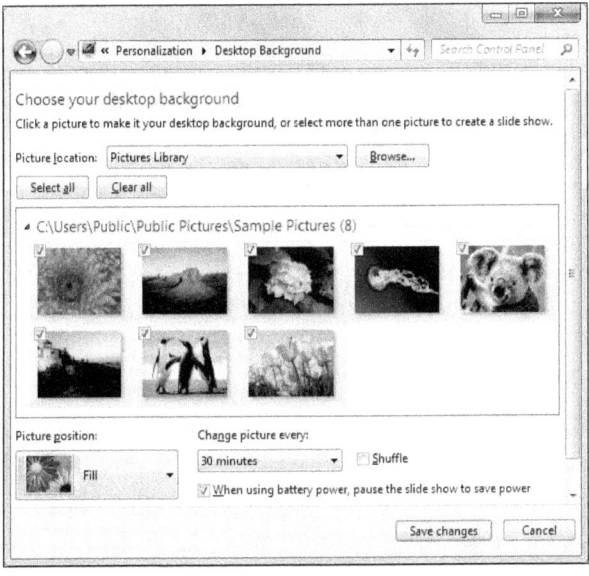

2   Choose a location from the "Picture location" drop-down list, and then click the picture or color that you want for your background. To select multiple pictures, use the checkboxes that appear when you point to each thumbnail image, or click "Select all" or "Clear all".

or

To use your own pictures, click Browse, find a picture folder on your computer or network, and then click OK. The folder appears in the "Picture location" drop-down list.

3   Choose an option from the "Picture position" drop-down list. Fill, Fit, and Stretch distort small images. If you're using your own small photos, try Tile or Center.

4   If you selected multiple images, choose a slideshow interval from the "Change picture every" drop-down list. To randomize the display sequence, select Shuffle.

5   Click "Save changes".

Desktop Background Tips

•   To advance to the next background image manually, right-click the desktop and then choose "Next desktop background".

•   You can use bitmap (.bmp/.dib) or JPEG (.jpeg/.jpg) files as background pictures.

•   If you choose Solid Colors from the "Picture location" drop-down list, the "More" link lets you pick a custom color.

•   To make any picture on your computer your desktop background, right-click the picture and then choose "Set as desktop background".

•   To use a web image as wallpaper, right-click the image in Internet Explorer and then choose "Set as background". The downloaded image appears in the "Picture location" list. Each new internet image that you define as a background replaces the old one.

•   To save a web image permanently and use it as wallpaper, right-click the image in Internet Explorer, choose "Save picture as", save the image in Pictures or a folder of your own, and then proceed as described.

•   Go to "Managing Visual Effects and Performance" on page 162 and experiment with "Use drop shadows for icon labels on the desktop" to see which setting makes your desktop icons' text labels easier to read against your background.

Resizing Desktop Images

If the photos from your digital camera are larger than your screen, here's how to trim them to use as wallpaper:

1   Right-click an empty area of your desktop and then choose "Screen resolution".

2 In the Resolution drop-down list, note the number of pixels (for example, 1024 × 768).

3 Find the icon or thumbnail of the image that you want to use for wallpaper, and hover the pointer over it until its file-information tooltip appears. (Alternatively, right-click the icon and then choose Properties > Details tab > Dimensions property.) Dimensions gives the image's width and height size in pixels (for example, 1600 × 1200).

If the image's dimensions exceed your computer's screen resolution, Windows fills your screen with the center portion of the image, and the edges go wherever leftover pixels go. This result is fine if the image edges are uninteresting. But if you want the uncropped image to be your wallpaper, make a copy and then use the Resize function of a graphics program (Windows Paint, GIMP, or Adobe Photoshop, for example) to shrink it to the same size as your screen (or close).

Setting the Screen Saver

A **screen saver** blanks the screen or shows images after a specified time passes without keyboard, mouse, or trackpad activity. Pressing a key, moving the mouse, or tapping the trackpad deactivates the screen saver. Screen savers were developed to prevent hardware damage to your display, but today's displays don't need that protection, so modern screen savers provide decoration or entertainment instead. A screen saver can also password-protect your computer and hide your screen when it takes effect.

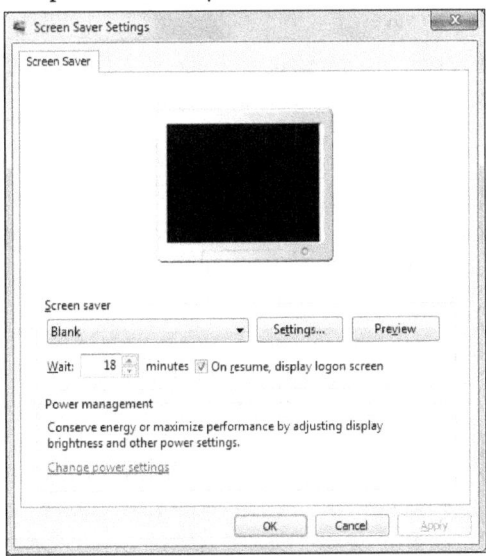

To set a screen saver:

1   Choose Start > Control Panel > Appearance and Personalization > Personalization > Screen Saver. Or right-click an empty area of the desktop and then choose Personalize > Screen Saver.

2   Choose a screen saver from the dropdown list. To turn off the screen saver, choose (None) from the list, click OK, and then skip the remaining steps.

3   Specify how long your computer must be idle before the screen saver activates. Try 15 to 20 minutes. (Wage slaves: set your screen saver's wait time carefully so your boss won't realize how long it's been since you did anything.)

4   Click Settings to see any options for the selected screen saver—to change color or animation style, for example.

5   (Optional) Select "On resume, display logon screen" to display a logon window when you begin using your computer after screen-saver activation. Your screen-saver password is the same as your user account password (page 8). If you have no account password, you can't set a screen-saver password.

6   Click Preview to see a full-screen preview of the screen saver. Press a key or move your mouse to end the test.

7   Click OK (or Apply).

To use personal pictures as a screen saver:

1   Make sure that you have two or more pictures in a folder on your computer (usually, your Pictures folder).

2   In the Screen Saver Settings dialog box, choose Photos from the drop-down list.

3   Click Settings to pick the folder containing your pictures and then set other options. The Photos screen saver scrolls through all the pictures and videos in the selected folder.

4   Click OK or Save in each open dialog box.

Tip: Appearances aside, screen savers—particularly complex ones such as 3D Text—waste power and processor time. To save resources, turn off your display manually or automatically after a certain period of inactivity. See "Conserving Power" on page 152.

Setting the Desktop Theme

If Windows' default appearance and sounds aren't to your taste, you can change them with a different desktop **theme**—a stored set of pictures, colors, icons, pointers, sounds, and other elements that redecorate your desktop. You can pick a predefined theme or create your own.

To set a theme:

1   Choose Start > Control Panel > Appearance and Personalization > Personalization. Or right-click an empty area of the desktop and then choose Personalize.

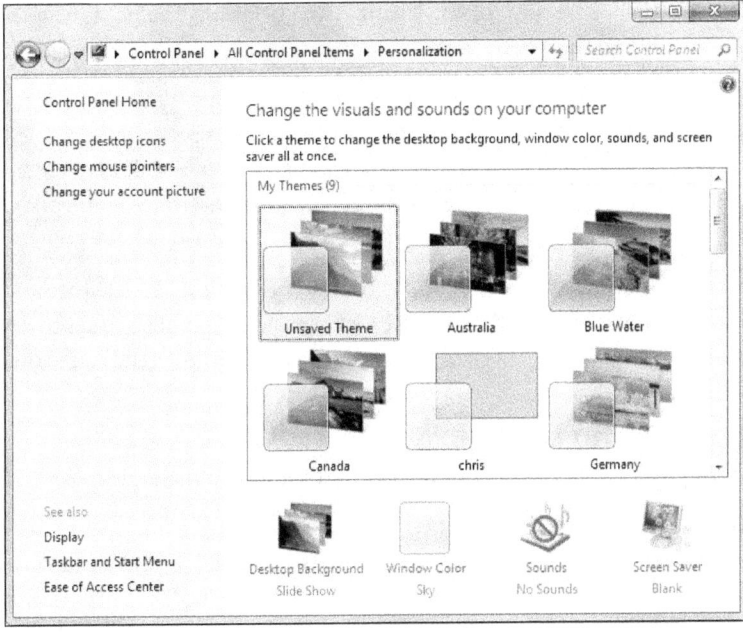

2   Select a theme in the list. Windows updates your desktop automatically when you select a theme.

To populate the theme list, Windows looks in \Users*user_name*\AppData\ Local\Microsoft\Windows\Themes and \Windows\Resources\Themes. Windows comes with a few themes, and you can get more by clicking "Get more themes online" (in the My Themes section of the themes list). Double-click a downloaded theme (.themepack file) to add it to your theme collection. See also "Turning Off Aero" on page 122.

3   Click Close.

To create a custom theme:

1   Choose Start > Control Panel > Appearance and Personalization > Personalization. Or right-click an empty area of the desktop and then choose Personalize.

2   Select a theme in the list as a starting point for creating a new one.

3   Choose the desired settings for Desktop Background, Window Color, Sounds, and Screen Saver.

4   When you're finished making changes, select your revised theme (in the My Themes section of the theme list), click Save Theme, type a theme name, and then click Save.

To save a custom theme as a file, right-click it (in the My Themes section of the theme list), choose "Save theme for sharing", type a theme name, and then click Save. Windows saves the theme as a .themepack file, which you can back up or share. Double-clicking a theme file activates it and adds it to the My Themes collection.

To delete a custom theme, right-click it and then choose "Delete theme". You can delete only themes that you created or installed—not the ones that Windows provides. (You can't delete a custom theme while it's the active theme.)

Configuring the Display

Windows lets you adjust your display hardware with these settings:

Screen resolution

Screen resolution is the amount (fineness) of detail in your screen's image, expressed in pixels wide by pixels high. (A **pixel**—or "dot"—is the smallest building block of the display.) Conventional screens have resolutions of 640 × 480 (largely useless except in emergencies), 800 × 600, 1024 × 768, and 1152 × 864. Modern widescreen displays have much higher resolutions.

Color quality

Color quality ranges from 16 ugly colors for archaic Standard VGA to 4 billion colors (32 bits per pixel) for the best displays and video cards. The number of colors available correlates to your resolution setting—most video cards display fewer colors at higher resolutions—so you may have to reduce resolution to get higher color quality. The available resolution and color choices adjust automatically. If your digital photos look blotchy, increase the color quality.

Refresh rate (CRT displays only)

Refresh rate is the frequency at which the screen is redrawn to maintain a steady image. Higher refresh rates yield less flicker. A refresh rate below 72 hertz, or 72 times per second, can tire your eyes if you look at the screen too long.

Color matching

Color matching ensures that colors are represented accurately and consistently across color printers, scanners, cameras, displays, and programs. Without color management, onscreen and printed colors may vary: orange can appear brown, green can appear blue, and so on. Graphic designers love color matching because it does away with trial and error in resolving color differences.

Color matching requires a separate **color profile** (.icc or .icm file) for each device connected to your computer. This profile conveys the device's color characteristics to the color management system every time colors are scanned, displayed, or printed. Color profiles installed with a display and video card are stored in the folder \Windows\System32\spool\drivers\color. If you have a separate color profile file, right-click it to install it or associate it with a device.

Professionals get accurate color on their displays by using separate hardware (colorimeters) but Windows' built-in Display Color Calibration wizard is good enough for everyday use. To run it, choose Start > Control Panel > Appearance and Personalization > Display > "Calibrate color" (on the left), and then follow the onscreen instructions.

LED, LCD, Laptop, and Tablet Displays

If you're using a flat-panel LCD (liquid crystal display), LED (light-emitting diode), laptop, or tablet display rather than a traditional bulky CRT (cathode ray tube) display, you can ignore some of the discussions here:

- LED/LCD displays produce sharp images only at **native**, or **optimal, resolution**, (and possibly some fractions thereof, depending on your model). Running at other resolutions makes the screen image blurry or blocky. The display's manufacturer will tell you the native resolution, but usually it's the maximum resolution available.

- The refresh rate doesn't apply to LED/LCDs, because they work with a continuous stream of light and pixels don't dim unless instructed to. CRT pixels begin to dim as soon as the electron gun's beam passes them.

- **ClearType,** Microsoft's font-smoothing technology, makes text appear sharper on LED/LCD and plasma screens. (Results vary on CRTs.) ClearType is turned on by default. To use the ClearType wizard, choose Start > Control Panel > Appearance and Personalization > Display > "Adjust ClearType text" (on the left), and then follow the onscreen instructions. More information about ClearType is at Microsoft Typography (*microsoft.com/typography/ClearTypeInfo.mspx*). See also "Managing Fonts" on page 158.

Changing Display Settings

Changing a display's settings affects all users who log on to your computer. Video-card memory largely determines the maximum resolution and color quality that you can use. To see how much video memory you have, choose Start > Control Panel > Appearance and Personalization > Display > "Adjust resolution" (on the left) > "Advanced settings" > Adapter tab > Adapter Information section. Better video cards have 256 MB or more of dedicated video memory—overkill for word processing and email but just enough for gaming and digital video. High-end video cards add extra tabs to this dialog box or install their own Control Panel tool or Start-menu item.

To see a display's properties, choose Start > Devices and Printers (or Start > Control Panel > Hardware and Sound > Devices and Printers), and then double-click the display's icon under Devices (see also "Managing Device Drivers" on page 302). To adjust the display for vision impairments, see "Accommodating Disabled Users" on page 145. For general information about installing and configuring hardware, see "Hardware & Drivers" on page 293.

To set screen resolution and color quality:

1   Choose Start > Control Panel > Appearance and Personalization > Display > "Adjust resolution" (on the left). Or right-click an empty area of the desktop and then choose "Screen resolution".

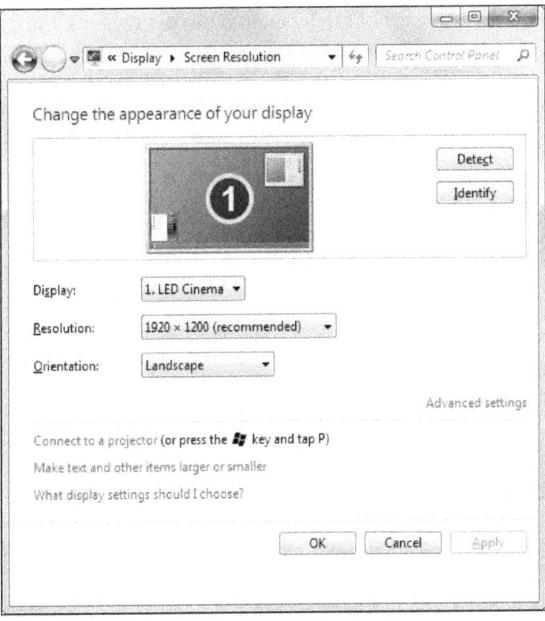

2   Choose a display size from the Resolution drop-down list.

3   To set the color quality, choose "Advanced settings" > Monitor tab > Colors drop-down list. Choose 16-bit or higher color; otherwise, photographic images will appear grainy (*dithered*).

4   Click Apply. Your screen turns black briefly and then refreshes with the new settings.

5   After your settings change, you have 15 seconds to accept the changes. If your new screen settings look good, click Yes; otherwise, click No or just wait to revert to your previous settings.

If you have more than one display, then the Screen Resolution window shows an icon for each display (click the Detect and Identify buttons if necessary). Click a display icon to activate it before choosing its resolution and color settings.

If you need a 256-color display to run an old DOS game or program, don't set your entire system to 256 colors even if that option is available. Instead, use the Compatibility feature; see "Running Older Programs" on page 244.

The "Advanced settings" link lets you view the hardware properties of your display and video card. You can adjust some settings, but you usually don't need to unless you're installing a new driver, setting color matching, or changing the refresh rate. The Troubleshoot tab lets you control graphics-hardware acceleration manually.

On CRT displays, don't always choose the maximum resolution available. If you spend most of your time typing memos or reading email, you may find that medium resolution reduces eyestrain. For general use, try 800 × 600 on a 15-inch display, 1024 × 768 on a 17-inch display, or 1152 × 864 on a 19-inch display.

To set the refresh rate (CRT displays only):

1   Choose Start > Control Panel > Appearance and Personalization > Display > "Adjust resolution" (on the left) > "Advanced settings" > Monitor tab. Or right-click an empty area of the desktop and then choose "Screen resolution" > "Advanced settings" (on the left) > Monitor tab.

    If you have multiple displays, click the icon of the target display while you're in the Screen Resolution window.

2   In the Monitor Settings section, choose a screen refresh rate from the drop-down list.

    To reduce eyestrain, choose the highest refresh rate that your display and video card support, but check the documentation or the manufacturer's website to find out what setting the hardware will accept.

    Don't clear "Hide modes that this monitor cannot display" to choose a higher refresh rate. A refresh rate that exceeds the capabilities of your display or video card can distort images or damage hardware.

3   Click Apply. Your screen turns black briefly and then refreshes with the new settings.

4   After your settings change, you have 15 seconds to accept the changes. If your new screen settings look good, click Yes; otherwise, click No or just wait to revert to your previous settings.

To manage color profiles:

1   Choose Start > Control Panel, type *color management* in the Search Control Panel box, and then select Color Management in the results list. Or choose Start > Control Panel, switch to icon view, and then click Color Management.

The profiles list shows all color profiles associated with the current display and video card (an empty profile list is fine for most people and everyday use—to learn more about color management, click "Understanding color management settings").

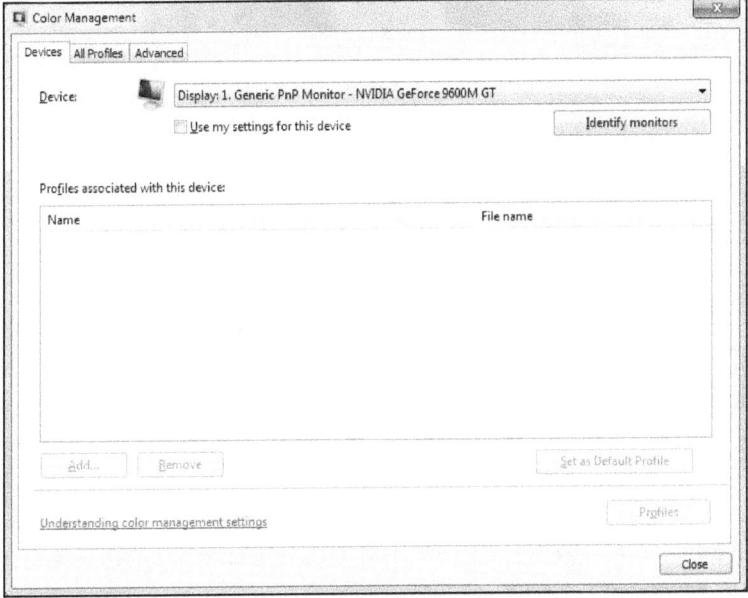

2   To add a color profile, click Add, and then use the Associate Color Profile dialog box to select a color profile to associate with the current display.

To remove a profile, select it and then click Remove.

To set a profile as the default for the current display, select it and then click Set as Default Profile.

3   Click OK in each open dialog box.

Scaling Text for Easier Reading

Dots per inch (dpi) is the standard way to measure screen and printer resolution—the more dots per inch, the better the resolution. By increasing dpi, you can make text, icons, and other screen items larger and easier to see. Decreasing dpi makes them smaller, fitting more on your screen. To adjust dpi scaling, choose Start > Control Panel > Appearance and Personalization > Display. Select one of the preset sizes or click "Set custom text size (DPI)" to set a specific size. Click Apply. Log off and then log on again to see the changes.

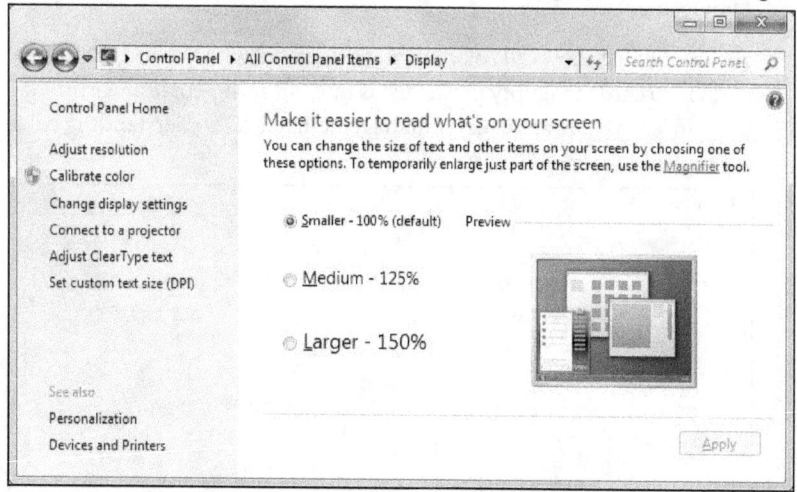

Configuring Sound and Audio Devices

Most computers have audio recording and playback devices such as sound cards, microphones, headphones, and speakers (built-in or external). Use Control Panel's Sound tool to configure these devices.

You can also customize system sound effects, which are audio clips (beeps, chords, or music snippets) associated with system events such as emptying the Recycle Bin or error messages.

Depending on your computer's audio hardware, you may see all or some of these devices (or others not listed here) in the Sound dialog box:

CD Player
> Controls the volume of audio CDs (if your CD drive is connected to the sound card directly with a cable).

Line In/Aux
> Controls the volume of the sound card's Line-In or Aux input (usually used to record from a stereo or other external playback device).

Microphone
> Controls the sound card's microphone input volume (usually used with a microphone or dictation headset).

Speakers/Headphones
> Controls the volume of your computer's headphones or external or built-in speakers (connected to a USB port, motherboard audio port, or a sound card).

SW Synth
> Controls the volume of music produced by the sound card's MIDI synthesizer or wavetable.

Wave Out Mix
> Controls sounds generated by Windows, games, MP3s, Windows Media Player, and many other programs.

To control sound volume:

1 Choose Start > Control Panel > Hardware and Sound > "Adjust system volume" (under Sound). Or right-click the Volume icon ◁)) in the taskbar's notification area and then choose Open Volume Mixer.

The Volume Mixer lets you adjust the master volume (at left) and, independently, the volume of individual programs that appear in the Applications section (at right).

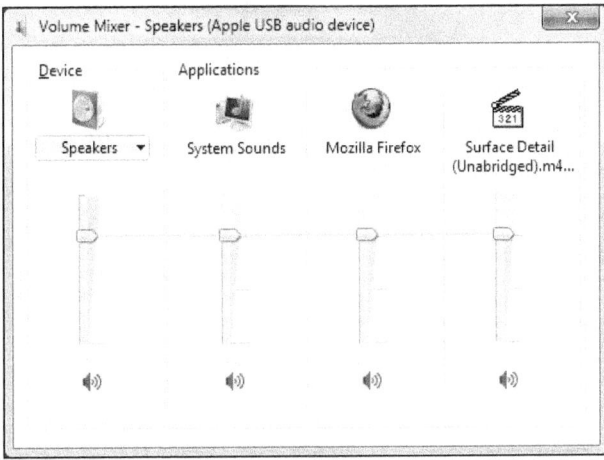

or

Click the Volume icon 🔊 in the taskbar's notification area. The slider controls the master volume for your speakers or headphones.

2   Drag the slider to lower or raise the volume, or click the Mute button 🔇 to turn off sound.

To see the current volume level and playback device:

• Hover the pointer over the Volume icon 🔊 in the taskbar's notification area. The current volume level is given on a scale from 0% (muted) to 100% (loudest).

Tip: If the Volume icon 🔊 doesn't appear in the notification area, right-click an empty area of the notification area, choose "Customize notification icons", click "Turn system icons on or off", and then turn on Volume.

To configure playback devices:

1   Choose Start > Control Panel > Hardware and Sound > Sound > Playback tab. Or right-click the Volume icon 🔊 in the taskbar's notification area and then choose "Playback devices".

2   Right-click a device (typically speakers or headphones) in the list and then choose a command to configure or test the device, or to inspect or change its properties.

3   Click OK in each open dialog box.

To configure recording devices:

1   Choose Start > Control Panel > Hardware and Sound > Sound > Recording tab. Or right-click the Volume icon 🔊 in the taskbar's notification area and then choose "Recording devices".

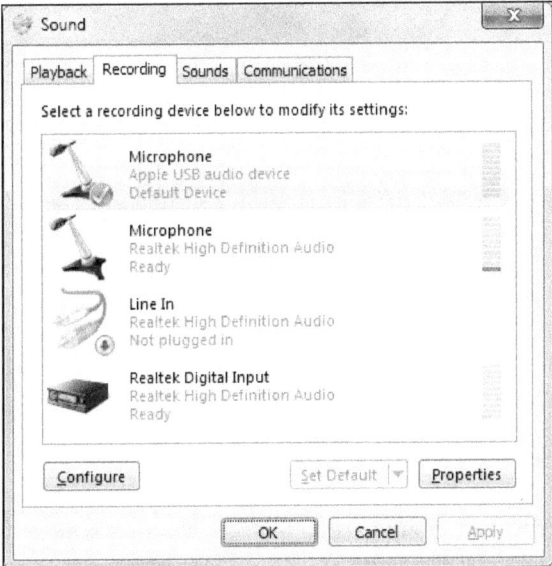

2   Right-click a device (typically a microphone or a line-in) in the list and then choose a command to configure or test the device, or to inspect or change its properties.

3   Click OK in each open dialog box.

To configure system sounds:

1   Choose Start > Control Panel > Hardware and Sound > Sound > Sounds tab. Or right-click the Volume icon ◁») in the taskbar's notification area and then choose Sounds.

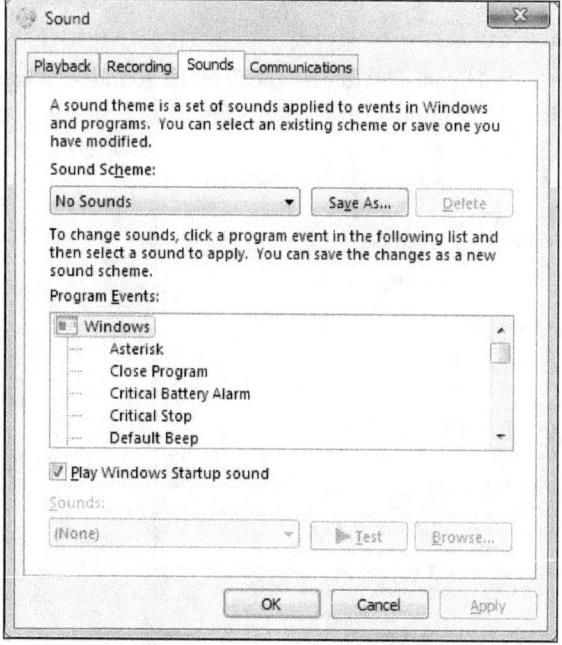

2   To choose a predefined group of sound effects, choose a scheme from the Sound Scheme drop-down list. You can choose (or mute) each sound individually or use a sound scheme to apply a group of sounds.

3   To change a sound for a particular event, click the event in the Program Events list, and then choose the sound from the Sounds drop-down list.

or

Select the event and then click Browse to select another sound file (in .wav audio format) on your system.

or

Choose (None) in the Sounds dropdown list to remove a sound.

4   To preview a sound for a particular event, select the event in the Program Events list and then click Test.

5 To save a changed sound scheme, click Save As, type a name, and then click OK.

6 To delete a custom sound scheme, select the scheme and then click Delete. You can delete only the schemes that you created or installed, not the ones Windows provides.

7 Click OK (or Apply).

Sound and Audio Tips

- To make an audio device's volume control appear even when it's not playing sound, right-click the Volume icon  in the taskbar's notification area and then choose "Volume control options". Select the checkboxes of any audio devices whose volume you want to adjust even when they're not playing sound. You can make sure, for example, that your speaker volume isn't explosively loud when you switch over from headphones.

- To make Windows mute or lower the volume of other sounds (such as music) automatically when you make a computer-based telephone call, choose Start > Control Panel > Hardware and Sound > Sound > Communications tab.

- Place .wav files in the folder \Windows\Media to have them appear in the system sounds list.

- To adjust sounds for hearing impairments, see "Accommodating Disabled Users" on page 145.

- To see an audio device's properties, choose Start > Devices and Printers (or Start > Control Panel > Hardware and Sound > Devices and Printers), and then double-click the audio device's icon. See also "Managing Device Drivers" on page 302.

- For general information about installing and configuring hardware, see "Hardware & Drivers" on page 293.

Setting the Date and Time

Keep your system time accurate, because Windows uses it to time-stamp files and messages, schedule tasks, and record events. (When your computer is shut down, the motherboard battery maintains the system time.)

The clock in the taskbar's notification area shows the system time. If the clock isn't visible, right-click an empty area of the notification area, choose "Customize notification icons", click "Turn system icons on or off", and then turn on Clock 🕘. Windows also includes a Clock gadget (page 106) that you can place on your desktop.

To set the date and time:

1   Choose Start > Control Panel > Clock, Language, and Region > Date and Time.

    or

    Click the clock in the notification area and then click "Change date and time settings".

    or

    Right-click the taskbar clock and then choose "Adjust date/time".

    or

    Choose Start, type *date and time* in the Search box, and then press Enter.

2   On the Date and Time tab, click "Change date and time", adjust the date and time as needed, and then click OK. To set the time in the Time box, type new numbers, press the up- and down-arrow keys, or click the small

up and down arrows. To change months, click the small arrow at the top of the calendar.

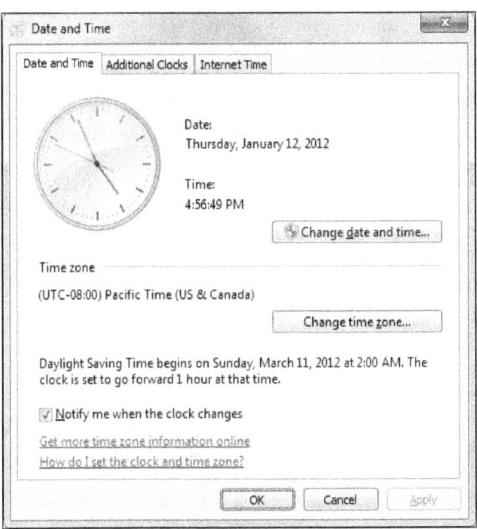

3   On the Date and Time tab, click "Change time zone", choose your time zone from the drop-down list, and then click OK. If your location doesn't use daylight saving time, clear "Automatically adjust clock for Daylight Saving Time". You don't have to be an administrator (page 8) to change the time zone.

4   On the Additional Clocks tab, you can add more clocks that show the date and time in other time zones. To view the clocks, click (or hover the pointer over) the clock in the notification area.

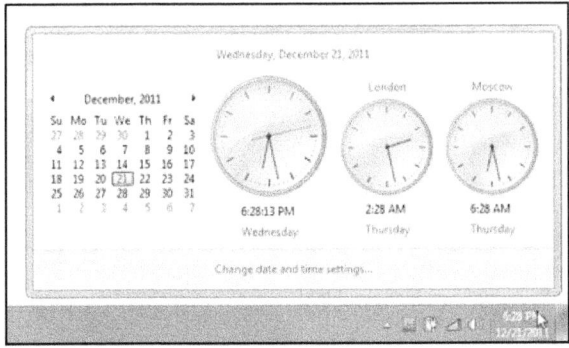

5   On the Internet Time tab, click "Change settings", select "Synchronize with an Internet time server" to synchronize your computer clock with a

highly accurate clock, and then type or choose any time-server address in the Server box. Once a week is the only interval you get unless you click "Update now". A time server won't synchronize your system time if your date is incorrect.

Internet-time synchronization occurs regularly only if you have a full-time internet connection such as DSL or cable. If you use dial-up, click "Update now" while you're connected to the internet to synchronize your clock immediately.

6 Click OK in each open dialog box.

Localizing Your System

Windows supports many international standards, formats, and languages. Use Control Panel's Regional and Language Options tool to adjust country-specific settings such as unit of measurement; currency, number, and date formats; and keyboard and display language.

To set formats for numbers, currencies, times, and dates:

1 Choose Start > Control Panel > Clock, Language, and Region > Region and Language > Formats tab. Or choose Start, type *region and language* in the Search box, and then press Enter.

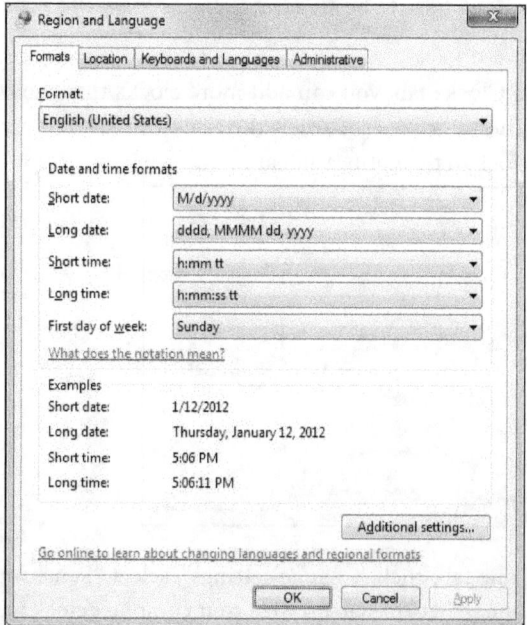

2   Choose a language from the Format drop-down list. The language affects how programs format numbers, currencies, times, and dates.

You can't save customized regional settings as though they were themes. If you customize and then choose another language in the list, you lose your customized settings.

3   To change individual settings, use the drop-down lists or click "Additional settings". The Examples section shows how selected settings affect the appearance of quantities.

4   Click OK in each open dialog box.

To set your current location:

1   Choose Start > Control Panel > Clock, Language, and Region > Region and Language > Location tab.

2   Choose your location from the "Current location" drop-down list.

Some programs and web services use this location to deliver to you local information such as news and weather. If your computer has a location sensor (GPS receiver), click the "Default location" link in this dialog box.

3   Click OK (or Apply).

To set the keyboard language:

1   Choose Start > Control Panel > Clock, Language, and Region > Region and Language > Keyboards and Languages tab.

2   Click "Change keyboards".

3   On the General tab, click Add, specify the language(s) and keyboard layout(s) to install, and then click OK.

The input language controls the language used when you type on your keyboard. You can click the Preview button to look at the keyboard layout of each language before you add it. Keyboard layouts rearrange the keys' character assignments. Pressing the [key on a U.S. keyboard with a German layout, for example, types the ü character.

4   On the Language Bar tab, set the location and appearance of the Language bar. The default location—the taskbar—is usually the most sensible place for the Language bar.

5   On the Advanced Key Settings tab, define a hotkey for each language. Hotkeys make it easy to switch among languages on the fly.

6   Click OK (or Apply).

7   To choose a language or keyboard layout to switch to, click the Language bar (on the taskbar), press the left Shift and left Alt keys at the same time, or press the language's hotkey (if you defined one).

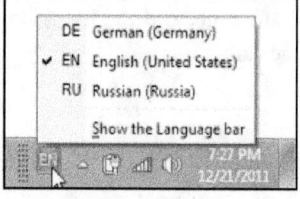

Tip: Use Character Map (page 261) to view the characters available on your keyboard.

To set the display language:

1   Choose Start > Control Panel > Clock, Language, and Region > Region and Language > Keyboards and Languages tab.

2   In the "Display language" section, choose a language from the list and then click OK. If you don't see a list of display languages, then you must install additional language files. Click "How can I install additional languages?" and then follow the onscreen instructions.

To set the preferred language for older programs:

1   Choose Start > Control Panel > Clock, Language, and Region > Region and Language > Administrative tab.

2   In the "Language for non-Unicode programs" section, click "Change system locale", choose your preferred language in the list, and then click OK. If an older program can't recognize your preferred language, Windows can swap the character set.

3   To apply your Regional and Language settings to all new user accounts or to system accounts, click "Copy settings", select the desired account checkboxes, and then click OK.

4   Click OK (or Apply).

Accommodating Disabled Users

Windows can be set up to assist disabled users. **Ease of Access** is Microsoft's umbrella term for tools that make a computer easier to use for people with poor eyesight, hearing, or mobility. **Ease of Access Center** is the main switchboard that teaches you about ease-of-access options and lets you turn them on or off.

The easiest way to learn about Ease of Access options is to answer a questionnaire that recommends settings based on your answers. If you prefer to skip the questionnaire, you can explore and set each option individually. Ease of Access options are also available on the Welcome screen (page 21).

Some Ease of Access tools are for everyone. Graphic designers and developers can use Magnifier for pixel-level design work, and On-Screen Keyboard is handy if you find yourself with a broken keyboard.

The main Ease of Access features are:

Magnifier
   Enlarges part of the screen in a small separate window while you work, leaving the rest of your desktop in a standard display. Keyboard shortcuts: Windows logo key+plus (+) and Windows logo key+minus (–).

Narrator
   Reads onscreen text aloud and describes some computer events (such as error messages) when they happen.

On-Screen Keyboard

Displays a picture of a keyboard with all the standard keys so you can type with mouse clicks or a joystick.

High Contrast

Makes things easier to read by increasing the contrast of colors. Keyboard shortcut: Press left Alt+left Shift+Print Screen (or PrntScrn).

Speech Recognition

Lets you give commands and dictate text by using your voice. See "Using Speech Recognition" on page 147.

Mouse Keys

Lets you use the arrow keys on your keyboard or the numeric keypad to move the pointer around the screen. Keyboard shortcut: Press left Alt+left Shift+Num Lock.

Sticky Keys

Lets you press key combinations, such as Ctrl+Alt+Delete, one key at a time. Keyboard shortcut: Press Shift five times.

Toggle Keys

Plays an alert each time you press the Caps Lock, Num Lock, or Scroll Lock key. Keyboard shortcut: Press Num Lock for 5 seconds.

Filter Keys

Removes unintentional repeated keystrokes when you hold down a key too long. Keyboard shortcut: Press right Shift for 8 seconds.

To open Ease of Access Center:

1 Choose Start > All Programs > Accessories > Ease of Access > Ease of Access Center.

   or

   Choose Start > Control Panel > Ease of Access > Ease of Access Center.

   or

   Choose Start, type *ease of access* in the Search box, and then press Enter.

   or

   Press Windows logo key+U.

Ease of Access Center starts by reading its own text aloud. You can mute it by clearing "Always read this section aloud".

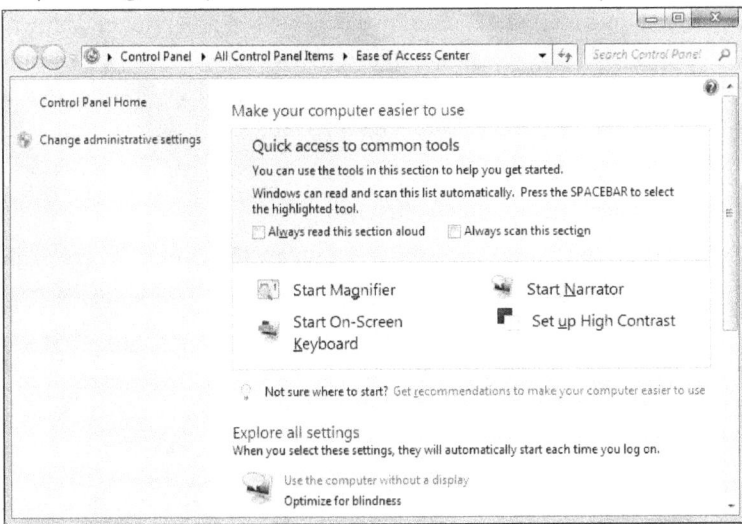

To use the Ease of Access questionnaire:

1   In Ease of Access Center, click "Get recommendations to make your computer easier to use".

2   Follow the onscreen instructions. When you finish the questionnaire, Windows presents you with a list of Ease of Access options that you can turn on or off.

To set Ease of Access options individually:

•   In Ease of Access Center, click the links under "Explore all settings". Each link takes you to a page of controls that lets you turn on or off related options.

Using Speech Recognition

Control Panel's Speech tool controls Windows' speech-recognition and text-to-speech (speech synthesizer) features.

Speech Recognition

Speech Recognition lets you speak into a microphone to control your computer; you can give commands that the computer will carry out or dictate text that will self-type on your screen. You can create a voice profile that trains your computer to understand the sound of your voice, word pronunciation, accent, and speaking manner. You can use speech recognition to dictate documents and messages, use your voice to control programs and browse the web, and avoid repetitive-strain injuries by reducing the use of your mouse and keyboard. Speech recognition works for nearly all applications that come with Windows, Microsoft Word, and Microsoft Outlook (but not Excel and PowerPoint).

To set up speech recognition for first use:

1   Choose Start > All Programs > Accessories > Ease of Access > Speech Recognition. Or choose Start, type *speech recognition* in the Search box, and then click Speech Recognition.

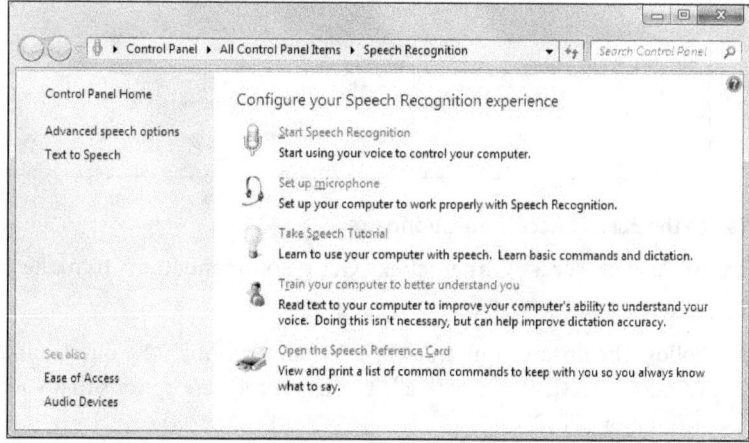

2   Click "Start Speech Recognition". The "Set up Speech Recognition" wizard opens.

Detour: Rather than using the wizard, you can instead set up the parts of speech recognition individually: click "Set up microphone", "Take Speech Tutorial", and "Train your computer to better understand you". Follow the onscreen instructions that appear after you click each link.

3   Follow the onscreen instructions. The wizard helps you set up your microphone, learn how to talk to your computer, and train your computer to understand your speech.

The speech tutorial takes about 30 minutes to complete. Make sure that you have enough uninterrupted free time to finish it.

To set speech options:

1 Choose Start > Control Panel > Ease of Access > Speech Recognition > "Advanced speech options" (on the left) > Speech Recognition tab.

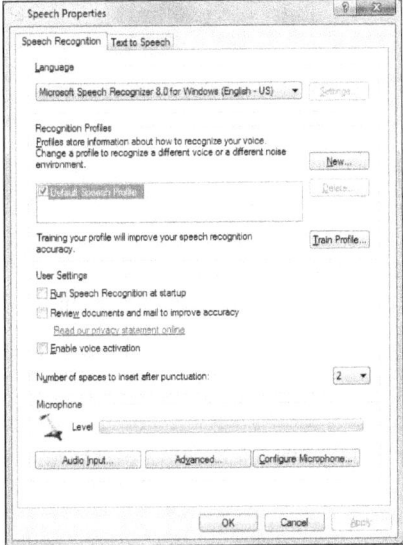

2 In the Language section, choose a speech-recognition engine from the drop-down list or click Settings (if available) to show additional engine properties.

3 In the Recognition Profiles section, click New to create a new recognition profile for your voice, and then follow the onscreen instructions when the wizard opens.

4 Under Microphone, set and configure your audio input device (page 134).

5 Click OK (or Apply).

To use speech recognition:

1 Choose Start > Control Panel > Ease of Access > Speech Recognition.

2 Click "Open the Speech Reference Card" to use a quick reference while you give commands and dictate text.

3 Switch back to Speech Recognition and then click "Start Speech Recognition". If you haven't yet set up speech recognition, then the "Set up Speech Recognition" wizard opens; see "To set up speech recognition for first use" above.

The most common way to use speech recognition is to dictate a document. Here's a quick example that starts WordPad, dictates the body of a document, names and saves the document, and then exits WordPad:

- "Start listening" (This makes the computer listen to you.)

- "Open WordPad"

- "This is a test of speech recognition period" (Remember to pronounce punctuation.)

- Say "File", then "Save as", then "My test document", and then "Save"

- "Close WordPad"

- "Stop listening" (This makes the computer stop listening to you.)

To correct mistakes while dictating text, say "Correct" plus the word that the computer typed by mistake, and then select the correct word in the list offered by Speech Recognition or repeat the correct word again. For example, if the computer misrecognized "speech" as "peach", say "Correct peach", and then select the right word in the list or say "speech" again.

When you say a command that can be interpreted in a few ways, the system displays a disambiguation interface to clarify what you intended.

Speak directly into your microphone, and make sure that it's properly attached and not muted. If your computer still can't hear you, check the input level on the Levels tab of the mic's Properties dialog box (see "Configuring Sound and Audio Devices" on page 134).

Text to Speech

Windows' Text-to-Speech (TTS) tool reads aloud onscreen text, buttons, menus, filenames, keystrokes, and other items by using a speech synthesizer. The only built-in program that reads to you is Narrator, which has its own voice controls (see "Accommodating Disabled Users" on page 145). You can find other TTS programs at *microsoft.com/enable*. In addition to a microphone, you'll need a sound card if your computer's motherboard doesn't have a built-in microphone jack. Use a high-quality microphone such as a USB headset microphone or an array mic. Get a mic with noise-cancellation technology if you work in a noisy place like a call center or trading floor.

To set text-to-speech options:

1 Choose Start > Control Panel > Ease of Access > Speech Recognition > "Advanced speech options" (on the left) > Text to Speech tab.

2 In the "Voice selection" section, choose one of the available TTS voices from the drop-down list or click Settings (if available) to display additional voice properties. The selected voice speaks the text in the "preview voice" box.

3 In the "Voice speed" section, drag the slider to adjust the voice's rate of speech.

4 Click Audio Output to set the preferred device for voice playback (page 134).

5 Click OK (or Apply).

Conserving Power

Environmental and money concerns make power management an issue for desktop as well as laptop users. Control Panel's **Power Options** tool lets you configure hardware features that reduce power consumption, affect how the power switch works, and extend the life of computer parts by turning them off or switching them to a low-power state.

To optimize your computer's power use, Windows uses a **power plan**—a collection of settings that reduces the power consumption of certain system devices or of your entire system. You can use the default power plans provided with Windows or create your own by using one of the default plans as a starting point. You can change settings for any of your custom plans or the default plans to, for example:

- Make your computer go to sleep (page 30) or turn off the display after a specified idle period.

- Adjust the brightness of your display (page 128).

- Require a password to unlock the computer when it wakes from sleep.

- Choose what your computer does when you press the power and sleep buttons on your computer's case or (for a laptop) close the lid.

Some computers may not be able to use all the Power Options features. Windows identifies your hardware configuration automatically and makes available only the settings that you can change.

To set a power plan:

1 Choose Start > Control Panel > Hardware and Sound > Power Options, and then select a power plan.

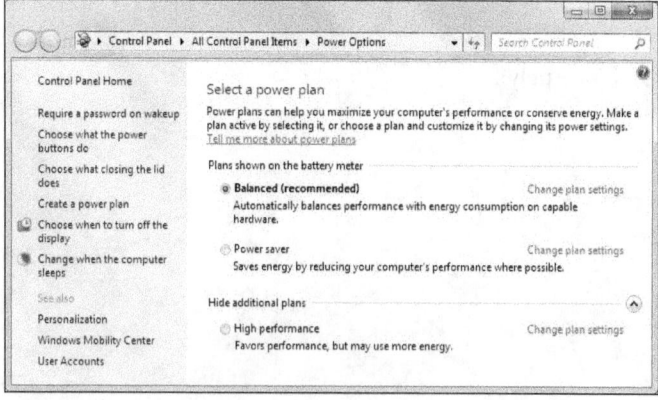

or

Choose Start, type *power options* in the Search box, press Enter, and then select a power plan.

or

If the Power (battery) icon 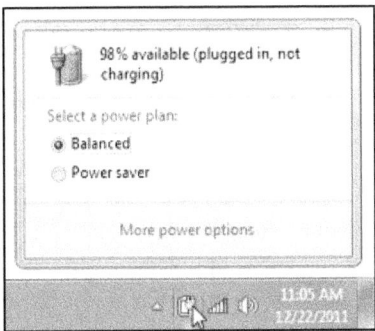 appears in the taskbar's notification area, click it, and then select a power plan.

The following built-in power plans are available (your computer's manufacturer or system administrator may have added others):

Balanced
Offers full performance when you need it and saves power during periods of inactivity. This plan is fine for most people's needs.

Power saver
Maximizes battery life by reducing system performance. If you're a laptop user, use this plan if you travel often and rely on battery power for long periods.

High performance
Maximizes system performance and responsiveness. If you're a desktop user, use this plan for processor-intensive tasks like editing video, playing 3D games, and doing engineering or scientific calculations.

To extend a battery's charge, use the "Power saver" power plan, reduce your display brightness, and unplug the USB and PC Card devices that you're not using. Note that if you're a domain member (page 9), your administrator can block you from changing the power plan.

The battery-shaped Power icon in the taskbar's notification area appears on all laptop computers. On desktop computers, it appears only if you're using a short-term battery, such as a UPS (page 157) that plugs into a USB port.

The Power icon responds to clicks, hovers, and right-clicks. Click the icon to see or change the power plan. Hover the pointer over the icon for a status report or right-click it for a shortcut menu. Choosing Power Options from the shortcut menu is a quick way to open the Power Options window. If your laptop has more than one battery, click the icon to see the charge remaining on each battery, or hover over the icon to see the combined charge.

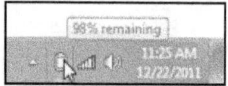

To show or hide the Power icon, right-click an empty area of the notification area, choose "Customize notification icons", click "Turn system icons on or off", and then turn on or off Power . (The Power option is unavailable if no battery is installed.) You can also open this dialog box from the Power icon's shortcut menu.

The Power icon is a graphical "fuel gauge" that tells you the battery's remaining power and charging state. If you've customized your power plan to let you know when your battery is low, that notification appears above the Power icon. System-intensive tasks (like watching video) drain a battery a lot faster than mundane ones (like texting). Over time you'll learn how accurate the battery meter is for your laptop, battery, and computing tasks.

The Power icon reflects the current state of your battery:

Power icon	Battery condition
	Your laptop is plugged in, and the battery is charging.
	Your laptop is plugged in, and the battery is fully charged.
	Your laptop isn't plugged in, and the battery is draining.
	The battery is low (yellow caution sign).
	The battery is critically low (red circled ×).
	Windows can't determine the battery charge (empty battery).
	Windows can't find a battery in the battery bay (red ×). Check the documentation that came with your battery or laptop to know when it's safe to remove or insert the battery.

To set low and critical battery behavior:

1 Choose Start > Control Panel > Hardware and Sound > Power Options.

2 Next to the selected plan, click "Change plan settings".

3 Click "Change advanced power settings".

4 On the "Advanced settings" tab, expand Battery.

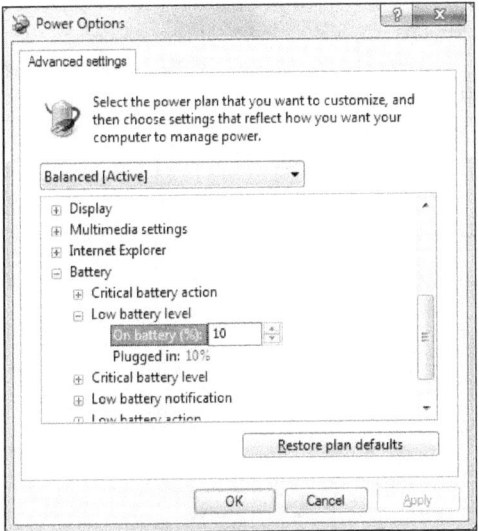

5 To set the charge levels at which battery notifications occur, expand "Low battery level" and "Critical battery level", and then choose the percentage that you want for each level. Windows monitors your battery's charge and warns you when it reaches low and critical levels. Don't set these levels so low that you won't have a chance to install a charged battery, find a power outlet, or save your work and turn off your laptop. Try 25% (low) and 10% (critical) initially.

or

To set what to do when a battery notification occurs, expand "Low battery action" and "Critical battery action", and then choose the action that you want for each level.

or

To turn on or off battery-level notifications, expand "Low battery notification", click "On battery", and then choose On or Off.

6 Click OK.

7 Click "Save changes".

To create your own power plan:

1 Choose Start > Control Panel > Hardware and Sound > Power Options.

2 Click "Create a power plan" (on the left).

3 On the Create a Power Plan page, select the plan that's closest to the type of plan that you want to create. If you want to create a plan to conserve power, for example, start with "Power saver".

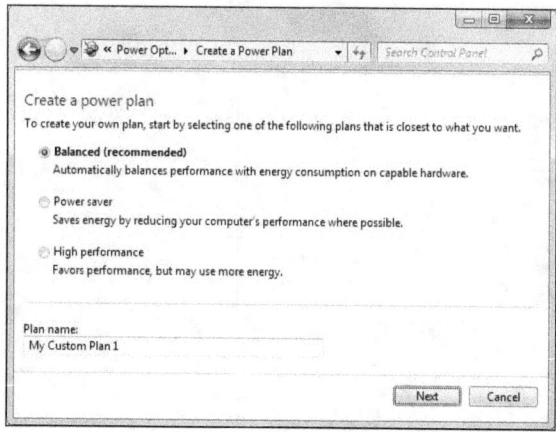

4 In the "Plan name" box, type a name for your plan, and then click Next.

5 On the Edit Plan Settings page, choose the display (page 128) and sleep (page 30) settings that you want to use when your computer is running on battery and when it's plugged in, and then click Create. The newly created plan automatically becomes the active plan.

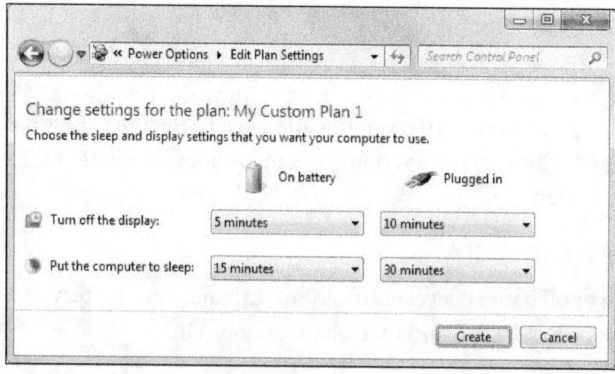

To change an existing power plan:

1 Choose Start > Control Panel > Hardware and Sound > Power Options.

2 Next to the plan that you want to change, click "Change plan settings".

3 On the Edit Plan Settings page, choose the new settings.

4 If you don't want to change any more settings, click "Save changes".

  or

  To change additional power settings, click "Change advanced power settings", and then complete steps 5 and 6.

5 Change the settings on the "Advanced settings" tab. Expand the category that you want to customize, expand each setting that you want to change, and then choose the values that you want to use when your computer is running on battery and when it's plugged in.

6 Click OK.

7 Click "Save changes".

To delete a power plan:

1 Choose Start > Control Panel > Hardware and Sound > Power Options.

2 If the active plan is the one that you want to delete, make a different plan the active plan.

3 Next to the plan that you want to delete, click "Change plan settings". You can't delete a built-in plan (Balanced, Power saver, or High performance).

4 On the Edit Plan Settings page, click "Delete this plan".

5 When prompted, click OK. You can't restore a plan after deleting it.

To configure system settings for power options:

1 Choose Start > Control Panel > Hardware and Sound > Power Options.

2 Click "Require a password on wakeup" (on the left).

3 Choose the settings for the power and sleep buttons, laptop lid, and password protection. These settings apply to all power plans. If any settings are unavailable, click "Change settings that are currently unavailable".

4 Click "Save changes".

Uninterruptible Power Supply

An **Uninterruptible Power Supply** (UPS) is a sealed backup battery—connected between the computer and the electrical outlet—that kicks in to keep your computer running if power fails. The UPS's capacity is expressed in minutes available to save your work and shut down normally during a power outage—about 5 minutes for cheaper UPSs and more than 30 minutes for better ones. UPSs also protect against power surges, spikes, and brownouts (low voltage), which damage hardware more than blackouts.

Don't forget to plug your display into the UPS. You can also plug in a power strip for extra sockets and keep your router, printer, and electric stapler safe too.

A UPS doesn't really *have* to interact with Windows, but Windows includes built-in support for monitoring that sounds power-failure alerts, displays remaining UPS-battery time, and—if power becomes very low—shuts down the computer automatically. A UPS that plugs into a USB port will install its driver and may come with its own power-management software.

Managing Fonts

A **font** is a collection of letters, numbers, punctuation, symbols, and other characters that describes a certain typeface, along with size, spacing, and other qualities. Windows includes dozens of fonts used to display text onscreen and in print. Most of these are **TrueType** or **OpenType** fonts, which look smooth and clear in all sizes and on all output devices. Windows also supports **PostScript** fonts (an older standard), with no need for Adobe Type Manager. You'll also find a few hideous bitmapped fonts, called **raster** fonts, included for compatibility with older programs. You manage fonts in the Fonts folder.

If you want a font that prints well and is easy to read on the screen, use a True-Type or OpenType font. If you need a large character set for language coverage and fine typography, use an OpenType font. For printing glossy magazines and professional-quality publications, use an OpenType or PostScript font.

For more font information, visit *microsoft.com/typography*. Look for a list of font foundries where you can buy high-quality fonts online. You can also download lots of free fonts, but they're rarely of good quality. (Make sure that you trust the source when you download a font.)

To open the Fonts folder:

- Choose Start > Control Panel > Appearance and Personalization > Fonts.

  or

  Choose Start, type *fonts* in the Search box, and then press Enter.

  or

  In Windows Explorer, open the folder \Windows\Fonts.

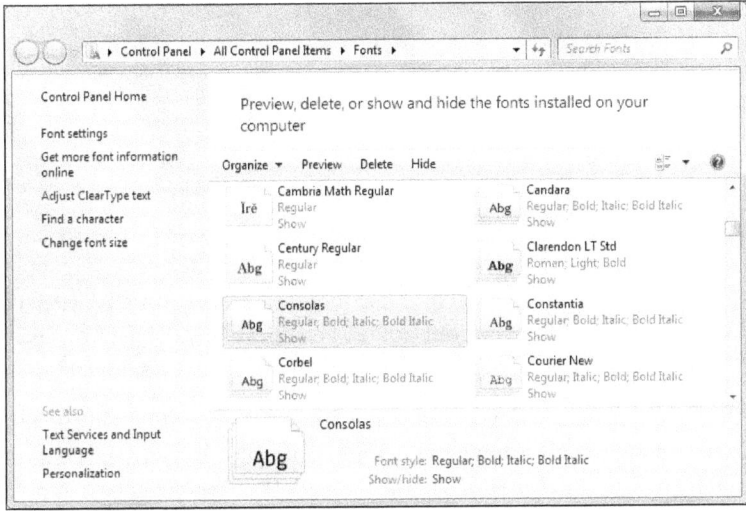

Font styles (regular, bold, italic, and so on) in the same font family appear in the Fonts folder as "stacks" rather than as individual icons.

Double-click a stack to see the individual fonts.

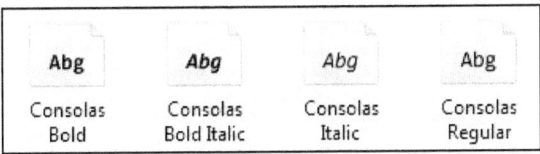

Double-click an individual font or a group of selected fonts to preview it in Font Viewer, which displays font statistics, the full alphabet, and a type sample at various sizes. Click Print to print a font sample.

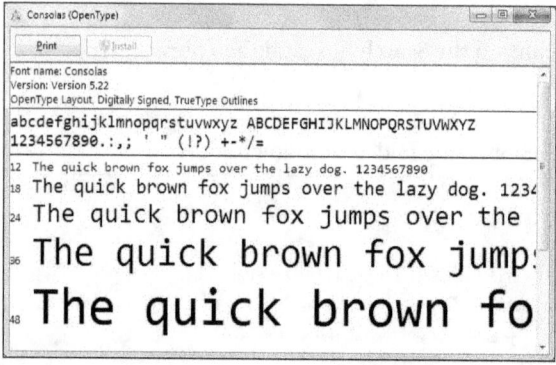

To install a new font:

- Right-click the font that you want to install and then choose Install (you can highlight and install multiple fonts at the same time). Alternatively, drag a font file into the Fonts folder. Font files generally have the filename extension .ttf (for TrueType fonts) or .otf (for OpenType fonts)

After a font is installed, it appears in your programs' Font dialog boxes and lists. To show or hide a font without uninstalling it, select it in the Fonts folder and then click Show or Hide (on the toolbar). If a new font appears unexpectedly in your Fonts folder, a recently installed program probably put it there. If you install a TrueType font and a PostScript font with exactly the same name, Windows won't know which one to access when you use it. Avoid installing different fonts with the same name; install only one.

To remove a font:

- In the Fonts folder, right-click the font's icon and then choose Delete. Alternatively, in the Fonts folder, select one or more font icons, and then press the Delete key or click Delete on the toolbar. (If you drag fonts from the Fonts folder to another folder, they're copied, not deleted.)

Font Tips

- Font Viewer displays only a predefined set of characters. To display every character in a font, use Character Map (page 261). To view fonts with a program other than Windows Font Viewer, right-click a font icon in the Fonts folder, choose Properties, and then click Change.

- To see only fonts for your language or save space by using font shortcuts, in the Fonts folder, click "Font settings" (on the left).

- To see each font's name, styles, and show–hide status, in the Fonts folder, choose 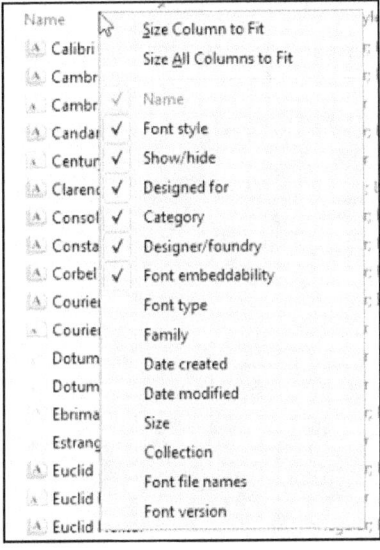 > Tiles (on the toolbar).

- To match the font names with their filenames and paths (page 179), in the Fonts folder, choose ▦ ▾ > Details (on the toolbar), right-click a column heading in the file list, and then select "Font file names". If a font icon has a shortcut arrow (page 110), then the font is installed but located elsewhere; the "Font file names" column tells you where.

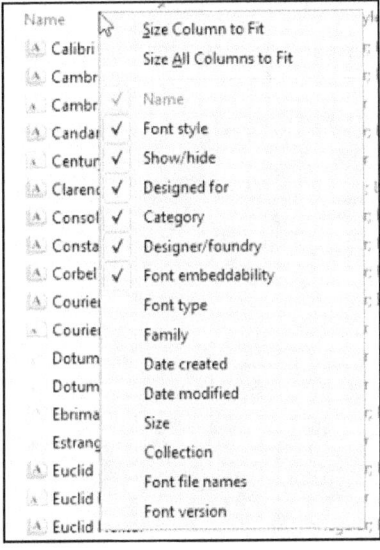

- To make onscreen fonts clearer, you can increase dpi scaling (click "Change font size" in the Fonts window) and use ClearType (click "Adjust ClearType text"). For details, see "Scaling Text for Easier Reading" on page 134. The Windows fonts designed to work well with ClearType include Constantia and Cambria (serif); Corbel, Candara, and Calibri (sans serif); Consolas (monospace); Gabriola (script); and Segoe UI (used throughout the Windows interface).

- Windows uses the font Segoe UI in menus, icons, and other screen elements. To change the Windows font, choose Start > Control Panel > Appearance and Personalization > Personalization > Window Color > "Advanced appearance settings". In the Item list, choose the part of Windows where you want to change the font, and then pick a font, size, and color.

Managing Visual Effects and Performance

The Windows interface offers many visual effects, such as animation, fading, and shadows. These effects can be entertaining or useful (or annoying), but they chew up processor time and can degrade performance noticeably (particularly if you're short on RAM, video processor speed, or battery power). Windows lets you turn off individual visual effects, perhaps making your system more responsive. It's worth experimenting.

To turn off visual effects:

1   Choose Start > Control Panel > System and Security > System > "Advanced system settings" (on the left).

2   On the Advanced tab, in the Performance section, click Settings > Visual Effects tab.

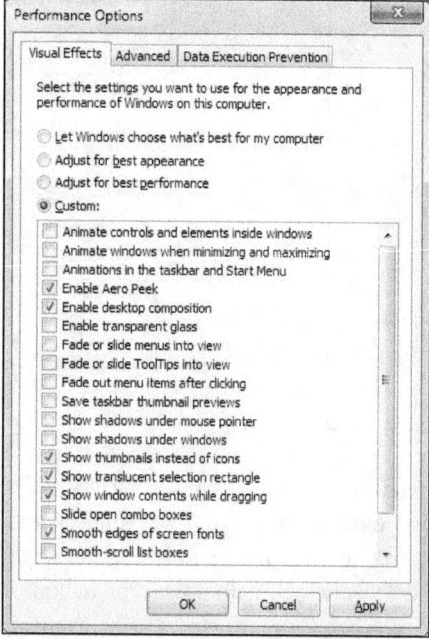

3   Select Custom, clear the checkboxes for the effects that you want to turn off, and then click OK in each open dialog box.

Tip: If you have a solid-color desktop background (page 123), you may be able to better read icon labels if you turn off "Use drop shadows for icon labels on the desktop". If you have an elaborate or photographic background, leave it turned on.

---

4   Files, Folders & Drives

Windows uses files and folders to organize your information so that you aren't overwhelmed by long file lists and can distinguish one set of content from another. A **file** is the basic unit of computer storage; it can be a program, a program's configuration data, a log that the computer itself maintains, or a document that you create or receive. You organize files in containers called **folders** (or **directories**), which can hold additional folders (called **subfolders**) to form a treelike hierarchy. Folders in turn are stored on **drives** (or **volumes**) such as disk drives, flash drives, CDs, DVDs, and network servers. Windows creates a few system folders to store its own files and settings but otherwise doesn't care how you structure your tree of folders and files. This chapter explains how to use Windows Explorer to navigate and manage your stored information.

Exploring Your Computer

The **Computer** folder is the window to your computer's data structure. The Computer folder shows the top-level folders and drives on your computer, including network drives and other connected storage devices. This window's appearance varies by computer and changes when you add or remove drives and devices.

From the Computer folder you can open files, folders, and drives on your computer, network, and connected devices, which are categorized as follows:

Hard Disk Drives
    Lists the hard drives (internal and external) installed on this computer.

Devices with Removable Storage

Lists USB flash drives, CDs, DVDs, floppy disks, tapes, and other removable media.

Portable Devices

Shows icons for connected cameras, smartphones, and other portable devices. It's not always clear whether a gadget should be classified as a portable device or removable storage.

Depending on how your computer is configured, more categories (such as Other and Network Drives) may appear.

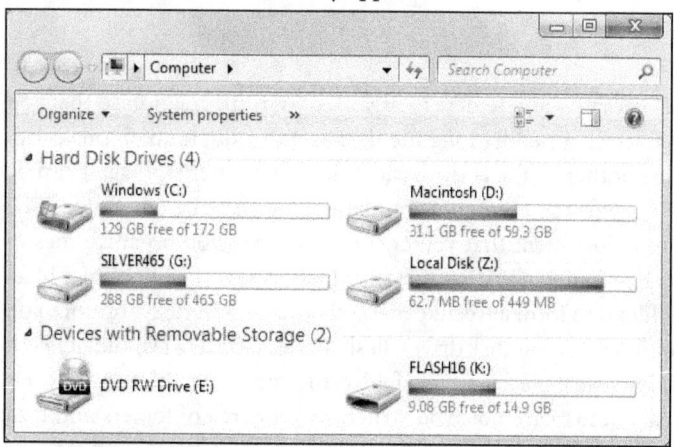

To see what's on your computer:

1 Choose Start > Computer, or press Windows logo key+E.

2 To see what's on a hard drive, in the Hard Disk Drives section, double-click the drive that you want to see.

   or

   To find a file or folder on a USB flash drive, CD, DVD, or other removable media, in the Devices with Removable Storage section, double-click the item that you want to see. (You'll get an error message if there's no media in the drive.)

   or

   To see what's on a portable device, in the Portable Devices section, double-click the device that you want to see. Windows may open an AutoPlay dialog box asking you what you want to do.

or

To see what's on a shared network drive, expand the Network folder (page 313) in the Navigation pane or choose Tools > Map Network Drive (tap Alt if the Tools menu isn't visible) and then browse to a network drive (ask your network administrator).

3   Keep double-clicking folders to burrow to the file or folder that you want. To return to the previous folder, press Backspace or click the Back button in the window's top-left corner.

Windows System Folders

The **system drive**, marked with a Windows logo ⊞ in the Computer folder, is the drive on which Windows is installed. If you double-click it, you can browse the top-level **system folders** that Windows Setup created during installation:

Program Files
Contains all the programs—Microsoft Word, Internet Explorer, or Adobe Photoshop, for example—that you, Windows Setup, your computer's manufacturer, or your administrator installed, along with all the support files needed to run those programs. In general, you shouldn't need (or want) to touch files in this folder.

Users
Contains a subfolder for each user account or for each user who has logged on to a network domain (page 9). These subfolders contain the users' personal settings and files. If you're not an administrator (page 8), you can't open or see other users' subfolders. The Public folder (page 320) stores files available to every user, administrator or not. (The Users folder was named Documents and Settings in some earlier Windows versions.)

Windows
Contains critical operating-system files. Look but don't touch. (The Windows folder was named WINNT in some earlier Windows versions.)

Drive Letters

Windows inherits its drive-naming conventions from the old DOS system. Drives are named by a letter followed by a colon.

- A: is the first floppy-disk drive (if present).

- B: is the second floppy-disk drive (if present).

- C: is the first hard drive or the first partition (page 356) of the first physical hard drive. This drive usually contains Windows itself if you have only one operating system on your machine.

- D: through Z: are assigned to other hard drives, partitions, USB flash drives, CD/DVD drives, mapped network drives (page 316), removable storage, and portable devices.

Windows assigns drive letters consecutively, but you can use Computer Management to change them; see "Managing Drives" on page 355.

Computer Folder Tips

- When you double-click a folder, Windows replaces the original window with a new one or opens a separate window atop the current one. Opening new windows makes it easy to move or copy files but clutters the screen quickly. To choose the behavior you prefer, in Computer, choose Organize (on the toolbar) > "Folder and search options" > General tab, and then select an option under "Browse folders".

- The horizontal separator for each category lists the number of drives or devices in that category. Click a separator to select all the icons in that category, or double-click it or click its arrow button ▶ to show or hide them.

  ◢ Hard Disk Drives (4)

- To make Computer appear as a submenu in the Start menu, right-click the Start button, choose Properties > Customize > Computer > "Display as a menu" > OK. Even when Computer is set to expand as a menu, you can still right-click its icon in the Start menu to open it in a window.

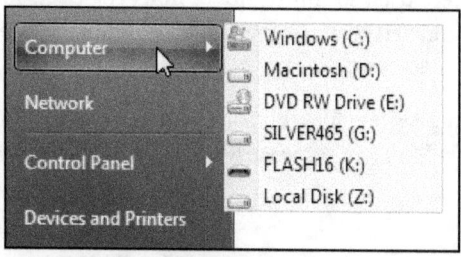

- To show the Computer icon on the desktop, open the Start menu, right-click Computer, and then choose "Show on Desktop".

- To rename a drive icon, right-click it and then choose Rename.

- Tiles view (available from the  button on the toolbar) shows you how much free space remains on each hard drive. In other views, right-click a drive icon and then choose Properties.

Your Personal Folder

Your **personal folder**, labeled with your user account name (page 8), is a convenient location for storing your files and folders in one place.

A unique personal folder is associated with the user account of whoever is logged on. Other users (besides administrators, page 8) can't see what's in your personal folder; neither can you see what's in theirs. The personal folder contains specialized subfolders, each of which is intended for the type of file that its name suggests, for example:

Downloads
> Files and programs downloaded from the internet.

My Documents
> Word-processing files, spreadsheets, presentations, personal databases, and text files.

My Music
> MP3s and digital music, downloaded or ripped from a CD.

My Pictures
> Digital pictures from a camera, scanner, or email message.

My Videos
> Videos and clips from your digital camera or camcorder, or video files downloaded or ripped from a DVD.

These folders are just helpful anchors to help you organize your files without having to start from scratch, but this storage scheme doesn't work when things get complicated. It's better to ignore file types and nest folders deeply. If you create a shallow or "flat" folder structure, then you're forced to use long, descriptive filenames rather than succinct ones. A flat structure also makes you fill each folder with so many subfolders that it's hard to discern the structure quickly. If you're, say, running an advertising campaign, it's more sensible to organize all the photos, graphics, copy, layouts, videos, and spreadsheets in a dedicated project folder rather than disperse them to the factory-installed subfolders.

You don't *have* to store your stuff in your personal folder (Windows doesn't care where you put your files), but doing that is a good idea because:

- It's easy to open from the Start menu, taskbar, Windows Explorer, Navigation pane, and other parts of Windows.

- Its specialized subfolders (My Music, My Videos, My Pictures) are optimized for faster searching and organizing, and are preset to display their contents best.

- It's indexed by Windows automatically so you can find files instantly by using a Search box.

- It's where programs expect you to save and open files.

- It segregates your programs (which are stored in \Program Files) and your work, preventing accidental document deletion when you remove or upgrade programs.

- It makes it easier to back up your work by archiving only your personal folder (and its subfolders) rather than folders scattered about your hard drive.

- It keeps your personal files private.

The file tagging, instant search, and library features *do* let you scatter related files around your hard drive and then quickly list them all in a single window. But any pro on a deadline will tell you that nothing provides utility and peace of mind like a well-designed folder hierarchy. To reduce clutter, don't store documents on the desktop. Reserve your desktop for shortcuts to your pending projects. In general, don't put anything—even shortcuts—in the root folder on the Windows drive (typically, C:\).

To open your personal folder:

1 Choose Start.

2 To open your personal folder, click your user name (below the icon in the top-right section of the menu). To open a personal subfolder, click one of the links below your user name (Documents, Pictures, or Music, for example).

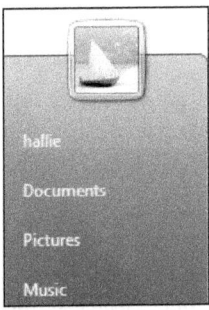

Moving the My Documents Folder

If you want to keep your latest files at hand, you can move your My Documents folder to a connected pocket hard drive or USB flash drive: in your personal folder, right-click My Documents, choose Properties > Location tab > Move, navigate to a new location, and then click Select Folder.

Windows updates all My Documents links in all folder windows to point to the new location. Programs use the new location as the default for storing new documents. (This trick works for any of the built-in personal subfolders, not just My Documents.)

Personal Folder Tips

- The path (page 178) to your personal folder is \Users*user_name*.

- To see your files in one place instead of opening different folders to see different kinds of files, see "Searching for Files and Folders" on page 211 and "Using Libraries" on page 224.

- If you back up (page 362) your personal folder regularly, it might be convenient to create a top-level folder—say, C:\nobackup—to store miscellaneous files and downloads that you don't want archived.

- To show or hide your personal folder and subfolders in the Start menu, right-click the Start button; choose Properties > Start Menu tab >

Customize; choose an option under Documents, Music, Personal folder, Pictures, or Videos; and then click OK.

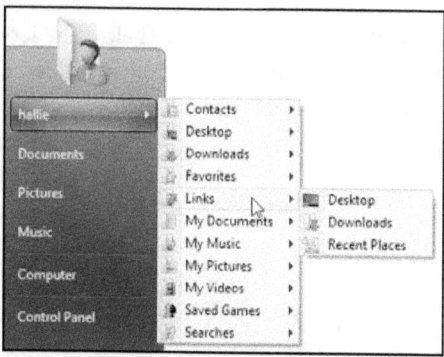

- Your personal folder contains a hidden folder named AppData, which stores your local (user-specific) settings and application data. You usually don't need to touch AppData, but you'll find tips on the web that refer to it. To view it, in any folder window, choose Organize (on the toolbar) > "Folder and search options" > View tab > select "Show hidden files, folders, and drives".

Using Windows Explorer

Windows Explorer, or simply Explorer, is the key tool for working with files and folders on your local machine or network. The term "folder window" actually refers to a Windows Explorer window. It's common to have several Explorer windows open at the same time, each one looking a little different depending on the settings and filters in effect for that folder. Microsoft presets folders to show their contents a certain way; you'll see panes show or hide themselves and icons grow or shrink or regroup, depending on which folder you click (you can change the view settings). Explorer windows work like other windows (page 54), but also have specialized parts.

Back and Forward buttons

Navigation pane

Address bar

Menu bar   Toolbar

Column
headings

Search box

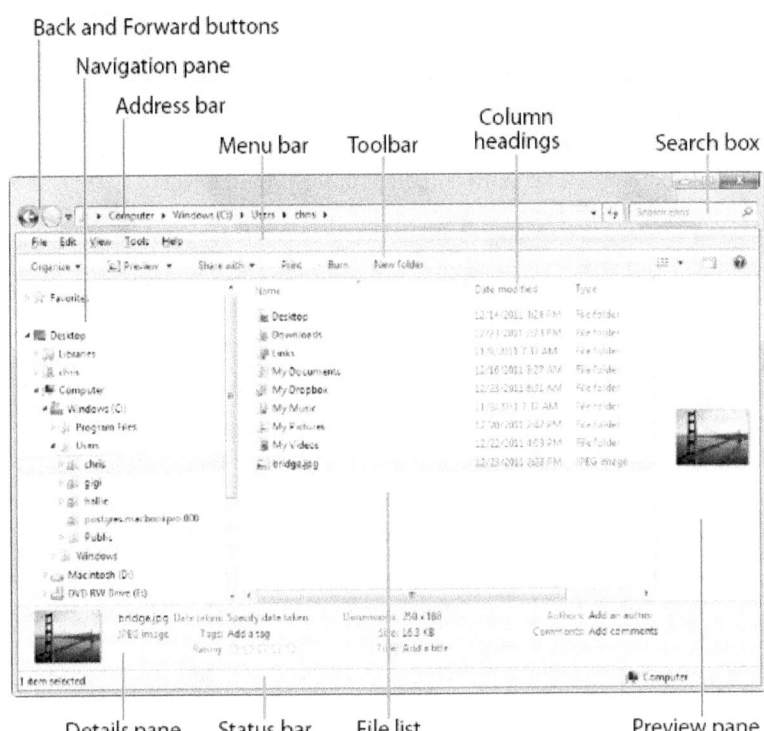

Details pane   Status bar   File list   Preview pane

Back and Forward buttons
   Moves among previously visited locations. See "Address Bar Tips" on
   page 179.

Navigation pane
   Lets you navigate directly to the folder that contains the files you want.
   Folders and drives are organized in an expandable treelike structure.
   To show or hide this pane, choose Organize (on the toolbar) > Layout >
   "Navigation pane". See "Navigation Pane" on page 180.

Address bar
   Shows or changes the current location. See "Address Bar" on page 177.

Menu bar
   Shows the classic folder menus. The menu bar is hidden by default. To
   show it, tap Alt. To always show it, choose Organize (on the toolbar) >
   Layout > "Menu bar" (or choose Organize > "Folder and search options" >
   View tab > select "Always show menus").

Toolbar

Shows the most frequently used commands. The Organize, Views , and Preview pane buttons always appear. The other buttons change to show only what's useful for what you've selected. If you click a picture file, for example, the toolbar shows different buttons than it would if you clicked a music file. (You can't hide this toolbar.)

Column headings

Determines what information appears in Details view and changes the way that the files in the file list are filtered and organized. See "" on page 185.

Search box

Finds files in the current folder and its subfolders. See "Searching for Files and Folders" on page 211.

Details pane

Shows details about the selection and lets you add or edit them. This pane is a shortened version of the Properties dialog box (page 65). To show or hide this pane, choose Organize (on the toolbar) > Layout > "Details pane". See "Tagging Files" on page 183.

Status bar

Shows settings and statistics about the selection. It's divided into sections that show different information. To show or hide the status bar, choose View > "Status bar" (tap Alt if the View menu isn't visible). The status bar displays a short explanation of any menu command that you point to.

File list

Shows the contents of the selected folder or files filtered by using column headings or the Search box.

Preview pane

Shows or plays the contents of the selected file. To show or hide this pane, choose Organize > Layout > "Preview pane", press Alt+P, or click (on the toolbar).

To open Windows Explorer:

- Click the Windows Explorer icon 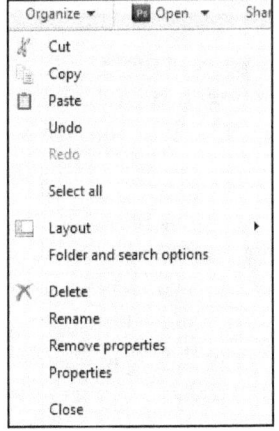 on the taskbar.

    or

    Choose Start > All Programs > Accessories > Windows Explorer.

    or

    Right-click the Start button and then choose Open Windows Explorer.

    or

    Choose Start, type *windows explorer* in the Search box, and then press Enter.

    or

    Press Windows logo key+R, type *explorer*, and then press Enter.

Tip: Click the Help button 🕐 on the toolbar to open Help and Support (page 71).

The Organize Menu

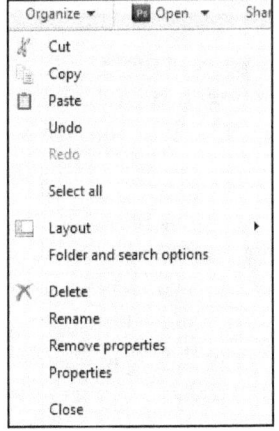

To open a menu of commands for managing your files and folders, click the **Organize** button on the toolbar. This menu shows the basic tasks: moving, copying, renaming, deleting, and so on. If you can't find what you want on the toolbar, try the menu bar (tap Alt if the menu bar isn't visible) or try right-clicking a file, folder, or an empty area of the window.

Folder Views

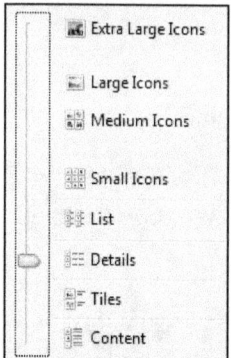

Each time that you click the **Views** button <img> ⏷ on the toolbar, it changes the size or arrangement of the file and folder icons in the folder window, cycling through List, Details, Tiles, Content, and Large Icons views. Click the down arrow ▼ on the button for more choices. The slider moves smoothly between **Extra Large Icons** and **Small Icons**. **List**, the most compact display, lists only the names of files and folders, preceded by small icons, across multiple columns. **Details** displays a columnar list of files, folders, and their properties (see "Using Column Headings" on page 186). **Tiles** displays medium icons with three lines of descriptive text that vary by file type. **Content** is a hybrid of Details and Tiles, with one icon per line.

You can also change views by right-clicking an empty area of the file list and then making a choice from the View submenu. Shortcut: Hold down the Ctrl key and spin your mouse wheel in either direction to cycle through all the views.

To make all folders of the same type use the same view, set up one folder the way you want it and then choose Organize > "Folder and search options" > View tab > Apply to Folders. Each folder remembers its own view when revisited. You can still apply distinct views to individual folders after clicking Apply to Folders. To return all folders of the same type to their default views, click Reset Folders.

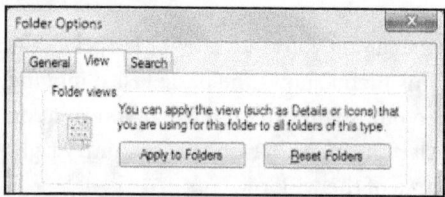

Folder Layout and Panes

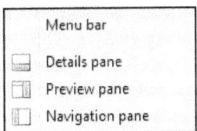

	Menu bar
	Details pane
	Preview pane
	Navigation pane

To show or hide the various panes of the folder window, click Organize (on the toolbar) and then use the Layout submenu. To resize panes, drag the vertical and horizontal separators. (When you hover the pointer over a separator, the pointer changes to a double-headed arrow.) The amount of information shown in the Details pane increases or decreases with the size of the pane.

Folder Searches

As you type in the **Search box**, the folder's contents are filtered to show only those files that match what you typed. The Search box doesn't automatically search your entire computer, however—only the current folder and its subfolders. If the folder view is already filtered (if it's showing files only by a certain author, for example), the Search box will search only within that limited view. For details, see "Searching for Files and Folders" on page 211.

Live Icons (Thumbnail Previews)

Sample Pictures

Live icons let you see a preview of a file's or folder's actual contents without having to open it (provided that previewing is supported for the file type or creating application). This feature improves on generic system and program icons. What's displayed depends on the type of file selected: the opening text of a text file or Word document, the first slide of a PowerPoint presentation, the first worksheet of an Excel spreadsheet, the first frame of a video, the album art of a song, or a scaled-down image of a photo. Folder icons show previews of the individual files that they contain. For example, a folder that contains photos shows high-resolution thumbnails of those photos. Larger icons provide clearer previews. The Details and Preview panes in Explorer show the same images as live icons.

Full-Screen View

To see Explorer in **full-screen view** with minimal clutter, press F11. The Address bar appears when you move your pointer near the top edge of the screen. Press F11 again to restore normal view.

Changing the Default Folder

Clicking the Windows Explorer icon on the taskbar usually opens a folder window showing your libraries (page 224), but you can modify the shortcut to open a folder of your choice initially.

To open Windows Explorer with a specific folder selected:

1   Right-click the Windows Explorer icon 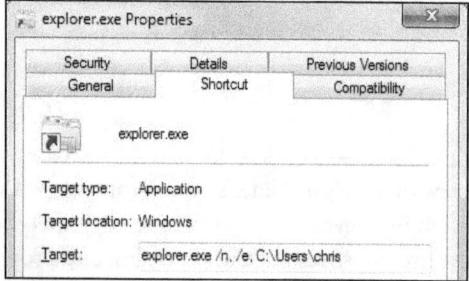 on the taskbar.

2   In the jump list, right-click Windows Explorer and then choose Properties > Shortcut tab.

3   In the Target box, type:

```
explorer.exe /n, /e, C:\myfolder
```

Replace *C:\myfolder* with the path (page 178) of the folder of your choice. The folder can be on a local, removable, or network drive. If *C:\myfolder* contains spaces, surround it with double quotes. The text *%windir%* can optionally precede *explorer.exe*.

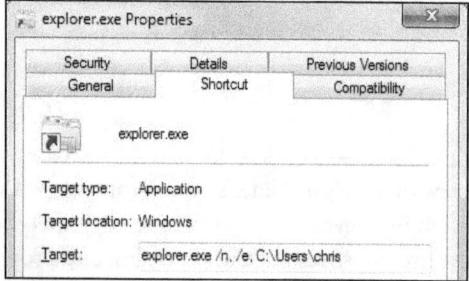

4   Click OK. When you click the shortcut, Explorer opens with the specified folder selected.

Another way to open Explorer in a specific folder: choose Start or press Windows logo key+R, type or paste the folder's path in the box, and then press Enter.

To make the Windows Explorer taskbar shortcut open the Computer folder (page 163), right-click Explorer's taskbar shortcut, right-click Windows Explorer on the jump list, choose Properties > Shortcut tab, and then change the Target to *%windir%\explorer.exe /root,::{20D04 FE0-3AEA-1069-A2D8-08002B30309D}*.

Printing Folder Listings

Windows Explorer lacks the simple capability to print the contents of a folder; the Print button on the toolbar or the Print command in the File menu, if it appears, prints the selected file, not the file list. You can create a file listing by using Command Prompt (page 262), however. At a prompt, use the cd command to change to the desired directory and then type:

```
dir /a /o:neg /-p > list.txt
```

This command creates the file *list.txt* in the current directory. Open list.txt in Notepad (or any text editor) for a printable list of the files and folders in the directory. To change the command to suit your preferences, search for *command-line reference* in Help and Support (page 71), and then look for the *dir* command and *command redirection*.

Navigating in Windows Explorer

You can use Windows Explorer's address bar or Navigation pane to move among the folders on your computer or network.

Address Bar

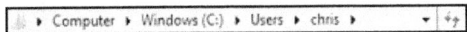

The **address bar** appears at the top of every folder window and displays your current location as a path or as a "breadcrumb trail" of links separated by arrows. The address bar shows your current location on the computer or on a network.

Tip: You can drag the small icon at the left edge of the address bar to create a shortcut (page 110).

To click a new location:

- To go directly to a location that's already visible in the address bar, click the link in the address bar.

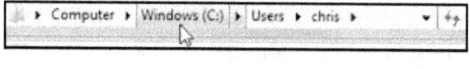

or

To go to the subfolder of a link that's visible in the address bar, click the arrow ▶ to the right of the link and then click the new location in the list. The boldface item in the list is the current link.

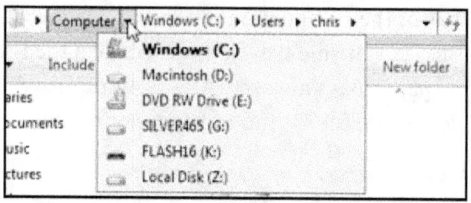

To type a new location:

1   Click an empty area in the address bar to the right of the text that displays the current location.

or

Click the small icon at the left edge of the address bar.

or

Press Alt+D.

The address bar changes to display the path (page 179) of the current location. (If you click accidently, press Esc to cancel and return to link notation.)

2   Type or paste the path of the new location and then press Enter.

or

To go to a common location, type its name and then press Enter. Valid location names include *Computer, Contacts, Control Panel, Documents, Favorites, Games, Music, Pictures, Recycle Bin*, and *Videos*.

Tip: You can also launch programs from the address bar. For example, type *cmd* or *notepad* or *excel* in the address bar and then press Enter.

Paths

Windows locates and identifies each file or folder by its unique address, called its **path**. A path lists the folders that lead from the **root** (topmost) directory of a drive to a particular file or folder. A backslash (\) separates folder and file names; in many situations, a forward slash (/) is also a valid separator. For example, C:\ represents the C drive's root directory. The path

C:\Users\Public\Pictures\Sample Pictures\Tulips.jpg

traces the route from the file Tulips.jpg to the C drive's root directory. For files on a network, the path can begin with a double backslash and a computer or server name instead of a local drive (\\someserver instead of C:, for example).

To see a path, right-click an icon and then choose Properties (the path is in the Location box). To copy a path, hold down Shift while you right-click an icon and then choose "Copy as path".

Address Bar Tips

- Like a web browser, Explorer records your recently visited locations, which you can revisit by clicking Back or Forward. Click the Recent Pages button (right of the Forward button) to jump directly to any of these locations. The checked item in the list is the current location.

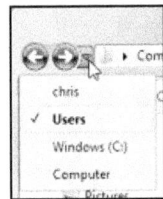

- Click the Previous Locations button ⊡ at the right edge of the address bar (or press F4) for a drop-down list of your location history, including web addresses. Click any list item to go to that location. To clear this list, choose Start > Control Panel > Network and Internet > Internet Options > General tab > Delete (under "Browsing history") > History > Delete.

- Click the Refresh button 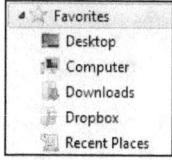 (or press F5) if some icons are badly drawn or if you think that the folder window is out of date (which happens sometimes for network locations).

- If the address bar is too narrow to display the entire location, click the chevron button « that appears to the left of it.

- If you type a web address (URL) in the address bar, Internet Explorer opens and displays the webpage.

Navigation Pane

By using the **Navigation pane**, you can navigate directly to the folder that contains the files you want. To show or hide the Navigation pane, choose Organize (on the toolbar) > Layout > "Navigation pane".

Favorites, at the top of the Navigation pane, offers one-click access to commonly used folders. Clicking a link shows its contents and takes you to its location in the folder list. Saved searches (page 223) and search connectors (page 219) appear in the Favorites list automatically.

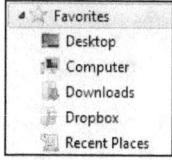

To customize the Favorites list:

- To reorder the list, drag links up or down.

  or

  To add a link, drag a folder or a saved search to the list. You can also drag folders from the lower part of the Navigation pane.

  or

  To rename a link, right-click it, choose Rename, type or paste the new name, and then press Enter. (Only the link is renamed, not the original folder or saved search.)

  or

  To remove a link, right-click it and then choose Remove. (Only the link is deleted, not the original folder or saved search.)

or

To restore the default list, right-click the word Favorites and then choose "Restore favorite links".

Desktop, below the Favorites list in the Navigation pane, represents your files, folders, and drives as a hierarchical structure called a **tree.** A fully expanded tree is unwieldy, so you can use the mouse or keyboard to collapse and expand individual branches selectively. To show or hide the tree, double-click Desktop in the Navigation pane. To set the default expansion options, choose Organize (on the toolbar) > "Folder and search options" > General tab > "Navigation pane" section.

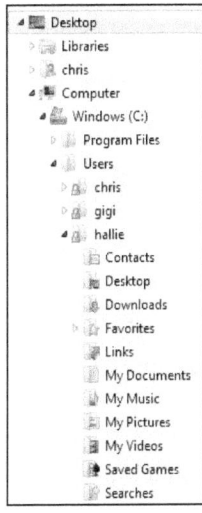

To navigate by using the folder tree:

- To show a folder's contents, click its icon in the tree. To expand or collapse a branch, click an arrow (▷ or ⊿) to the left of an icon in the tree.

Folder Tree Keyboard Shortcuts
You can use keyboard shortcuts to navigate the folder tree quickly. See also "General Keyboard Shortcuts" on page 230.

To	Press
Expand or collapse the selected branch	Right arrow or left arrow
Jump to parent branch without collapsing	Backspace
Open the parent folder	Alt+up arrow

To	Press
Revisit recently visited folders	Alt+left arrow (back) or Alt+right arrow (forward)
Move up visible branches	Up arrow
Move down visible branches	Down arrow
Expand all branches below the selection	* (on numeric keypad)
Go to a visible branch	The branch's initial letter
Cycle through visible branches with same initial letter	The initial letter repeatedly
Cycle through the parts of a folder window	Tab or F6

Navigation Pane Tips

- A security prompt may appear when you try to navigate to some folders. If it does, type an administrator password (page 8) or confirm the action.

- If no arrow appears next to an icon, that branch can't be expanded further because it has no subfolders.

- If the Navigation pane is too narrow to show its contents, drag the right edge of the pane to widen it. If you point to a partially hidden folder, a pop-up label displays its full name.

- Press F5 to refresh the display if you notice that a folder or drive is missing or that an arrow appears next to a folder that has no subfolders (which happens sometimes for network folders).

Tagging Files

Every file has properties—bits of information about the file, some of which you can edit (for details, see "Properties" on page 65). Windows also lets you create tags. **Tags** are properties that you can attach to your files to help you find and filter them. Unlike predefined properties, a tag can be anything you choose and, when created and attached to a file, becomes one of the file's properties. Like predefined properties, tags aren't part of the actual contents of a file; they're **metadata** (data about data).

The easiest way to add tags is to use the Details pane in Windows Explorer (if the pane isn't visible, choose Organize (on the toolbar) > Layout > "Details pane"). You can also add or change file properties when you save a file (in Word, Excel, and other Office programs, the Save dialog box lets you type tags and other properties). If you share files, you can remove the properties that you don't want others to see.

You can apply multiple tags to a single file or apply a single tag across multiple files. You can also add tags by using Windows Live Photo Gallery or Windows Media Player. You can't add tags to text (.txt), RTF (.rtf), AVI (.avi), bitmap (.bmp), and some other types of files. To use tags and other properties to find files, see "Searching for Files and Folders" on page 211.

To add or change properties by using the Details pane:

1   Click a file or select a group of files to apply properties to.

2   In the Details pane at the bottom of the folder window, click the property that you want to change, type the new property, and then click Save. To add more than one entry for the same property, separate the entries with a semicolon (;). To rate a file by using the Ratings property, click a star. Some intrinsic properties—such as Size, Dimensions, and Date Created—are read-only.

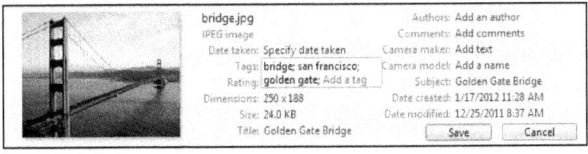

Tip: To resize the Details pane, drag the horizontal separator at the top edge of the pane. You can also right-click an empty area of the pane and then make a choice from the Size submenu.

To add or change properties that don't appear in the Details pane:

1 Right-click a file or a group of files and then choose Properties. (For more ways to open the Properties dialog box, see "Properties" on page 65.)

2 In the Properties dialog box, click the Details tab, click the properties box that you want to change, and then type a word or phrase. To add more than one entry for the same property, separate the entries with a semicolon (;). To rate a file by using the Ratings property, click a star. If you don't see any text for the property that you want to add, point to the place where you would expect to see it, and a box will appear. Scroll down the list to see and change a large number of properties.

3 Click OK (or Apply).

To add or change properties when saving a file:

1 In the program that you're using, choose File > Save (tap Alt if the File menu isn't visible).

2 In the Save As dialog box, type tags and other properties in the appropriate boxes.

3 Type a name for the file and then click Save.

To remove properties:

1 Right-click a file or a group of files and then choose Properties.

2 In the Properties dialog box, click the Details tab.

3 Click "Remove Properties and Personal Information". The Remove Properties dialog box opens.

   Select "Create a copy with all possible properties removed" and then click OK. This option lets you keep the original file with all its properties and make a copy with all the properties removed that you can share.

   or

   Select "Remove the following properties from this file", select each property to remove (or click Select All), and then click OK.

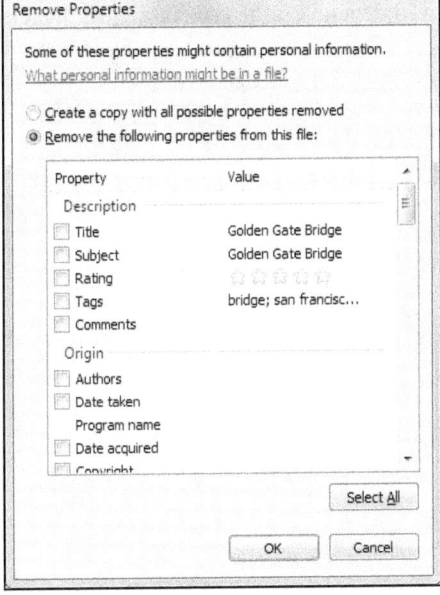

Filtering, Sorting, Stacking, and Grouping Files

Windows offers many options that control how the file list is filtered and organized in an Explorer window.

Using Column Headings

Column headings, which appear in Details view (page 174) atop the file list in Windows Explorer, are more useful than their appearance suggests. You can:

- Reorder columns by dragging column headings left or right.

- Resize a column by dragging the right edge of its heading left or right.

- Make a column width match its widest entry by double-clicking the right edge of its column heading (or right-clicking a column heading and choosing Size Column to Fit or Size All Columns to Fit).

By default, the columns displayed depend on the type of files in the folder—music folders show "Album", for example, and document folders show "Date modified"—but you can choose which columns appear.

To choose which column headings to show:

1   In Windows Explorer, click the View button on the toolbar and then choose Details view.

2   Right-click any column heading.

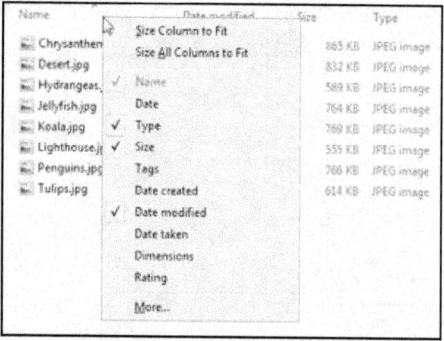

3   Select or clear a heading name on the menu to show or hide it. (You can't hide the Name column.)

or

Click More, select or clear the headings to show or hide, and then click OK. The Choose Details dialog box lists dozens of properties, many of which apply only to specific file types. You can also reorder headings and set their widths here, but it's more cumbersome than dragging the headings directly.

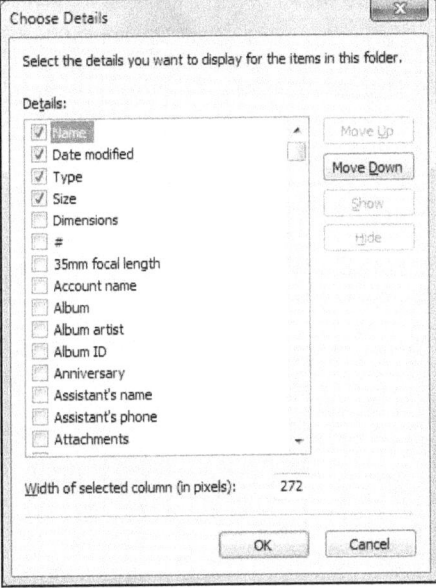

Filtering Files

You can also use column headings to filter files. When you **filter** a folder's contents by its file properties (such as filename, date, author, or tag), only files with those properties are displayed. Filtering helps you find files that have something in common. To see only the files written by a particular author, for example, filter by that person's name. You can filter sorted, grouped, or stacked files.

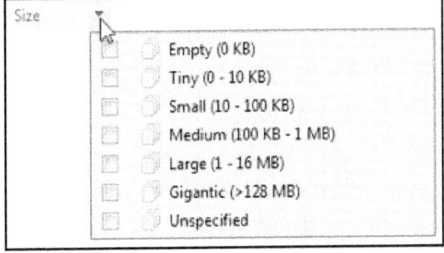

To filter files:

1 Open the folder that contains the files you want to filter.

2 In Details view, click the arrow ⌄ to the right of the heading that you want to filter by. Options vary by column heading and the contents of the folder.

3 Click the name of the property that you want to filter by. To filter by two or more properties, select the checkbox for each property. A check mark appears in the column heading when filtering is applied.

Calendar Filtering

You can filter a column that contains dates by a specific date or a range of dates.

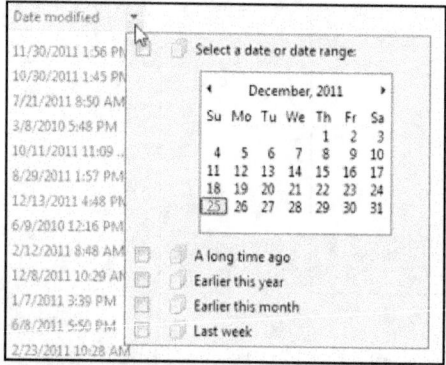

To go back or forward a month
Click the ◄ or ► arrow.

To jump to a month of this year
Click the month name to see all 12 months, and then click the one you want.

To jump back or forward by years
Double-click the month name to see decades or triple-click to see centuries. Click the ◄ or ► arrow to move through the years (1601–9999) and then drill down to the desired month and year.

To specify a date or date range
Select the desired month and year and then click a particular date, or drag (in any direction) through a range of consecutive dates.

Tip: To specify dates in a search, see "Advanced Searches" on page 219.

Sorting Files

By default, Windows Explorer sorts files alphabetically by name (listing all folders first, followed by all files), but you can sort them by any column heading.

To sort files:

1 Open the folder that contains the files you want to sort.

2 In Details view, click the heading of the column to sort by. To reverse the sort order, click it again.

or

In any view, right-click an empty area of the file list and then choose from the "Sort by" submenu.

Subtle shading indicates the sort column ⌈ Name ▾ ⌉. A small arrowhead above the column name points up for ascending sort or down for descending sort. You can sort filtered, stacked, or grouped files. In the Computer folder (page 163), you can sort by the drives' free space or total size.

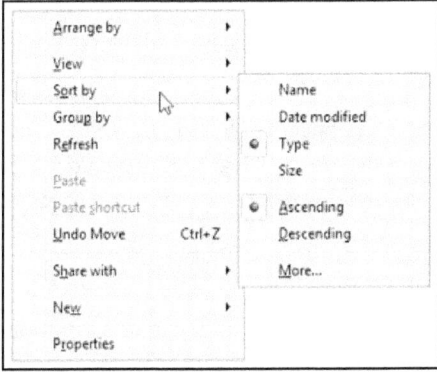

Stacking Files

In a library (page 224), you can arrange files into **stacks** that correspond to a column heading, such as Type. If you stack by Author, for example, you'll see one stack for each author. If you want to see only the files written by a particular author, open (double-click) that author's stack. The same document can appear in multiple stacks (a document with multiple authors, for example, will appear in the stack of each collaborator).

To arrange files in stacks:

1   Open the library that contains the files that you want to stack.

2   In any view, right-click an empty area of the file list and then choose from the "Arrange by" submenu. To unstack, choose "Arrange by" > Folder.

Grouping Files

Whereas a stack hides the files it contains behind an icon, a **group** lists all the files in that particular group. When you group files by Author, for example, several groups appear, each one displaying all the files written by a particular author.

To group files:

1   Open the folder that contains the files you want to group.

2   In any view, right-click an empty area of the file list and then choose from the "Group by" submenu.

Unlike stacked files, grouped files appear in the original folder. You can click the horizontal separator at the top of each grouping category to select all the files in that category or double-click the separator to hide them.

Customizing a Folder

You can apply folder templates and custom images to folders. Customization isn't available for libraries (page 224) and the Windows and Programs Files system folders (page 165).

To customize a folder:

1   In Windows Explorer, open the folder that you want to customize.

2   Right-click an empty area of the file list and then choose "Customize this folder".

    or

    Choose View > "Customize this folder" (tap Alt if the View menu isn't visible).

3   Choose a folder template from the drop-down list, and then specify whether you want the template applied to all subfolders as well. The template choice determines the view setting (Details, Large Icons, and so on) and column headings for the folder. The General Items template is for generic folders. Other templates are designed for document, photo, video, and music folders.

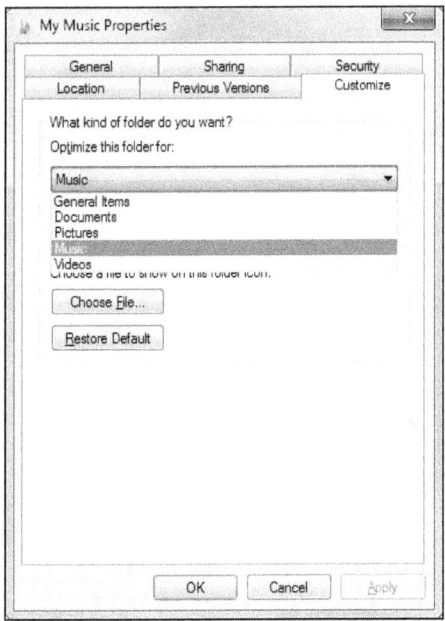

4 To replace the standard folder icon, click Change Icon, and then navigate to and select an icon.

5 Click OK (or Apply).

Setting Folder Options

Windows offers many options that control how folders appear and behave (some of which have default values that can make Windows harder to use or drain your laptop battery faster). These options affect all Explorer windows.

To set folder options:

1 In Windows Explorer, choose Organize (on the toolbar) > "Folder and search options" > View tab.

or

Choose Start > Control Panel > Appearance and Personalization > Folder Options > View tab.

or

Choose Start, type *folder options* in the Search box, press Enter, and then click the View tab

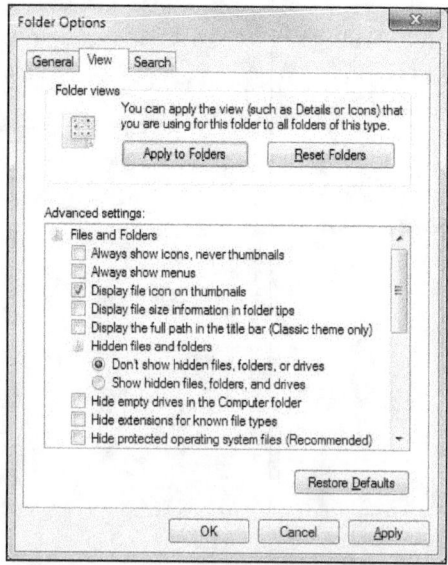

2 Select the desired options (described below).

or

To restore the options to their factory settings, click Restore Defaults.

Changes affect all Explorer windows.

3 Click OK (or Apply).

Always show icons, never thumbnails
Always shows static icons of files instead of their thumbnail previews (page 175). Turning off this option may speed your computer a little and (for laptops) drain the battery slower.

Always show menus
Turn on this option if you prefer always to see the classic menus above the toolbar. The menu bar is hidden by default. If this option is turned off, tap Alt to show the menus.

Display file icon on thumbnails
Turn on this option to overlay miniature file-type icons on thumbnail previews (applies if the option "Always show icons, never thumbnails" is turned off).

Display file size information in folder tips
Turn on this option to show size information in the folder tip that pops up temporarily when your pointer hovers over a folder icon. If you turn it off, you still get pop-up information; to turn off folder tips, choose the folder option "Show pop-up description for folder and desktop items".

Display the full path in the title bar (Classic folders only)
When this option is turned on, taskbar buttons and the Alt+Tab pop-up window show the selected folder's full path: C:\Users\hallie\Documents instead of only Documents, for example.

Hidden files and folders/Hide protected operating system files (Recommended)
By default, Windows hides critical files that it doesn't want you to move, delete, or rename. If you show these files, they appear as dimmed icons so that you remember to leave them alone. Technically, a hidden file has its Hidden attribute set. You can view (or change) this attribute in the General tab of the file's Properties dialog box (page 65).

Hide empty drives in the Computer folder

By default, Windows shows every connected drive in the Computer folder (page 163). You can declutter the window by turning on this option to hide unused, empty drives.

Hide extensions for known file types

By default, Windows hides file extensions (.docx for Word files and .exe for programs, for example). Beginners may be tempted to leave this option on to make Windows appear less intimidating, but everyone should turn it off for the reasons given in "Associating Documents with Programs" on page 254.

Launch folder windows in a separate process

By default, only one copy of explorer.exe is ever in memory, handling all Explorer windows, the Start menu, the desktop, and much more. Turn this option on to open a new program instance for each Explorer window so that if one instance crashes, the rest don't. For technical reasons, if the "wrong" one crashes, you may be left without a Start menu and desktop (though Windows can usually recover by itself). To conserve power and memory, favor turning off this option.

Show drive letters

Turn off this option if you want to hide the drive letter (page 165) of each drive or device in the Computer folder (page 163). Drive letters are useful in many situations (particularly if you need technical support); you should turn on this option unless you want to see only the friendly name of each drive.

Show encrypted or compressed NTFS files in color

Turn on this option to show EFS-encrypted and NTFS-compressed files and folders in identifying colors. Turn off this option to turn all files the same color. See "Encrypting File System" on page 347 and "NTFS Compression" on page 207.

Show pop-up description for folder and desktop items

Turn on this option to see pop-up information about almost any icon that you point to. Turn it off if the little pop-up boxes bug you.

Show preview handlers in preview pane

Turn off this option to never show the contents of files in the Preview pane. Turning off this option may speed your computer a little and (for laptops) drain the battery slower.

Use check boxes to select items

Turn on this item to add checkboxes to file views to make it easier to select multiple files. This option is useful if it's difficult for you to hold the Ctrl key while clicking to select multiple files. Tablet and touchscreen users like this setting because it makes it easier to select multiple files with a stylus or finger. Checkboxes appear when you hover the pointer over a file or folder. To select all the files, select the box in the Name column heading (in Details view).

Use Sharing Wizard (Recommended)

Turn on this option to use the friendly File Sharing wizard when you share your files. Experienced network administrators may prefer to turn off this option. See also "Sharing Files" on page 320.

When typing into list view

When the file list is active in a folder window, this option determines whether your keystrokes are used to select files in the list or are redirected to the Search box to filter the files in the list. Try both settings to see which one you prefer.

Creating Folders

You can create a folder inside another folder, on the desktop, at the root of a hard drive, or on an external or network drive. If you're creating a hierarchy of folders, see "Your Personal Folder" on page 167 for advice on organizing your files and folders.

To create a folder:

1   In Windows Explorer, open the folder where you want to create a subfolder.

2   Right-click an empty area of the file list and then choose New > Folder.

or

Press Ctrl+Shift+N.

or

Choose File > New > Folder (tap Alt if the File menu isn't visible).

or

To create a new folder on the desktop, right-click an empty area of the desktop and then choose New > Folder.

3 Type or paste a name for the new folder and then press Enter. While editing, you can use the keyboard shortcuts for Cut, Copy, Paste, Undo, and Select All (Ctrl+X, Ctrl+C, Ctrl+V, Ctrl+Z, and Ctrl+A, respectively).

Tip: The New submenu also lets you create new empty documents, depending on which programs are installed.

Naming Files and Folders

You can rename a file or folder to make its name longer, shorter, or more explicit.

To rename a file or folder:

1 In Windows Explorer, select the file or folder that you want to rename.

2 Right-click the file or folder and then choose Rename

or

Press F2.

or

Choose File > Rename (tap Alt if the File menu isn't visible).

or

Click the file or folder's name (not its icon) twice, slowly (don't double-click).

3 Type or paste a new name and then press Enter or click outside the name area. While editing, you can use the keyboard shortcuts for Cut, Copy, Paste, Undo, and Select All (Ctrl+X, Ctrl+C, Ctrl+V, Ctrl+Z, and Ctrl+A, respectively).

Naming Rules

A file or folder name can contain up to 260 characters, including the extension (the part after the last dot). Spaces and punctuation are permitted but names can't contain these characters: \ / : * ? " < > |.

The 260-character limit actually applies to the complete path (for example, C:\downloads\myfile.txt). Avoid using very long filenames.

A folder can't contain two items with the same name. Windows is case-insensitive (it considers *MyFile.txt* and *myfile.txt* to be identical), but it preserves the case of each letter that you type.

If you select multiple items and rename one of them, say, *MyFile.txt*, Windows renames the others *MyFile-(1).txt*, *MyFile-(2).txt*, and so on. If you bulk-rename a bunch of files accidentally, press Ctrl+Z repeatedly to revert to the original names.

For major surgery on filenames, search the web for *windows file renamer*. File renamers let you find and replace a static phrase or an arbitrary pattern in a set of filenames, add dates and sequence numbers to filenames, and preview your changes before you commit them.

File Naming Tips

- You can also rename a file or folder in the General tab of its Properties dialog box (page 65).

- Press Esc while editing to revert to the original name.

- You can't rename the system folders Program Files, Users, or Windows.

- In applications, you can rename files and folders in the Open and Save dialog boxes.

- If the folder option (page 192) "Hide extensions for known file types" is turned on, Windows tracks the file association automatically.

- You can rename a library (page 224) by using the same method.

Moving and Copying Files and Folders

You can move or copy files and folders to reorganize your folder structure, make backup copies in a safe location, or move files to the Public folder (page 320) to share them with other users. To copy or move items, you must select (highlight) their icons (page 52).

To move or copy items by choosing a destination:

1   In Windows Explorer, select the item(s) that you want to move or copy.

2   To move the items, choose Edit > Move to Folder or, to copy the items, choose Edit > Copy to Folder (tap Alt if the Edit menu isn't visible).

3   Navigate to the destination folder, and then click Move (or Copy).

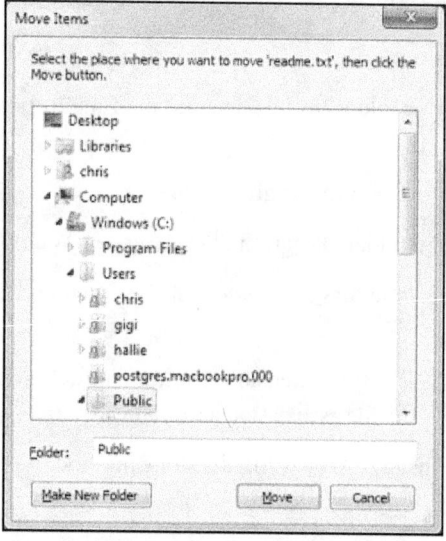

To move or copy items by using cut, copy, and paste:

1   In Windows Explorer or on the desktop, select the item(s) that you want to move or copy.

2   To move the items, press Ctrl+X (or right-click a selected item and then choose Cut).

    To copy the items, press Ctrl+C (or right-click a selected item and then choose Copy).

3   Select the destination folder, drive, or window.

4   Press Ctrl+V (or right-click an empty area and then choose Paste).

To move or copy items by dragging:

1 Make sure that the destination folder, drive, or window is visible.

2 In Windows Explorer or on the desktop, select the item(s) that you want to copy or move.

3 Right-drag the items to the destination, and then release the right mouse button.

   If you drag to the Navigation pane, the destination folder in the folder tree darkens as the pointer moves on or close to it. If you hover briefly over a folder that contains subfolders, it will expand.

4 Choose "Move here" or "Copy here" from the shortcut menu.

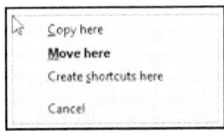

Move and Copy Rules

When you drag an icon, a small label appears when you arrive at the new location, telling you whether you're moving, copying, or creating a shortcut.

If you use the left mouse button and drag normally to copy or move items (bypassing the shortcut menu), the rules that determine what happens are:

• If you drag an item to another place on the same drive, it's moved.

• If you drag an item from one drive to another, it's copied.

• To copy an item instead of moving it, hold down Ctrl while dragging.

• To move the item instead of copying it, hold down Shift while dragging.

• To create a shortcut (page 110) to the item instead of moving or copying it, hold down Alt while dragging.

• If you drag a system icon such as Computer or Control Panel, it's never moved or copied; instead, a shortcut is created.

If that's too much to remember, always *right*-drag to copy or move items; it's easier and surer.

Robocopy and RichCopy

robocopy ("robust copy") is a command-line tool (page 262) that's more powerful than the traditional *copy* and *xcopy* commands. It's especially useful for copying large folder structures across a network (for backups and mirroring) because if the network goes down, robocopy doesn't quit—it waits to continue where it left off (you can configure the wait time).

Type *robocopy /?* at a command prompt for usage and options. If you prefer point-and-click to the command line, you can find a graphical front end for robocopy at "Utility Spotlight: Robocopy GUI" at *technet.microsoft.com/en-us/magazine/2006.11.utilityspotlight.aspx*. An even more powerful tool, RichCopy, is available at "Utility Spotlight: RichCopy" at *technet.microsoft.com/en-us/magazine/2009.04.utilityspotlight.aspx*.

Moving and Copying Tips

- If you move or copy an item to a folder that already has an item with the same name, Windows asks you what to do. You can overwrite the file in the destination folder, cancel the operation, or complete the operation but rename the file being moved or copied so that its name doesn't conflict with the other file.

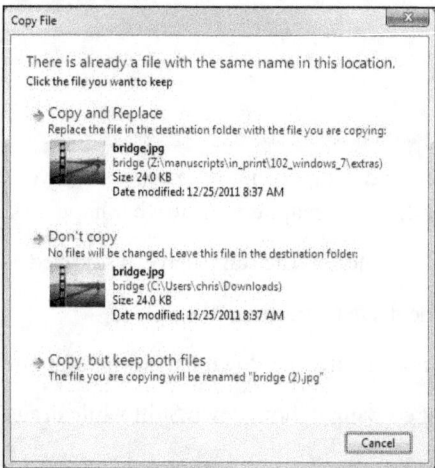

- You can move or copy items anywhere on your computer or network, so long as you have privileges to do so. If a security prompt appears, type an administrator password (page 8) or confirm the action.

- If you copy an item to the folder in which it already exists (which is a fast way to duplicate an item), Windows creates a duplicate named "*item_name* - Copy".

- You can drag items between Explorer windows, or cut or copy from one window and paste to another.

- Items appear dimmed when they're cut, but they don't actually move until you paste them somewhere. Press Esc to cancel a cut.

- Press Esc during a drag to cancel it.

- To drag to a minimized or hidden folder: drag an item and then hover over the Windows Explorer button on the taskbar; wait a second until the target folder's pop-up thumbnail appears; hover over the thumbnail until the full-size target folder opens; and then drop the item in that folder.

- During long move or copy operations, the Windows Explorer button on the taskbar shows a progress bar.

- To drag to a crowded desktop: drag an item and then hover over the Show desktop button ▌ (on the right edge of the taskbar), wait a moment until all the windows minimize, and then drop the item anywhere on the desktop.

Sending Files and Folders

One of the handiest file-management tools is the "Send to" menu, which lets you send a copy of a file or folder quickly to:

- A compressed (zipped) folder (page 209)

- Your desktop (as a shortcut)

- Your Documents library (or any folder or library)

- Another person via fax or email

- A USB flash drive, an external or mapped drive, or a CD/DVD for burning

- Other destinations, depending on the programs installed

The "Send to" menu is often faster than dragging and dropping. Windows adds destinations for removable storage automatically.

To send an item:

1   In Windows Explorer or on the desktop, select the item(s) that you want to send.

2 Right-click one item, choose "Send to", and then choose a destination from the submenu. To move an item instead of copying it, hold down Shift when you right-click (holding down Shift also reveals hidden "Send to" destinations).

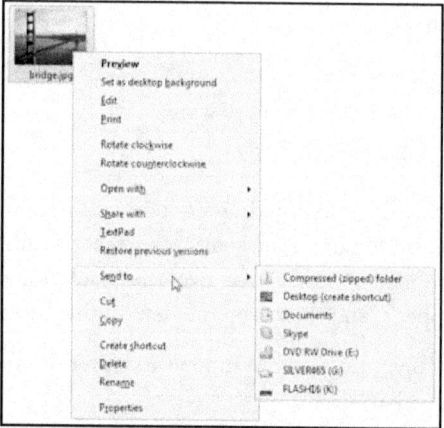

If you perform the same file-management tasks regularly, you can add your own destinations to the "Send to" menu by adding new shortcuts to your SendTo folder (which is hidden by default). Every user account has a its own SendTo folder. The destination determines what happens to the item being sent. If the destination is a program, for example, the program is launched with the selected file open. For folder and drive destinations, items are copied. A printer shortcut prints documents with no need to open their associated applications.

To add a destination to the Send To menu:

1 Choose Start > Computer > Local Disk (C:) > Users > *user_name*. If Windows is installed on a drive other than C, choose that drive instead. Look for the drive with the Windows logo ⊞.

2 Make sure that hidden files and folders are visible by choosing Organize (on the toolbar) > "Folder and search options" > View tab > "Show hidden files, folders, and drives" > OK.

3 Choose AppData > Roaming > Microsoft > Windows > SendTo.

The full path of your current location is C:\Users*user_name*\AppData\ Roaming\Microsoft\Windows\SendTo.

4 Add the desired shortcuts to the folder, or right-click an empty area and then choose New > Shortcut.

You can create "Send to" shortcuts to local drives as well as to shared folders on your network. If you have many destinations, you can nest folders to create "Send to" sub-submenus. Trick: if you put a shortcut to the SendTo folder inside the SendTo folder itself, you can create destinations quickly by sending them to the SendTo folder.

5 Close the window when you're done adding shortcuts. (Don't forget to rehide hidden files and folders.)

Deleting Files and Folders

When you delete a file or folder, it's not actually erased but compressed and stored in the **Recycle Bin** on the desktop. The Recycle Bin is a safeguard from which you can restore (undelete) items if you change your mind or delete them permanently. The Recycle Bin's icon tells you whether it contains deleted items or is empty.

To delete items:

1 In Windows Explorer or on the desktop, select the item(s) that you want to delete.

2 Choose Organize (on the toolbar) > Delete.

or

Press Delete.

or

Right-click one item and then choose Delete.

or

Drag the items to the Recycle Bin.

3 If an "Are you sure?" message appears, click Yes. If you're deleting one item, Windows gives you a thumbnail preview of it. For multiple items, you're given a count but no preview. (To suppress "Are you sure?" messages, right-click the Recycle Bin, choose Properties, and then clear "Display delete confirmation dialog".)

To delete selected items without sending them to the Recycle Bin, press Shift+Delete (do so with care). You can bypass the Recycle Bin so that all deleted files are erased immediately (good for using a public computer): right-click the Recycle Bin, choose Properties, and then choose "Don't move files to the Recycle Bin. Remove files immediately when deleted." Items deleted from network drives and removable storage (such as pocket hard drives and USB flash drives) bypass the Recycle Bin, as do deletions via the command-line del and erase commands.

Tip: You can also delete items within Open and Save dialog boxes.

A few things may stop you from deleting a file or folder:

- You lack the proper privileges to delete it. If you didn't create it, you may not be able to delete it, even if it's in the Public folder (page 320). Ask the file's owner to delete it.

- A program is currently using the file. Find the program and close it. (Closing only the file but leaving the program running might not release the file lock immediately.) If you're not the only person logged on, someone else might be using the file.

- If you delete all the files in a folder but can't delete the folder itself, close all open programs and then try to delete the folder. If this doesn't work, restart the computer and then try to delete it again. The folder probably wasn't deleted because it was locked by another program or system utility.

To empty the Recycle Bin:

1 Double-click the Recycle Bin icon.

   Details view (click ⊞ ▾ on the toolbar) tells you when items were deleted and where from.

2 To remove all items, click "Empty the Recycle Bin" (on the toolbar).

   or

   To remove some items, Ctrl+click each item to remove, and then press Delete.

or

To remove one item, click it and then press Delete (or right-click it and then choose Delete).

3   Click Yes in the "Are you sure?" message.

Tip: To empty the Recycle Bin quickly without inspecting its contents, right-click its icon on the desktop and then choose "Empty Recycle Bin". (You can't suppress the "Are you sure?" message.)

To restore items from the Recycle Bin:

1   Double-click the Recycle Bin icon.

2   Ctrl+click the items that you want to restore (or click only one item).

3   To restore items to their original locations, click "Restore the selected items" (or "Restore this item") on the toolbar. Alternatively, right-click a selected item and then choose Restore.

or

To restore items to a specific location, drag them out of the Recycle Bin to the target folder or the desktop.

Tip: To restore everything in the Recycle Bin, make sure that nothing is selected and then click "Restore all items" on the toolbar.

The Recycle Bin stores deleted items until it runs out of space, at which point the items are removed automatically, oldest first, to accommodate new items. By default, the size of the Recycle Bin folder is 10 percent of the hard drive, but you can change that percentage. Each drive has its own Recycle Bin. If you have more than one drive or have a partitioned drive, you can set each drive's junk limit independently.

To change the Recycle Bin's capacity:

1   Right-click the Recycle Bin icon and then choose Properties.

2   Click a drive in the list, choose "Custom size", and then specify how much drive storage (measured in megabytes) to allocate to the Recycle Bin.

On high-capacity drives, 10 percent is a lot of space. On a 500 GB drive, for example, 10 percent is 50 GB of junk. Unless you have a lot of music or video files, 2 GB or 3 GB should be enough.

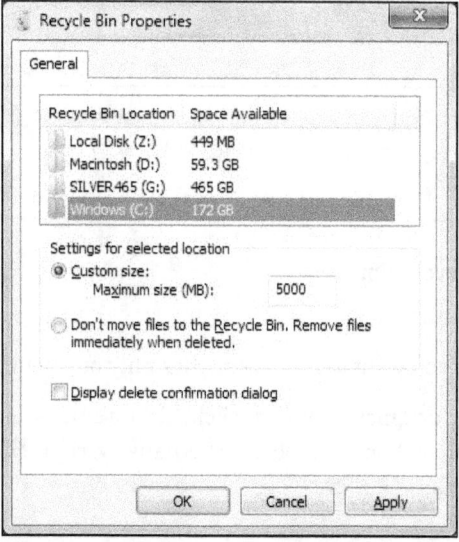

3 Click OK (or Apply).

Tip: To hide the Recycle Bin or change its icon, choose Start > Control Panel > Appearance and Personalization > Personalization > "Change desktop icons" (on the left).

Deleting Files Securely

Deleting files doesn't actually destroy their data; it just makes the data harder to find. When you empty the Recycle Bin, Windows doesn't erase files but *marks* them as deleted, making them invisible to you and to programs but leaving their data intact on the drive. Only when Windows needs drive space later will it overwrite deleted files with newly created ones. On a large or sparsely populated drive, deleted files may survive for weeks before Windows reclaims the space.

To recover deleted files, use an undelete utility soon after you've emptied the Recycle Bin. A web search for *windows undelete files* turns up scores of free solutions. Don't restore deleted files to the same drive that you're recovering them from, or you might overwrite other files that you want to restore.

Conversely, use a **file shredder** to make your files *un*recoverable. File shredders—useful if you're selling your computer or expecting a search warrant—overwrite deleted files or entire drives with random data. Shredders let you overwrite one time (to defeat forensic software) or many times (to defeat an electron microscope). To shred files, use Eraser (*trac.heidi.ie*) or DBAN (*dban.org*); they're free.

Note that Windows' *format* (formerly *fdisk*) command won't shred files. To utterly destroy data, dismantle the drive with a precision screwdriver, smash the platters or surfaces, and then throw the pieces in a river (or burn them).

Compressing Files and Folders

Compressing files and folders reduces the space that they occupy on your drives. Windows offers two compression schemes: Microsoft's proprietary NTFS compression and industry-standard zip files. You can use either scheme or both; each has its relative advantages. NTFS compression is simple, transparent, and suitable for everyday use, whereas zip files are best for:

- Emailing large attachments

- Archiving files that you no longer need regularly

- Transferring files over the internet or via FTP

- Gaining the maximum amount of drive space

- Compressing encrypted files

NTFS Compression

Some important points about **NTFS compression** are:

- It's available on only NTFS-formatted drives, not FAT or FAT32 drives. To determine whether a drive is NTFS-formatted, choose Start > Computer, right-click the drive, and then choose Properties. The file system appears on the General tab.

- You can compress individual files and folders or an entire NTFS drive.

- It's easy to use but doesn't save much drive space compared with zip compression.

- NTFS-compressed files and folders act normally in Explorer, programs, and dialog boxes. Windows decompresses and compresses files invisibly and on the fly when you open and close them, at the cost of a small (probably not noticeable) performance hit.

- Don't compress system files (page 165) in the Windows folder, because they're used frequently.

- If you send an NTFS-compressed file to a non-NTFS drive (via email or dragging, for example), Windows expands it to its normal size automatically and invisibly. A file sent to an NTFS-compressed folder or drive is compressed automatically.

- NTFS-compressed files can't be EFS-encrypted (page 347), but you can encrypt zip files.

Compressing an entire hard drive may take hours. Close all programs before you start; otherwise, Windows halts midprocess to ask you to quit a program.

To NTFS-compress a file, folder, or drive:

1 Close all files to be compressed.

2 To compress individual files or folders, select their icons in Windows Explorer, right-click one of the selected items, choose Properties > General tab, click the Advanced button, select "Compress contents to save disk space", and then click OK. (If the Advanced button is missing, then the selected file or folder isn't on an NTFS drive.) The Advanced Attributes dialog box won't let you choose both compression and encryption.

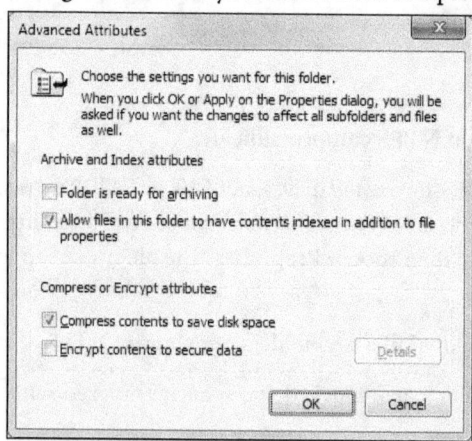

or

To compress a drive, right-click its icon in the Computer folder (page 163), choose Properties > General tab, select "Compress this drive to save disk space", and then click OK.

3   In the Confirm Attribute Changes dialog box, indicate whether you want to compress subfolders too (usually, you do).

Tip: To display compressed files and folders in a different color in Windows Explorer, choose Organize (on the toolbar) > "Folder and search options" > View tab > select "Show encrypted or compressed NTFS files in color".

Zip Files (Archives)

Some important points about zip files are:

- A **zip file**, also called an **archive**, is a collection of files compressed and combined into a single file. An archive looks like a folder, except with a zipper. An archive has a .zip filename extension (page 254).

- You can create archives on any drive, not just NTFS-formatted drives. Archives stay compressed when you send them elsewhere. Mac and Unix users can work with them too.

- Zipping squashes files much smaller than NTFS compression does. Zipping most image, video, music, and PDF files won't save space because they're already compressed, but program, webpage, text, word-processing, spreadsheet, database, bitmap, TIFF, and WAV audio files shrink a lot.

- Though they're actually files, archives behave like folders in several ways. Double-click an archive to see what's in it. Double-click a document in the archive to open a read-only copy of it, or extract it from the archive to work with the original.

- Details view (click ☰ ▾ on the toolbar) provides compression information about each file. The Ratio column tells you how much smaller a zipped file is relative to its uncompressed size. (The closer the ratio is to 100%, the more compressed the file is.)

To create an empty zip file:

1 In Windows Explorer, select where you want to create the new zip file.

2 Choose File > New > "Compressed (zipped) folder" (tap Alt if the File menu isn't visible).

or

Right-click an empty area of the file list and then choose New > "Compressed (zipped) folder".

3 Type or paste a name for the new zip file (keeping the .zip extension, if it appears) and then press Enter.

Tip: To create an empty zip file on the desktop, right-click an empty area and then choose New > "Compressed (zipped) folder".

To create a zip file containing copies of existing files or folders:

1 In Windows Explorer, select the file(s) or folder(s) that you want to archive.

2 Right-click one of the selected items and then choose "Send to" > "Compressed (zipped) folder".

3 Type or paste a name for the new archive (keeping the .zip extension, if it appears) and press Enter.

To add files or folders to a zip file:

1 In Windows Explorer, find the zip file that you want to add files or folders to.

2 Right-drag the item(s) into the zip file, release the right mouse button, and then choose Copy Here or Move Here.

To extract files and folders from a zip file:

• To extract only some files or folders, double-click the zip file to open it and then drag the files or folders to a new location, where they return to their original sizes.

or

To extract all files and folders, right-click the zip file and then choose Extract All. The Extract Compressed (Zipped) Folders wizard lets you specify a destination folder and, optionally, open it after extraction.

WinZip and WinRAR

If you zip files only occasionally, Windows' built-in tools work fine; otherwise, get a copy of WinZip (*winzip.com*) or WinRAR (*win-rar.com*), superior utilities that can:

- Zip and email in a single step

- Create self-extracting (.exe) archives that unpack themselves automatically when double-clicked

- Use wildcard file specifications—like *.docx (Word files) or *.mp3 (MP3s)— to bulk-add files to an archive instead of adding them one by one

- Split large archives across drives for easy reassembly later

- Encrypt and password-protect archives

- Work with many compression standards, not just zip

WinZip/WinRAR and zip files can coexist. When installed, WinZip/WinRAR takes over the .zip filename extension (page 254) and becomes the main way to handle zip archives. A more capable but proprietary compression format is RAR (.rar files). It's used mostly on file-sharing networks.

Searching for Files and Folders

Even if you organize your files and folders logically, sooner or later you'll need to find something: a newly installed program, a downloaded file, a file or folder whose location you forgot, or a particular photo among thousands. Often, you'll also want to find all files that meet certain criteria: all or part of a filename, files containing a specific phrase, documents written by a given author, photos taken on a certain date, and so on.

The Search feature returns results instantly and is available systemwide. You'll find Search boxes in, for example, the Start menu, Control Panel, every folder window, Help and Support, Windows Live Photo Gallery, and Windows Media Player.

When you type in a Search box [Search   🔎], Windows returns a results list or filters the view based on what you're typing. You can type things like file and folder names, program names, text contained within a document, and file tags and properties. Common properties that you can type in the Search box include:

Filename

Type part or all of the filename that you're looking for. To find a file named *Golden Gate Bridge.jpg*, for example, you can type *Gol* or *bridge*.

Kind of file

The kind is typically *Document, Picture,* or *Music.* To find all your text, word-processing, spreadsheet, and presentation files, for example, type Document.

Type of file

The last few letters of the filename, called the filename extension (page 254), identify the file type. Common types include doc or docx (Word document), xls or xlsx (Excel spreadsheet), ppt or pptx (PowerPoint presentation), jpg (JPEG image), mp3 (music/audio file), txt (plain-text file), rtf (formatted-text file), and zip (compressed zip file). Type the file extension. To find only MP3 files, for example, type *mp3* or (for more accurate results) **.mp3*.

Tags

Tags are words or phrases that you apply to your files to describe them. Type any tag to see a list of files for which that tag has been added. See "Tagging Files" on page 183.

Author

Type the name of the person who created the file to see a list of files by that author.

Search is context sensitive, basing its results on your current location and activity. Searching from the Start menu finds stuff in all your files, folders, and programs; searching from Control Panel finds only Control Panel tasks; and searching from a folder window finds items only in that folder and its subfolders.

General Search Tips

• The keyboard shortcuts for Cut, Copy, Paste, Undo, and Select All work in the Search box (Ctrl+X, Ctrl+C, Ctrl+V, Ctrl+Z, and Ctrl+A, respectively).

• In a Search Results window, you can press F5 to update the results list. If you've deleted a file or folder or changed it so that it no longer meets the search criteria, it disappears from the list (or appears in it if the change meets the criteria).

- Search text is case-insensitive: Search considers *Boulder, boulder,* and *BOULDER* to be the same search term.

- For best results, type from the start of a word. If you're looking for *bicycle,* type *bic* rather than *cycle.* Words start after any of these characters: *space* . - _ & \ / ( ) { } [ ].

- You don't have to wait until a search ends to open or use a file in the results list.

- You can use **wildcard characters** to represent one or more filename characters when you don't know what the real character is or don't want to type the entire name. The ? character substitutes for any single character, and the * character substitutes for zero or more characters. Type **.do?x,* for example, to find all filenames that end in *.docx* (Word documents) or *.dotx* (Word templates). *chapter*.docx* finds all Word documents that begin with the word *chapter,* followed by any characters (or no characters).

- If you're not searching for an exact phrase, you can omit noise words from your search text. Type *connect internet* instead of *connect to the internet.*

- If you're looking for related files, finding them by using column headings (page 186) might be better than using Search.

Searching from the Start Menu

The Search box is in the bottom-left corner of the Start menu (page 82). It searches your computer for files, folders, and programs (including Control Panel programs), based on the filename, the program title (*excel,* for example), text in the file, tags (page 183), and other file properties. It looks at your personal folder, offline files, email, contacts, calendar events, internet favorites, and browsing history. (It doesn't search the private files of other users.) To change the scope of the search, right-click the Start button, choose Properties > Customize, and then turn on or off the Search options:

Search other files and libraries
  "Don't search" excludes nonindexed locations from searches. "Search with public folders" includes everyone's Public folders in searches. "Search without public folders" excludes everyone's Public folders in searches.

Search programs and Control Panel
  Turning off this option omits these items from the results when you use the Start-menu Search box.

To search from the Start menu:

1   Click the Start button (or tap the Windows logo key) and then type text in the Search box. You don't need to click inside the Search box before you begin typing; just type. As you type, items that match your text superimpose themselves on the Start menu. The results list narrows as you type more characters.

2   To open an item in the results list, click it or use the arrow keys to select it and then press Enter. If Search has already autoselected the item that you're looking for, just press Enter.

or

To open a folder with a complete list of results, click "See more results".

or

Right-click an item in the results list to show its shortcut menu.

or

To cancel the search, press Esc, backspace over the search text, or click the × in the Search box.

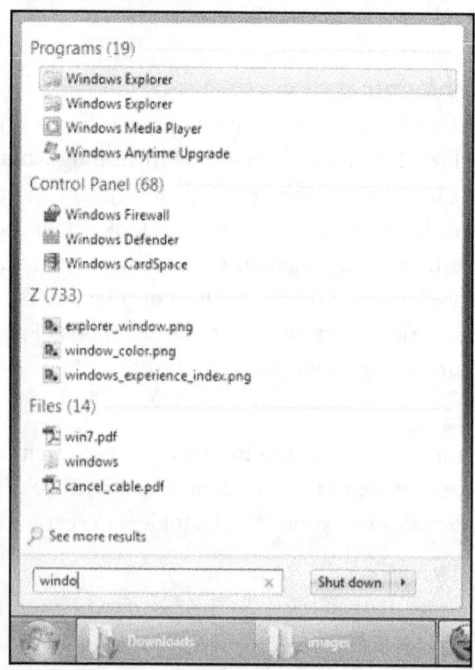

Start Menu Search Tips

- Typing all or part of a program name in the Start menu's Search box is often the fastest way to launch that program.

- Point (without clicking) to an item in the results list for a pop-up tip showing that item's file and folder details.

- You can drag an item from the results list into a folder or window, to the desktop, or into the Recycle Bin.

- To jump to a search result's actual location (instead of opening it), right-click it in the results list and then choose "Open file location".

Searching from Control Panel

A Search box is in the top-right corner of Control Panel (page 117). Use it to search for Control Panel tasks. Search works best in Category view, which is the default view. Control Panel searches find only tasks that you can access in Control Panel; they don't search your files, applications, or other parts of Windows.

To search from Control Panel:

1   Choose Start > Control Panel.

  or

  Choose Start, type *control panel* in the Search box, and then press Enter.

  or

If Control Panel is already open, press Ctrl+E.

2   Type text in the Search box. You don't need to click inside the Search box before you begin typing; just type. As you type, tasks that match your text appear in the Control Panel window. The results list narrows as you type more characters.

3   To open a task in the results list, click it, or tab to it and then press Enter.

or

To cancel the search, press Esc, backspace over the search text, or click the × in the Search box.

Searching from a Folder Window

A Search box is in the top-right corner of every folder window. Use it to search in the current folder and all its subfolders, no matter how deeply nested. These searches are useful if a folder contains hundreds of files or subfolders. Search bases its search on filenames, text in files, tags (page 183), and other file properties. See also "Using Windows Explorer" on page 170.

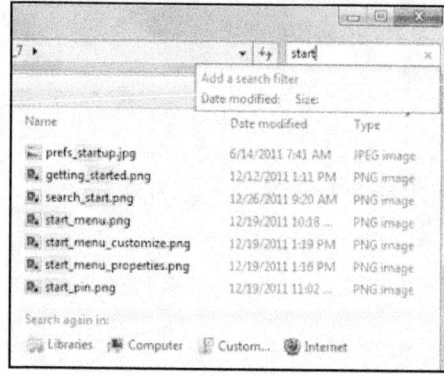

To search from a folder window:

1   In Windows Explorer, navigate to the folder that you want to search.

2   Click or tab to the Search box (or press Ctrl+E or F3) and then type text. As you type, the contents of the folder are filtered to match your text. The small pop-up window that appears below the Search box lets you choose previous search terms or refine the current search.

3   When you see the file or folder that you want, stop typing.

or

Click one of the "Search again in" links to change the scope of the search.

or

To cancel the search, press Esc, backspace over the search text, or click the × in the Search box. The folder window goes back to its unfiltered state.

Folder Search Tips

- For privacy reasons, only your own files are searched. To search for files belonging to another user, navigate to \Users*user_name* and then search as an administrator (page 8).

- To summon a search window from anywhere, press Windows logo key+F.

- To refine a search by using filters (page 187), click the links in the "Add a search filter" section of the Search box's pop-up window.

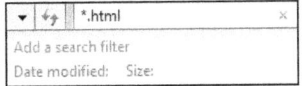

- To resize a Search box, drag its left edge.

- If you can't find a file that you know is on your computer, choose Start > Control Panel, switch to icon view, choose Troubleshooting > System and Security > Search and Indexing, and then follow the onscreen instructions to troubleshoot Search.

- Network locations, USB flash drives, external drives, memory cards, CDs, DVDs, and other removable storage aren't indexed, so searching them is slow compared with searching on your computer. If Windows complains that it can't reach a location, check your network connection or the drive. If you're searching a location that's not indexed, you may have to press Enter to start the search.

- Windows continually updates the index with the latest information about files on your computer. If you search while the index is being updated, your results may not be up to date for files that you've created or changed recently. Wait a few seconds for the index to update.

- To specify more search locations, click Custom in the "Search again in" section of the search results list. You may want to add search locations for system and program files, which aren't included in the index, to make routine searches faster. Navigate the location tree by clicking the small arrows. Use the checkboxes to include a place in the search or omit a place from the search. For some network or deeply nested places, it might be quicker to type or paste the location in the box and then click Add. The more locations that you add, the slower the search becomes.

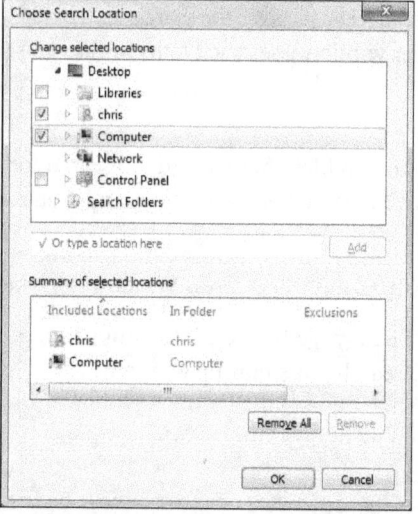

- To change the default behavior of Search, choose Organize (on the toolbar) > "Folder and search options" > Search tab. These settings reduce or expand the scope and type of searches and can make them much faster or slower.

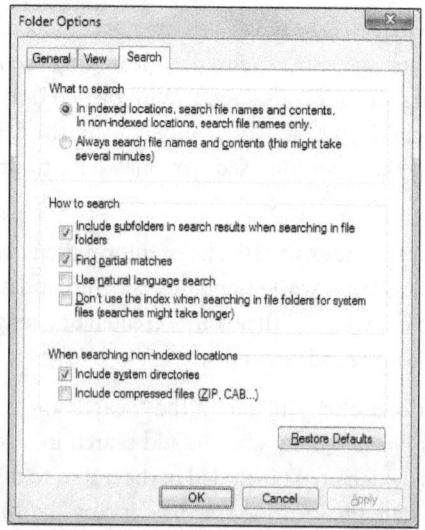

Federated Search

Federated search expands search beyond your computer and network to the internet. By downloading and installing **search connectors** (.osdx files), you can use Windows' Search box to search websites and online databases that support the OpenSearch standard. Windows Explorer's search features, including preview thumbnails, work with federated search. To get started, search the web for *federated search* or *search connector*. Google, YouTube, Twitter, and Flickr, for example, provide search connectors. Installed connectors are saved in your Searches folder (in your personal folder) and added as links to the Favorites list in Explorer's Navigation pane.

Advanced Searches

Search results can be too broad. Type *summer* and you may get photos tagged with *Summer in Boulder,* songs by Donna Summer, a file named *My Summer Vacation.docx,* a computer game named *_summer,* and a 1917 novel by Edith Wharton.

To search more selectively, you can filter your search in the Search box by specifying which file property to search: separate the name of the property and the search term with a colon (:). Type *name:summer* to find only files that have the word *summer* in the filename, for example. *tag:summer* finds only files tagged (page 183) with the word *summer. modified:2012* finds files changed at any time during that year (or *modified:1/1/2012* for that particular date).

You can filter on any property that appears in the column headings of a folder window. To see the complete list of properties, right-click any column heading in Details view and then click More. For details, see "Filtering, Sorting, Stacking, and Grouping Files" on page 186.

Boolean and other search operators let you combine search words by using logic. Type *AND, OR,* and *NOT* in uppercase. You can combine boolean and property filters:

- *author:tim AND hill* finds files that are authored by *tim* and any files that have *hill* in the filename or in any file property

- *author:(tim AND hill)* finds only files authored by both names (note how parentheses change the meaning)

- *author:"tim hill"* finds only files authored by someone with this name exactly

The advanced search operators are:

word1 AND word2
> Finds files or properties that contain both *word1* and *word2*, even if those words aren't next to each other. *small AND town* finds files that contain both those words.

word1 OR word2
> Finds files or properties that contain either *word1* or *word2*. *small OR town* finds files that contain either of those words.

NOT word
> Finds files or properties that don't contain word. *small NOT town* finds files that contain *small* but not *town*.

Quotes
> Finds files or properties that contain an exact phrase. *"small town"* finds files in which *small* and *town* are right next to each other, in that order.

Parentheses
> Finds files or properties that contain the specified words. *(small town)* finds files in that contain both those words in any order. Expressions in parentheses are evaluated before expressions outside them. If parenthesized expressions are nested, the innermost expressions are evaluated first.

> (greater than)
> Finds files or properties that are greater than a value or later than a date. *modified:>1/1/2012* finds files changed after that date.

< (less than)
> Finds files or properties that are less than a value or earlier than a date. *size:<1.5 MB* finds files smaller than 1.5 megabytes. *created:<yesterday* finds files created more than two days ago.

Natural-Language Search

Natural-language search lets you type search text the way you talk. You don't have to type *AND*, *OR*, and *NOT* in uppercase. *kind:music artist:(beethoven OR mozart)* is equivalent to the natural-language search *music by beethoven or mozart*. You can use tags and properties in your search text. Some examples:

- email from joe sent last month

- documents modified today

- documents created yesterday

- pictures of hawaii taken June 2010

- jazz music rated ****

To turn on natural-language search:

- Choose Start > Control Panel > Appearance and Personalization > Folder Options > Search tab > select "Use natural language search".

When natural-language search is turned on, you still can use the Search box in the normal way, with property names, colons, parentheses, and search operators.

Indexes

Windows invisibly and continually keeps track of the files on your computer by compiling an **index**, which stores the filename, date modified, size, file type, author, tags, properties, and other information. This index lets Windows do very fast searches; when you search, Windows consults the index instead of scanning your entire drive.

By default, Windows indexes the most common files on your computer, including all the files in your personal folder (such as Documents, Pictures, Music, and Videos), email, offline files, contacts, calendar events, internet favorites, and browsing history. It doesn't index program files and system files, because you rarely need to search them.

If you frequently search in locations that aren't indexed, your searches may be slow. You can add those locations to the index to speed future searches. Bigger indexes make for slower searches, however, so you shouldn't index any more than you have to (Windows usually scans the entire index every time you search). You can't turn off the index or index network locations.

To add or remove index locations:

1   Choose Start > Control Panel, switch to icon view, and then choose Indexing Options. The currently indexed locations are shown in the "Index these locations" list.

2   To add new files or locations to the index, click Modify, click "Show all locations", and then select the checkboxes in the "Change selected locations" list. To include a folder but not all its subfolders, expand the folder and then clear the checkbox next to any folder that you don't want to

index. These folders appear in the Exclude column of the "Summary of selected locations" list.

or

To remove a location from the index, clear its checkbox in the "Change selected locations" list.

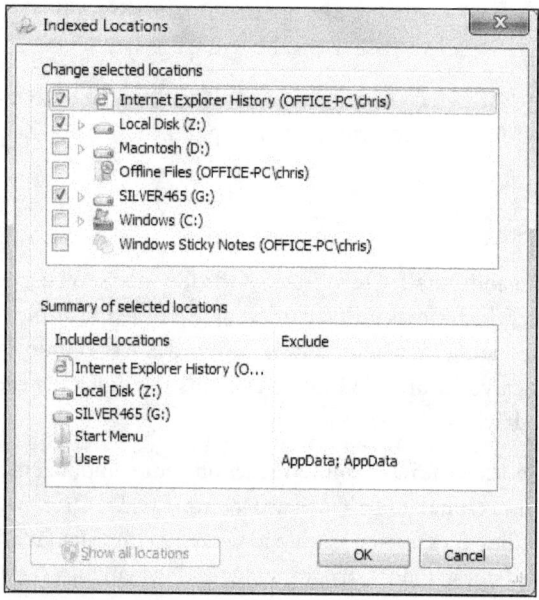

3 Close each open dialog box.

For advanced index management, click the Advanced button in the Indexing Options dialog box. The Index Settings tab lets you rebuild the index or change the drive or folder where it's stored. The File Types tab lets you search for a file type that's not currently being indexed (handy if you use an unusual file type that the index doesn't recognize). Usually, your index requires no maintenance. But if Windows can't find files that you know are in an indexed location, you may need to rebuild the index. This takes a long time to complete, so avoid rebuilding until you have given the index a few hours to self-correct.

Saving Searches

If you work regularly with a certain group of files and do the same search repeatedly to find them, you can save your search results. With a **saved search**, you don't have to keep rebuilding the same search manually. Just open that search. Windows repeats the search and lists the most-current files that match the original search criteria.

To save a search:

1   Press Windows logo key+F or, in any folder window or on the desktop, press F3.

2   Find your files (see "Searching for Files and Folders" on page 211).

3   When the search completes, click "Save search" (on the toolbar).

4   In the "File name" box, type a name for the search, and then click Save. The search is saved by default in your Searches folder (inside your personal folder). You can also add searches to this folder by dragging them from the file list. The Searches folder also contains search connectors (page 219).

To open a saved search:

- In Windows Explorer, click the search in the Favorites section of the Navigation pane, or double-click a saved search in your Searches folder.

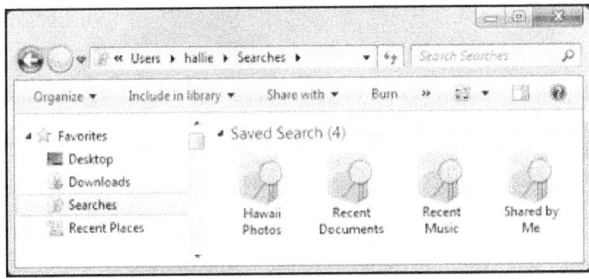

Double-clicking a saved search doesn't actually open it; it runs it and then displays the results in a folder window. Each saved search is a special file with the filename extension .search-ms, stored by default in the Searches folder in your personal folder. Right-click a saved search, and you'll see that you can copy, move, delete, rename, and share it, like any other file. What you can't do easily is *edit* it—if you save a flawed search, you'll have to rebuild it from scratch. To see what's inside a search file (XML code), right-click it, choose "Open with", and then open it in Notepad (or any text editor). For details, read the Microsoft article "Saved Search File Format" at *msdn.microsoft.com/en-us/library/bb892885.aspx*.

Using Libraries

A **library** is a collection of files, folders, and other items assembled from various locations. Libraries are superficially similar to folders—you open them to view and manage things—but libraries don't actually *store* things. Instead, they monitor locations that you specify and present their contents arranged the way you want. If you keep your music files on your local hard drive and on an external hard drive, for example, you can create a library (or modify the default Music library) to see all the files in one window.

Windows has four default libraries: Documents, Pictures, Music, and Videos. (Links to default libraries appear in the right column of the Start menu.) If those aren't enough, you can create new ones. A library can include folders in these locations:

- The Windows drive and all internal hard drives

- External hard drives (while they're connected)

- USB flash drives that appear in the Computer folder (page 163) in the Hard Disk Drives section (if the flash drive appears in a different section, consult the device manufacturer to see whether it can be changed)

- Network drives that have been indexed (page 221) or made available offline (right-click a network folder and then choose "Always available offline")

- Drives on different computers in your homegroup (page 322)

A library *can't* include removable media (CDs and DVDs), saved searches (page 223), and search connectors (federated searches, page 219).

You can customize a library by removing or adding (up to 50) folders, or **library locations**. If you copy, move, or save an item to a library, it's stored in the default save location, which you can change. You can optimize a library's display options for certain types of files (pictures or music, for example).

To create a library:

1 In a folder window, click Libraries in the Navigation pane. The Libraries folder contains the default libraries and any libraries that you've created. Expand a library in the Navigation pane to see which folders (locations) it includes. Right-clicking the Libraries folder or an individual library shows commands that are mostly the same as those of ordinary folders.

2 Click "New library" on the toolbar, or right-click an empty area in the folder and then choose New > Library.

3 Type or paste a name for the library and then press Enter.

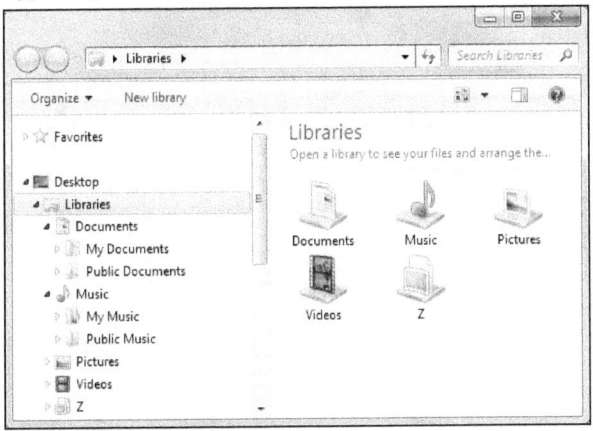

To customize a library:

1 Right-click the library in the navigation pane and then choose Properties.

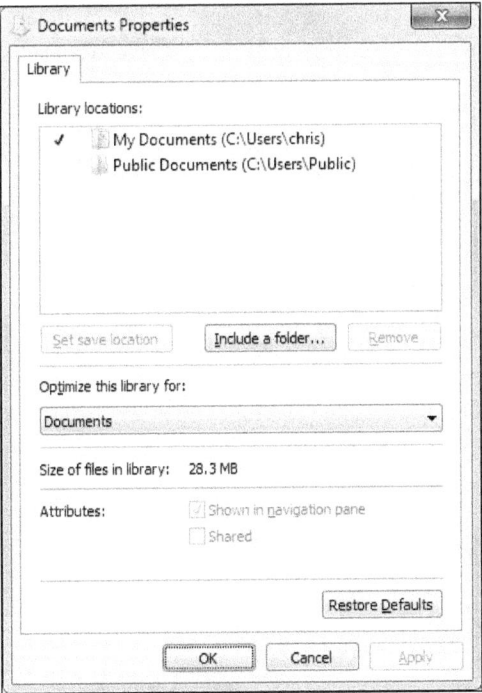

2 To add or remove library locations, click "Include a folder" or "Remove".

or

To set the default save location, click an (unchecked) folder in the "Library locations" list and then click "Set save location".

or

To optimize the library for a certain file type, choose that file type from the "Optimize this library for" drop-down list.

or

To restore a default library to its original state, click Restore Defaults.

3 Click OK (or Apply).

Library Tips

- To show or hide the Library pane in Windows Explorer, choose Organize (on the toolbar) > Layout > "Library pane". This command appears only if you're in a library or the Libraries folder. The Library pane appears below the toolbar. When a library is selected, you can click the "Includes" link to add or remove library locations or set the default save location. Click the "Arrange by" link to stack (page 189) the library's icons.

- Quick way to add (or remove) a library folder: right-click the folder in the Navigation pane or file list and then choose "Include in library" (or "Remove location from library").

- Deleting a library itself doesn't delete its original files and folders (because they're stored elsewhere), but deleting files or folders within a library does delete the originals from their original locations. If you add a folder to a library and then later delete that folder or disconnect its drive, the library can't access it.

- To restore a deleted default library, right-click the Libraries folder and then choose "Restore default libraries".

Burning CDs and DVDs

If your computer has a CD or DVD recorder, you can copy—or **burn**—files to a writeable disc. By default, Windows burns discs in the **Live File System** (UDF) format, but you can also use the **Mastered (ISO)** format.

Live File System (UDF) discs:

- Work like floppy disks or USB flash drives, meaning that you can copy files to disc immediately by dragging them

- Let you keep a disc in the burner and copy a few files at a time when you need to

- Let you delete individual files or reformat the disc to free space on CD-RW, DVD-RW, and DVD-RAM discs

- Don't need additional hard-drive space during burning

- Don't have a long recording step

- May need to be closed before you can use them in other computers

- Are compatible with only Windows XP and later

Mastered (ISO) discs:

- Are what most of the world uses

- Are convenient if you want to burn a large collection of files (always use this format when you're archiving backups)

- Don't copy files immediately, meaning that you need to select the entire collection of files that you want to copy to the drive and then burn them all at the same time

- Need temporary free hard-drive space at least the size of the files to be burned

- Have a long recording step

- Don't need to be closed

- Are compatible with older computers and devices such as CD players and DVD players

To burn a disc by using the Live File System (UDF) format:

1   Insert a writeable CD or DVD into your computer's disc burner.

2   If an AutoPlay dialog box appears, click "Burn files to disc".

3   In the Burn a Disc dialog box, type a title for this disc, choose "Like a USB flash drive", and then click Next. It might take a few minutes for Windows to format as Live File System. When the formatting completes, an empty disc folder opens.

4   Open the folder containing the files that you want to burn, and then drag the files into the empty disc folder. As you drag files into the disc folder, they are copied automatically to the disc.

To burn a disc by using the Mastered (ISO) format:

1   Insert a writeable CD or DVD into your computer's disc burner.

2   If an AutoPlay dialog box appears, click "Burn files to disc".

3   In the Burn a Disc dialog box, type a title for this disc, choose "With a CD/DVD player", and then click Next. An empty disc folder opens. A burn folder looks and acts like a normal folder. Down-arrow badges on the icons indicate that the files have not yet been burned to disc.

4   Open the folder containing the files that you want to burn, and then drag the files into the empty disc folder.

5   On the toolbar, click "Burn to disc". When Windows finishes burning the files to the disc, the burner tray opens, and you can remove the disc. Then you can use it in other computers or CD/DVD players.

Closing a Live File System disc makes it compatible with other computers and devices. (Mastered discs automatically are compatible with other computers and don't need to be closed.) You need to close only CD-R, DVD-R, and DVD+R discs (but not rewriteable discs, which end in RW). Discs that have not been closed can still be used in other disc burners but not in CD-ROM and DVD-ROM drives. Windows closes a disc automatically when you eject it.

To close a disc:

•   Press the Eject button on your computer's burner drive.

    or

    Choose Start > Computer, right-click the burner drive, and then choose Eject.

    It may take a few minutes to close the disc.

Tip: To close a disc manually, choose "Close session" from the burner drive's shortcut menu. To stop closing discs automatically, click Global Settings in the burner drive's Properties dialog box and then clear the checkboxes.

If you're using a CD-RW, DVD-RW, DVD+RW, or DVD-RAM disc, you can erase it and then write to it many times. Live File System discs let you delete one or more files. Mastered discs are an all-or-nothing erase.

To erase all files on a disc:

1   Insert a rewriteable CD or DVD into your computer's disc burner.

2   Choose Start > Computer, right-click the burner drive, and then choose "Erase this disc".

   or

   In a disc folder, click "Erase this disc" (on the toolbar).

3   Follow the onscreen instructions.

To erase some files on a disc:

1   Insert a rewriteable CD or DVD into your computer's disc burner.

2   Choose Start > Computer.

3   Double-click the burner drive to display its contents.

4   Select the files or folders that you want to delete.

5   Press Delete.

Disc Burning Tips

- If you change your mind about burning a Mastered disc after you've selected files to burn, you can delete the temporary files to recover hard-drive space. To delete the files, open the disc folder, select the files, and then click "Delete temporary files" (on the toolbar).

- To configure your disc burner, choose Start > Computer, right-click the burner drive, and then choose Properties > Recording tab. This tab lets you pick a default burner (if you have more than one) and choose the "scratch" drive for storing temporary files during Mastered burns. You can also turn off disc autoejection. (Temporary files are stored by default in the hidden folder \Users*user_name*\AppData\Local\Microsoft\Windows\Burn\Temporary Burn Folder.)

- You can put a shortcut (page 110) to your burner on your desktop and then drop files on the shortcut.

- Burners are finicky; during a Mastered burn, don't use other programs or stomp around the room. When the burn completes, test the disc immediately to see whether you can use it. (If you can't, you have a bicycle reflector.)

- To burn music CDs (for use with conventional CD players), use Windows Media Player. To burn multimedia DVDs with video, photos, and audio, use DVD Maker.

- To burn a **disc image**, or **ISO file**, to a disc, double-click the .iso file (or right-click it and then choose "Burn disc image").

General Keyboard Shortcuts

The following keyboard shortcuts apply to the desktop (page 81), Computer folder (page 163), Windows Explorer (page 170), and other programs. See also "Folder Tree Keyboard Shortcuts" on page 181.

To	Press
Show the top of the active window or folder list	Home
Show the bottom of the active window or folder list	End
Copy/Cut/Paste	Ctrl+C / Ctrl+X / Ctrl+V
Undo	Ctrl+Z
Delete or move the selected item(s) to the Recycle Bin	Delete
Delete the selected item(s) permanently, bypassing the Recycle Bin	Shift+Delete
Copy the selected item	Ctrl while dragging item
Move the selected item	Shift while dragging item
Create a shortcut to the selected item	Ctrl+Shift (or Alt) while dragging item
Rename the selected item	F2
Move the insertion point to the beginning of the next word	Ctrl+right arrow

To	Press
Move the insertion point to the beginning of the previous word	Ctrl+left arrow
Move the insertion point to the beginning of the next paragraph	Ctrl+down arrow
Move the insertion point to the beginning of the previous paragraph	Ctrl+up arrow
Highlight a block of text	Ctrl+Shift+arrow key
Select more than one item in a window or on the desktop, or select text within a document	Shift+arrow key
Select all contents	Ctrl+A
Search for a file or folder	F3
Create a new folder	Ctrl+Shift+N
Show the properties of the selected object	Alt+Enter
Close the active item or quit the active program	Alt+F4
Open the shortcut (or control) menu for the active window	Alt+spacebar
Close the active document in programs that allow you to have multiple documents open at the same time	Ctrl+F4
Switch among open windows	Alt+Tab
Use the arrow keys to switch among open windows	Ctrl+Alt+Tab
Cycle through windows in the order in which they were opened	Alt+Esc
Cycle through window panes or desktop elements	F6
Show the address-bar list in Computer or Windows Explorer	F4
Toggle full-screen mode on and off	F11
Show the shortcut menu for the selected item	Shift+F10 or Application key 📇

To	Press
Show the Start menu	Ctrl+Esc
Show a menu	Alt+underlined letter in the menu name
Carry out a menu command	Underlined letter in the command name in an open menu
Activate the menu bar in the active program	F10
Open the next menu to the right or open a submenu	Right arrow
Open the next menu to the left or close a submenu	Left arrow
Refresh the active window	F5
View the folder one level up in Computer or Windows Explorer	Backspace
Cancel the current task	Esc
Prevent the CD/DVD from playing automatically	Shift when you insert a disc into the drive

Windows Logo Key Shortcuts

To	Press
Show or hide the Start menu	Windows logo key
Show the System Properties dialog box	Windows logo key+Break
Show the desktop (reveal gadgets)	Windows logo key+D
Minimize all windows	Windows logo key+M
Restore minimized windows	Windows logo key+Shift+M
Open Computer folder	Windows logo key+E
Search for a file or folder	Windows logo key+F
Search for computers on a network	Windows logo key+Ctrl+F
Show Windows Help and Support	Windows logo key+F1
Lock your computer if you're on a network domain or switch users if you're not	Windows logo key+L

To	Press
Open the Run dialog box	Windows logo key+R
Cycle through windows on the taskbar	Windows logo key+T
Open Ease of Access Center	Windows logo key+U
Cycle through running programs by using Flip 3D (Aero interface only)	Windows logo key+Tab
Use the arrow keys to cycle through running programs by using Flip 3D (Aero interface only)	Windows logo key+Ctrl+Tab
Peek at desktop gadgets	Windows logo key+spacebar (press and hold)
Bring all gadgets to front	Windows logo key+G
Open Windows Mobility Center (on laptops)	Windows logo key+X
Select the first icon in the notification area	Windows logo key+B
Open the corresponding icon on the taskbar	Windows logo key+number key (1, 2,...)
Maximize the active window	Windows logo key+up arrow
Vertically maximize the active window	Windows logo key+Shift+up (or down) arrow
Minimize the active window (or restore it if it's maximized)	Windows logo key+down arrow
Minimize all but the active window	Windows logo key+Home (press again to restore)
Dock the active window against the screen's edge	Windows logo key+left (or right) arrow
Move the active window to the adjacent display	Windows logo key+Shift+left (or right) arrow
Zoom in/out	Windows logo key+(+/−)
Choose an external-display option	Windows logo key+P
Use OneNote Screen Clipping Tool (OneNote required)	Windows logo key+S

5

Programs & Documents

Windows is a launching pad for programs, or **applications** (apps, for short). Microsoft and sound design enforce substantial consistency, so you can apply knowledge of a few common operations to many programs. Most programs share user-interface elements—scrollbars, copy-and-paste operations, menus, ribbons, buttons, dialog boxes, and so on—as well as setup and management options. Windows provides consistent ways to manage programs and **documents**, which are self-contained pieces of work (files) that you create with programs.

Installing Programs

How you install a program depends on where its installation files are located. Most shrink-wrapped programs are installed from a CD or DVD. Windows' AutoPlay feature runs the Setup program automatically when you insert the disc into the drive. You can also install programs that you've downloaded from the internet or from a local network.

Keep these points in mind before you install a new program:

- If you have a third-party (non-Microsoft) antimalware program, turn it off (page 344).

- You must be an administrator (page 8) to install programs.

- Your computer's manufacturer may have added software—Microsoft Office or a PDF reader, for example—at the factory. Check the Start > All Programs menu before you install new stuff.

- Most installations go smoothly, though Windows' security features won't let some poorly designed or malicious programs harm your system by installing outdated drivers or system files that Microsoft knows to be dangerous.

- If you upgraded from an earlier version of Windows, Windows Setup configured your existing programs to run; you don't have to reinstall them. If an older program doesn't run, see "Running Older Programs" on page 244.

Installing from Disc
To install a program from CD or DVD:

1 Insert the program's installation or setup disc.

   If a security prompt appears, type an administrator password or confirm the action.

2 If the program launches an install wizard, the AutoPlay dialog box will appear, and you can choose to run the wizard.

   or

   If a program doesn't start to install, check the installation instructions that came with the program (or on the publisher's website). If you can't find instructions, browse through the disc and then open the program's setup file, usually named *setup.exe* or *install.exe*.

3 Follow the onscreen instructions. Install wizards usually make you pick a language, specify a destination folder, accept a license agreement, choose which components to install, and type a serial number or product key.

Installing from the Internet
The internet is the preferred (or only) distribution method for many software vendors. You can use Internet Explorer or any web browser to download thousands of commercial, shareware, demo, and free programs (and updates) from vendors' websites and from independent sites.

To install a program from the internet:

1 In your web browser, click the link to the program.

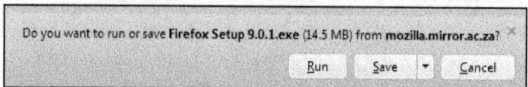

2 To install the program immediately, click Open or Run, and then follow the onscreen instructions.

or

To install the program later, click Save and then download the installation file to your computer. (To install the program, double-click the file and then follow the onscreen instructions.) The Save option is safer because you can scan the downloaded file for malware if you don't trust the website. It also leaves a copy of the program on your hard drive if you have to reinstall.

In either case, if a security prompt appears, type an administrator password or confirm the action.

By default, Internet Explorer and other Windows-aware browsers store downloads in your Documents library or the Downloads folder inside your personal folder (page 167). You can use the Save dialog box to pick a different place.

Downloaded programs are usually executable (.exe) files, which run when you double-click them and start installation automatically. If the download is a zip file (page 209), extract its files, and then look for a read-me file (*readme.txt* or *readme.html*) or double-click the installer program (usually named *setup. exe* or *install.exe*) among the extracted pieces. You can delete these pieces after you install (keep the original zip file if you need it).

Installing from a Network

If you're on a large network at work or school, your network administrator probably set up an internal webpage with instructions for installing licensed software from the network. If not, you can use Control Panel.

To install a program from a network:

1 Choose Start > Control Panel > Programs. Click "Add programs from your network" (provided that your administrator has enabled it).

2 Select a program from the list and then click Install.

3 Follow the onscreen instructions.

If a security prompt appears, type an administrator password or confirm the action.

Shortcuts to a Program

Any program that you (or any administrator) installs is available to all users by default; its shortcuts (page 110) appear in everybody's All Programs menu. Sometimes shortcuts end up in your personal All Programs menu because you (inadvertently) told Setup to do so or because Setup gave you no choice.

Windows inspects two folders to build the All Programs menu: one for All Users and another for the logged-on user (for details, see "Managing All Programs Items with Folders" on page 89). To make a program available to everyone (instead of only you), do the following:

1   Choose Start > All Programs.

2   Right-click the item (icon) that you want everyone to be able to access and then choose Copy.

3   Click Back, right-click All Programs, and then choose Open All Users.

4   In the Navigation pane or file list, right-click the Programs folder and then choose Paste.

Now the program appears in everyone's All Programs menu. If this method doesn't work, or if a program requires per-user settings, log on to each user account and rerun Setup.

Installation Tips

*   During lengthy installations, you can switch to other programs and hover your pointer over the installer's taskbar button to check its progress. A live progress meter appears in the pop-up thumbnail.

*   If you're installing an older DOS-based program from a floppy disk, try running it in Command Prompt (page 262).

*   To configure AutoPlay for program discs, choose Start > Control Panel > Hardware and Sound > AutoPlay > "Software and games" drop-down list. Choose what happens when you insert a program disc. The default setting, "Ask me every time", launches the AutoPlay dialog box.

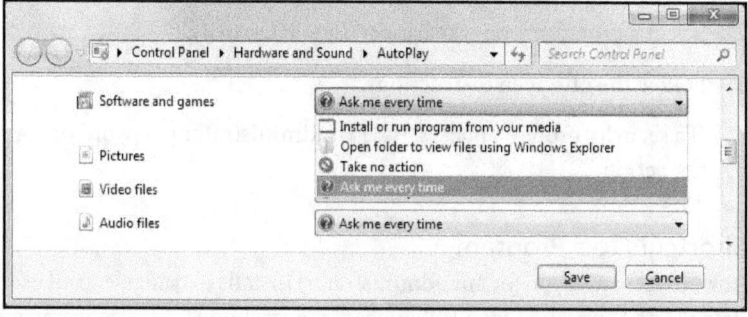

- Software publishers create install wizards with Microsoft's Windows Installer or with third-party programs such as InstallShield or Wise Installer, so sometimes you'll see those program names in title bars.

- After installation, the program's shortcuts are highlighted in color in the Start > All Programs menu. To turn off highlighting, right-click the Start button, choose Properties > Customize, clear "Highlight newly installed programs", and then click OK.

- If an installation goes very badly, see "Restoring Your System" on page 359.

Removing Programs

When you install a program, it scatters its components all over your folder structure, not just in the Program Files subfolder it creates. Only an unwanted program's uninstall utility can remove it completely. Don't just delete the program's folder; if you do, you'll leave behind shortcuts, support files, hidden folders, registry entries, and other litter on your hard drive.

You can uninstall a program if you no longer use it or if you want to free up space on your hard drive. You can also change the program's configuration by adding or removing certain components. (Some programs don't offer this option, in which case your only choice is to uninstall.)

Always exit the program that you're going to remove. If you're using fast user switching (page 25), make sure that no other logged-on users are using the program.

To uninstall or change a program:

1 Choose Start > Control Panel > Programs > Programs and Features.

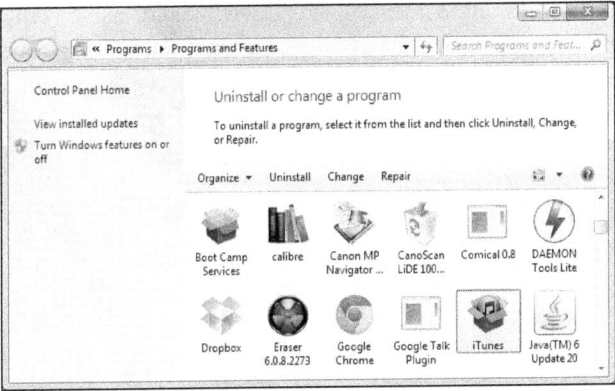

2 To uninstall the program, select the program and then click Uninstall (on the toolbar).

or

To change or repair the program, click Change or Repair (on the toolbar).

The buttons on the toolbar change depending on what uninstall/change/repair options the selected program provides. Big packages like Microsoft Office and Adobe Creative Suite provide the most options.

3 Confirm the removal or change if a dialog box appears.

If a security prompt appears, type an administrator password or confirm the action.

Windows runs the program's uninstall or change utility (which varies by program).

4 Follow any onscreen instructions.

Most uninstallers display a progress bar, explain what they're removing or not removing, and tell you whether you must restart your computer to complete the removal.

You may get a midprocess message asking whether Windows should remove a shared file that other programs may need. Warnings of this type can look a bit dire, but ignoring them rarely produces ill effects.

The folder that contained the program may persist after uninstall completes, usually because it contains documents created by the program. Games, for example, sometimes leave keyboard-binding and saved-game files. If you don't need those documents, you can delete the folder and its files safely.

If a program that you want to uninstall isn't listed, look for removal instructions in the program's read-me file (if any) or at the publisher's website. Or search the web for uninstall and the program's name. As a last resort, drag the program's folder into the Recycle Bin.

Turning Windows Features On or Off

Some programs and features that are included with Windows must be turned on before you can use them, whereas others, turned on by default, can be turned off if you don't need them.

In early versions of Windows, turning off a feature uninstalled it. Now all features remain stored on the Windows drive, so you can turn them back on when you want. Turning off a feature doesn't free drive space.

To turn Windows features on or off:

1   Choose Start > Control Panel > Programs > Programs and Features > "Turn Windows features on or off" (on the left). To learn about a feature, hover the pointer over it for a pop-up description.

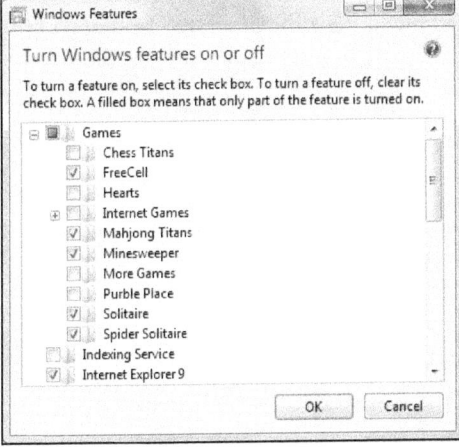

2   In the list, select or clear the checkboxes to turn features on or off. Some features are grouped in folders, which you can double-click to see. If a checkbox is partially selected or dark, then some of the items inside are turned on and others aren't.

3   Click OK.

Launching Programs

Windows gives you many ways to launch (open) a program.

To open a program:

- Choose Start > All Programs and then click the program's icon.

  or

  Choose Start, type the program's name in the Search box, and then click it in the results list. You need to type only part of a program's name for it to appear in the results list. Windows highlights the most relevant result; if that's the program you're looking for, just press Enter.

  or

  On the left side of the Start menu, click the program's icon (if it's pinned).

  or

  On the taskbar, click the program's icon (if it appears).

  or

  Choose Start > Computer > Local Disk (C:) > Program Files. In the program's subfolder, double-click the program's icon (.exe file).

  or

  Right-click the program's icon and then choose Open.

  or

  Press the keyboard shortcut that you assigned to the program's icon.

  or

  Press Windows logo key+R, type the program's name, and then press Enter. You may have to include the full path (page 178). The Run dialog box may seem old-fashioned, but for many experienced users and rapid typists, it's the fastest way to open a program or document. Press F4 for a drop-down history of previous commands. (You can also open a program or document from a command prompt just as you can from the Run dialog box.)

  or

  Type the program's name in the address bar (page 177) of any folder window and then press Enter.

Tip: You can use any of these methods to open a document with its associated program. If you created the document *stuff.docx* in Microsoft Word, for example, double-click the document's icon to start Word and open that document automatically.

Opening the All Programs Menu

When the Start menu is open (tap the Windows logo key or press Ctrl+Esc), you can open the All Programs menu in the following ways:

- Click All Programs.

- Hover the pointer over All Programs for a few seconds.

- Press the up-arrow key to highlight All Programs and then press Enter, the right-arrow key, or the spacebar.

After All Programs is open, you can open any item without using the mouse: use the up- and down-arrow keys (or type the first few letters of a program or folder name) to highlight the desired item, and then press Enter.

If you open a folder (instead of a program) in All Programs, the folder's contents are listed indented beneath the folder. To open or close a folder, click it. To open a folder via the keyboard, use the up- and down-arrow keys to highlight it and then press Enter or the right-arrow key. To close it, press Enter again or the left-arrow key. Most Setup programs put an icon in the All Programs menu or on the desktop. To move these icons, see "Using the Start Menu" on page 85.

Launching Programs Automatically

The Start > All Programs > Startup folder contains programs that open automatically every time that you start Windows. To save yourself a few clicks or keystrokes every time you log on, you can place your own shortcuts to programs or documents in this folder.

To open an item each time that you start Windows:

1 Choose Start > All Programs, right-click Startup, and then choose Open.

Choose "Open all users" (instead of Open) to change the Startup folder that applies to all users, not only yourself (the All Users Startup folder is more restrictive about what shortcuts it accepts). The All Users Startup folder might have a few icons already, put there by programs when they were installed.

2 In Windows Explorer or Computer, navigate to the drive, folder, program, or document that you want to open automatically.

3 Right-drag the item to the Startup folder and then choose "Create shortcuts here". From now on, the item opens each time that you start your computer or log on.

For an uncluttered desktop, open startup programs as taskbar buttons rather than as windows. Right-click a Startup shortcut, choose Properties > Shortcut tab, and then choose Minimized from the Run list. To identify startup programs, press Windows logo key+R, type *msconfig.exe*, and then press Enter. You can use the Startup tab's checkboxes to isolate startup problems and disable unwelcome startup programs.

Running Older Programs

If you've upgraded from an earlier Windows version, you probably still need to run your older programs. The current version of Windows can still run many of them, even those written for Windows 3.1/95 and DOS, but if it has trouble running a program that used to run fine under your old copy of Windows, you can try changing the **compatibility mode**.

To run a troublesome older program:

1 Right-click a program's executable (.exe) file or shortcut icon and then choose Properties > Compatibility tab.

2 Change the compatibility settings for the program.

3 Click OK.

The next time you open the program, Windows tries to run it by using your settings.

Windows Virtual PC

You can use **Windows Virtual PC** (*microsoft.com/virtualpc*) to run multiple operating systems at the same time on the same computer and then switch among them with a click. Each OS runs in a virtual machine (VM), which emulates a standard computer and its hardware. VMs often are used to run older programs that don't work in the latest version of Windows or test new or beta versions of operating systems.

Running 16-Bit Programs

Windows 3.1 and DOS programs are called **16-bit programs**. Programs written for Windows 95, NT, and later are called **32-bit programs**. The 16-bit programs run slowly because the current version of Windows runs them in a leakproof, emulated space called a **virtual machine** that draws on a common memory pool.

To run DOS programs, choose Start > All Programs > Accessories > Command Prompt (page 262). If Windows displays an incompatibility message when you try to install or run a 16-bit program, don't ignore it. Either find an update or try Windows Virtual PC.

Compatibility Tips

• If you want to be stepped through the process, use the Program Compatibility wizard: choose Start > Control Panel > Programs > "Run programs made for previous versions of Windows" (under Programs and Features).

• Never try to coerce obsolete hardware-dependent system utilities to run. Upgrade to the latest version of your virus scanner, backup program, partitioning tool, disc burner, or whatever.

• The high-end editions of Windows have **Windows XP Mode**, a fully functioning copy of Windows XP SP3 running in a virtual machine provided by Windows Virtual PC.

Switching Programs

You'll probably have multiple programs running simultaneously so that you can juggle, say, a word processor, email program, and web browser. You have several techniques for switching programs.

To switch among running programs:

- If the program's window is visible in the background, click it. (But click an empty area, not a button or menu, lest you activate it accidentally.)

   or

   Click the program's taskbar button. (The brightest button indicates the active program.)

   or

   Hold down Alt, press Tab repeatedly until the desired window is highlighted in the pop-up list, and then release both keys (or click an icon in the list to display that window). This gesture is called **Alt-tabbing**. The icons in the Alt+Tab list represent open windows. If you're using the Aero interface (page 122), the icons are live previews. Hold down Alt and press Tab repeatedly to highlight a window. If you press and release Alt+Tab quickly, you swap between only two windows instead of cycling through them all.

   or

   Hold down Alt, press Esc repeatedly until the desired program appears, and then release both keys.

   or

   Hold down the Windows logo key, press Tab repeatedly until the desired window comes to the front of the stack, and then release both keys (or click any part of any window in the stack to display that window). This feature is called **Flip 3D** and works only if you're using the Aero interface. If you release the Tab key but keep the Windows logo key pressed, you can use the arrow keys or mouse wheel to cycle through open windows.

Switching Tips

- If you press and release Ctrl+Alt+Tab or Ctrl+Windows logo key+Tab, you can use the arrow keys or Tab to cycle through open windows and then press Enter to activate a window.

- Flip 3D, Alt+Tab, and Alt+Esc cycle backward through programs if you hold down Shift. You can press or release Shift at any time to toggle forward and backward cycling.

- Alt+Esc—unlike Alt+Tab and Flip 3D—has no pop-up window, doesn't cycle through minimized programs, and doesn't swap between two programs. (It simply sends the active program to the bottom of the pile.)

Exiting Programs

When you finish using a program, you should exit (or quit or close) it to get it out of your way and to let Windows reclaim its memory for other use. Before exiting, the program prompts you to save any unsaved work.

To exit a program:

- Choose File > Exit.

    or

    In Windows Explorer, choose File > Close. (Tap Alt if the File menu isn't visible.)

    or

Activate the program's window and then press Alt+F4.

or

Click the program's Close button .

or

Double-click the program's icon (visible or invisible) at the left edge of the title bar.

or

Right-click the program's taskbar button and then choose "Close window" (or "Close all windows").

or

Activate the program's window, press Alt+spacebar, and then press C.

Killing Unresponsive Programs

Programs that crash/freeze/lock up/hang are said to be "not responding" in Microsoftese; you can move the pointer within the program's window, but the program itself won't respond to clicks or keystrokes. An unresponsive program rarely forces you to restart your computer. Instead, use Task Manager to send the frozen program to its grave.

Before you kill a program, make sure that it's really not responding. Wait a minute or two; Windows may be struggling to allocate extra memory. If you're running a Visual Basic macro in Microsoft Excel or Word, for example, the program may appear frozen while VB has control. Global reformatting or a find-and-replace operation on a long document can keep a word processor hypnotized for minutes. An open dialog box or message box may prevent you from doing anything else in the program; look for one hiding behind another window.

To kill an unresponsive program:

1   Right-click an empty area of the taskbar and then choose Start Task Manager.

or

Press Ctrl+Shift+Esc.

or

Press Ctrl+Alt+Delete and then click Start Task Manager.

or

Choose Start, type *taskmgr* in the Search box, and then press Enter.

2   On the Applications tab, select the name of the unresponsive task.

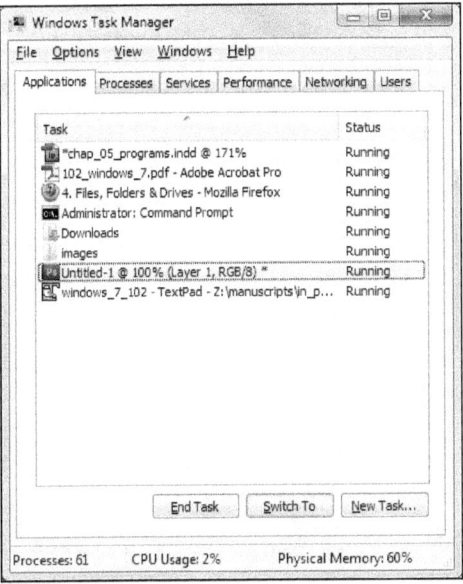

3   Click End Task.

4   If a message box appears, confirm the operation.

It may take Windows a few seconds—or minutes—to kill the program. After Windows terminates the program, you can launch it again immediately without repercussions.

Tip: As an alternative to killing programs via Task Manager, you can use the *tskill* command-prompt program (page 262), which allows more control than Task Manager. For usage and syntax, type *tskill /?* at a command prompt or search for *tskill* in Help and Support (page 71).

Next Steps

If killing an unresponsive program as described doesn't work, you still have these options, in order of preference:

- Click the Processes tab in Task Manager, click the program's image name, and then click End Process.

- Exit all other programs and log off.

- If you can't log off but other users are logged on (via fast user switching, page 25), right-click another user in Task Manager's Users tab, choose Connect to switch to that user, and then use Task Manager to log off (Disconnect) yourself.

- If none of these measures works, press your computer's reset or power button.

Saving Documents

Most applications let you save your work as documents, which you can return to later, print, send to other people, back up, and so on. Nearly all programs use Windows' standard Save dialog box. The first time that you save a document, Windows asks you to name it and pick a folder to store it in. (Two files in the same folder can't have the same name.)

To save a document:

1 Choose File > Save (or press Ctrl+S).

   or

   To save a copy of a file under a different name or in a different folder, choose File > Save As.

   (Tap Alt if the File menu isn't visible. If the program has a ribbon instead of menus, click the tab at the ribbon's left edge.)

2 Click Browse Folders. The dialog box expands to show the Navigation pane.

3 Use the address bar or Navigation pane to choose the folder to save the file to (for details, see "Navigating in Windows Explorer" on page 177). Alternatively, type the file's full path (page 178) in the "File name" box, and then skip the next step.

4 In the "File name" box, type the name of the file.

You can use the Cut, Copy, Paste, Undo, and Select All keyboard shortcuts (Ctrl+X, Ctrl+C, Ctrl+V, Ctrl+Z, and Ctrl+A, respectively) while editing. For file-naming rules, see "Naming Files and Folders" on page 196.

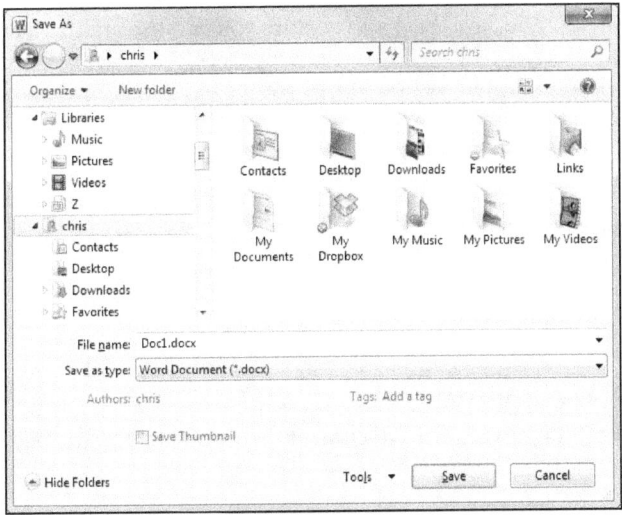

5   To save a file in a format other than the program's default (native) format, choose a target format from the "Save as type" drop-down list.

This feature lets you, say, save a Word document as PDF (.pdf), text (.txt), Rich Text Format (.rtf), or HTML (.html) so that users without Word can open it in a PDF viewer, text editor, WordPad, or a web browser.

6   Click Save.

Read-Only Files

You can prevent yourself (and others) from making accidental changes to a file by making it **read-only**. To change a file to read-only, right-click the file, choose Properties > General tab, select the "Read-only" checkbox (or clear it to make the file **read-write**), and then click OK. Read-only files can't be changed, but they can be copied, moved, renamed, or deleted.

Save Tips

*   In the file list, you can click a document to make its name appear in the "File name" box, and then click Save to overwrite the existing document or edit the name to save a new document. The latter technique saves typing when you're saving similarly named documents.

- The file list acts like an Explorer window. You can right-click any file or folder to, say, rename or delete it. You even can drag items into and out of this box or use the standard navigation keys.

- You must close the Save dialog box before you can use another part of the program.

- Some older programs use the old-style Save dialog box, with Windows XP–style navigation features.

- You can't save your work in some utility and game programs, such as Calculator and Solitaire.

- Some programs can autosave your work at a regular time interval that you set. Check the program's Options (page 79).

Opening Documents

You have several ways to reopen a document that you've already named and saved.

To open a document:

- In the program that created the document, choose File > Open (or press Ctrl+O), navigate to the document, and then click Open. The Open dialog box works like the Save dialog box (page 250).

    (Tap Alt if the File menu isn't visible. If the program has a ribbon instead of menus, click the tab at the ribbon's left edge.)

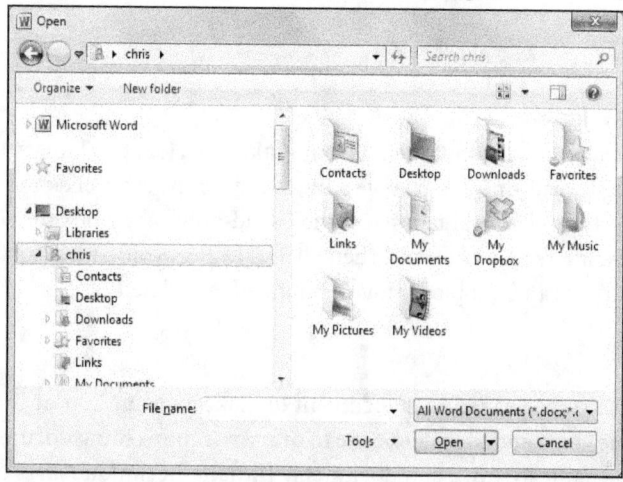

or

Choose Start, type the document's name in the Search box, and then click it in the results list.

or

In Windows Explorer or on the desktop, double-click the document's icon (or select it and then press Enter).

or

If the document was opened recently, choose it from the Start > Recent Items menu.

or

Press Windows logo key+R, type or paste the document's full path (page 178), and then press Enter.

or

Right-click the document's parent program (if it appears) on the taskbar and then select the document in the jump list.

Access Denied

If Windows denies you access when you try to open a file or folder, it may be that:

- The file is encrypted. To check whether it's encrypted, right-click the file and then choose Properties > General tab > Advanced button. If "Encrypt contents to secure data" is selected, see the person who created the file. If you encrypted the file, you might have done so in another user account. For details, see "Encrypting File System" on page 347.

- You don't own the folder. To take ownership, right-click the folder and then choose Properties > Security tab > Advanced button > Owner tab > Edit button. If a security prompt appears, type an administrator password or confirm the action. Click your name or group in the "Change owner to" list. If you want to own the files and subfolders too, select "Replace owner on subcontainers and objects". Click OK in each open dialog box.

Open Tips

- You can also open a document by using any of the techniques described in "Launching Programs" on page 242.

- Like the Save dialog box, the Open dialog box must be closed before you can use another part of the program.

- To open a file that's not associated with a particular program, right-click the file, choose Open With, and then select the name of a program. For details, see "Associating Documents with Programs" on page 254.

- If you open a document that somebody else already has open, the program usually will warn you or open a read-only copy of the document (unless it's a multiuser document such as a database).

Associating Documents with Programs

When you double-click a Word document, Windows launches Word—rather than, say, your browser or Photoshop—because a document's **file type**, or **file format**, is embedded in its filename, as the few characters following the name's last dot. These characters, called an **extension** or **filename extension**, link a document to a program. The link between a file type and its default program is an **association**. For example, the extension of the file readme.txt is .txt, denoting a plain-text file that will open in your text editor (Notepad, or whatever text editor you've specified). The extension of my.novel.docx is .docx, which tells Windows that the file is a document in the Microsoft Word file format. (Words in long filenames generally are separated by spaces, dots, or hyphens.)

Some notable extensions are:

- .avi, .mkv, .wmv, and .mp4 for movies, TV shows, and videos

- .jpg, .gif, .png, .tif, and .bmp for photos, artwork, and pictures

- .mp3 for music and audio books

- .pdf, .epub, and .mobi for books, magazines, and documents

- .txt for plain text

- .rtf for formatted text

- .html for webpages

- .otf and .ttf for fonts (page 158)

- .iso and .cue/.bin for disk images

- .url for links to webpages

- .doc and .docx for Microsoft Word documents

- .xls and .xlsx for Microsoft Excel spreadsheets

- .ppt and .pptx for Microsoft PowerPoint presentations

- .mdb and .accdb for Microsoft Access databases

- .psd for Adobe Photoshop documents

- .exe for programs (executable files)

- .dll for system and support files

- .zip for compressed zip files (page 209)

- .tmp for (program-created) temporary files

For a comprehensive list of extensions, go to *fileinfo.com*.

It's easy to set the default program for all files of the same type. You can change the program that opens all your digital photos from Picasa to Photoshop, for example, without having to change any .jpg files. If a newly installed program hijacks an association to become a file type's unwelcome default, you can reverse the change. (This misbehavior is less common than it used to be; now, installers usually let you manually set a program's associations.)

It may seem odd that the ability to open a file depends partially on something as easy to mistype as its filename, but when you rename a file in Windows, its name is selected only up to the last dot, letting you type a new name without accidentally changing the extension. If you do edit the extension, you're prompted to confirm the change. Changing an extension won't alter the file's contents or format, but it will change how Windows interacts with the file. Renaming a webpage file from *index.html* to *index.txt*, for example, causes the file to open by default in your text editor instead of your browser.

Hidden Extensions
Windows hides filename extensions by default, which is why the file *Maui.jpg* appears as only *Maui* in a folder or on the desktop. Extension-hiding may make your screen look friendlier, but it also forces you to discern a file's type from its (possibly tiny) icon or the containing folder's (possibly invisible) Type column. Instead of seeing merely *LoveLetter*, show extensions to see *LoveLetter.avi* (a movie), *LoveLetter.pdf* (a book), or *LoveLetter.exe* (a virus?) and anticipate which program will launch when you open the file.

If extensions are hidden, the file *love-letter-for-you.txt.vbs* appears without the *.vbs*, looking like a harmless text file while actually carrying a hostile Visual Basic script. Millions opened this file in 2000, infecting themselves and millions more via email with the ILOVEYOU worm. Even with extensions showing, the file

FreeMP3s.txt   .exe

will appear to be harmless if the embedded spaces hide the .exe extension in a narrow column.

To show or hide filename extensions for all files:

1 Choose Start > Control Panel > Appearance and Personalization > Folder Options.

   or

   In Windows Explorer, click Organize (on the toolbar) > "Folder and search options".

   or

   Choose Start, type *folder options* in the Search box, and then press Enter.

2 In the Folder Options dialog box, click the View tab, clear or select "Hide extensions for known file types", and then click OK.

Unregistered Extensions

Windows come with a list of **registered** extensions for built-in programs. When you install a new program, it registers its own extensions. The default program for .jpg files, for example, on a fresh copy of Windows is Windows Photo Viewer. Install Microsoft Excel and it registers itself as the default program for .xls and .xlsx files, among others.

If you double-click a file that has an unregistered extension, you're prompted to specify a compatible program. To find file types, extensions, and programs, go to *fileinfo.com* or read Wikipedia's list of file formats at *wikipedia.org/wiki/ list_of_file_formats*. Files that have no extension are usually text files containing release notes or support files not meant to be opened (support files display as random-looking garbage in a text editor).

Managing Associations and Extensions

Windows maintains a master list that pairs each filename extension with its default program. A file's Properties dialog box (page 65) shows its file type and associated program (and other metadata). You can override the default program for specific files.

Note: If a filename has an unregistered extension, Windows shows the complete name even if extension-hiding is turned on.

To open a specific file with a nondefault program:

1   Right-click the file, choose the desired program from the "Open with" submenu, and skip the remaining steps.

    or

    If the desired program isn't listed in the "Open with" submenu, choose "Open with" or "Open with" > "Choose default program".

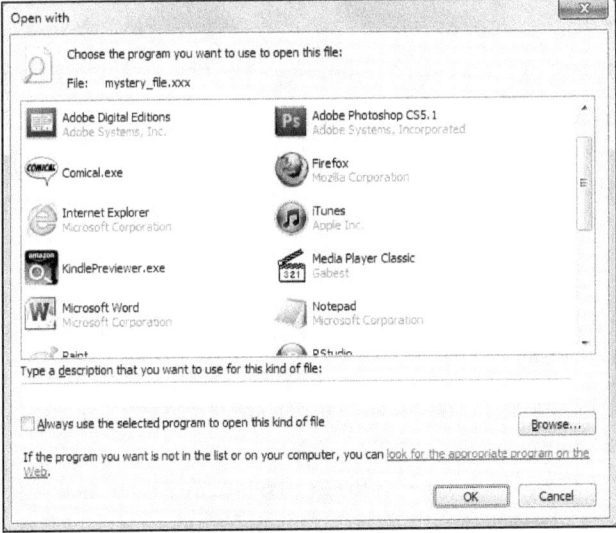

2   In the "Open with" dialog box, select the desired program (if it isn't listed, click Browse and then select it).

3   Clear "Always use the selected program to open this kind of file".

4   Click OK.

To change the default program for all files of a specific file type by using a file:

1 Right-click any file of the target file type and, from the shortcut menu, choose "Open with" or "Open with" > "Choose default program".

2 In the "Open with" dialog box, select the new default program (if it isn't listed, click Browse and then select it).

3 Select "Always use the selected program to open this kind of file".

4 Click OK.

To change the default program for all files of a specific file type by using the program:

1 Choose Start, type *default* in the Search box, and then click "Set your default programs" (under Control Panel) in the results list.

   or

   Choose Start > Control Panel > Programs > Default Programs > "Set your default programs".

2 In the Set Default Programs window, select the new default program.

3 To set the program as the default for *every* file type that it can open, click "Set this program as default". For example, you can set a media player to open all your video and audio files.

   or

   To set the program as the default for *some* file types, click "Choose defaults for this program", select the checkboxes for the desired file types, and then click Save.

To change the default program for all files of a specific file type by using the filename extension:

1 Choose Start, type *associated* in the Search box, and then click "Change the file type associated with a file extension" (under Control Panel) in the results list.

   or

   Choose Start > Control Panel > Programs > Default Programs > "Associate a file type or protocol with a program".

2   In the Set Associations window, select the filename extension in the list, and then click "Change program".

3   In the "Open with" window, select the new default program (if it isn't listed, click Browse and then select it).

4   Click OK and then Close.

To open a file that has an unregistered extension (or no extension):

1   Double-click the mystery file.

2   If you don't know which program can open the file, select "Use the Web service to find the correct program" to try to look up the extension on Microsoft's website. If Microsoft draws a blank, refer to one of the websites listed in "Unregistered Extensions" on page 256.

or

To open the file in a program that's installed on your computer, select "Select a program from a list of installed programs", click OK, select a compatible program in the "Open with" window, select "Always use the selected program to open this kind of file" (if you want), and then click OK.

Installing Windows Live Essentials

Windows used to come with programs for photo management, video editing, email, instant messaging, and more, but now you must download and install these (free) programs—called **Windows Live Essentials**—as a separate step after you set up Windows and connect to the internet.

Before you install, open Start > All Programs to check whether your computer's manufacturer or your administrator has already installed Windows Live programs on your computer.

To install Windows Live Essentials:

1   Click the Internet Explorer icon on the taskbar or choose Start > All Programs > Internet Explorer.

2   Go to *download.live.com*.

3   Choose your language, if necessary.

4   Click the Download link.

5   In the download dialog box, click Run.

6 If a security dialog box appears, confirm the action.

7 In the Windows Live Essentials dialog box, select the programs that you want to install, and then click Install. You can install any or all of the Windows Live programs.

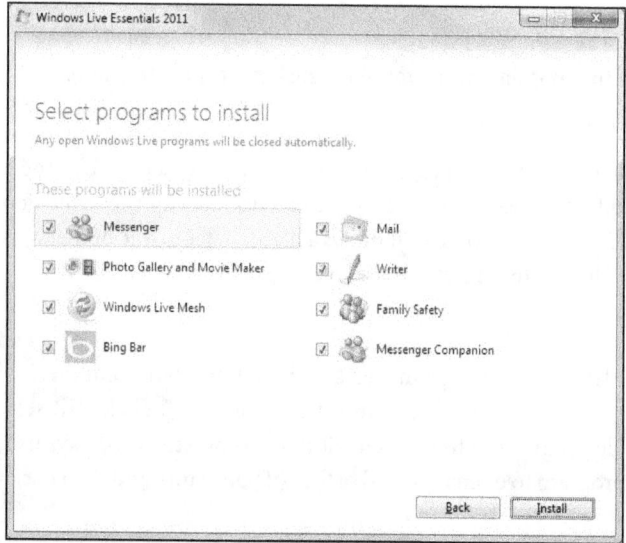

8 Follow the onscreen instructions. When the installation is complete, the programs appear in Start > All Programs > Windows Live.

Tip: To uninstall Windows Live Essentials programs, rerun the installer from the Windows Live webpage or choose Start > Control Panel > Programs > Programs and Features > Windows Live Essentials > Uninstall/Change.

Applications & Utilities

Windows teems with free programs that are part of the standard Windows installation. These programs include major applications like Internet Explorer and small utilities for specialized tasks. The All Programs menu (page 87) lists the programs installed on your computer, and most utilities are in All Programs > Accessories (see also "Launching Programs" on page 242). To get program-specific help for a program, use its Help menu (or press F1). This section describes programs that aren't covered elsewhere in this book.

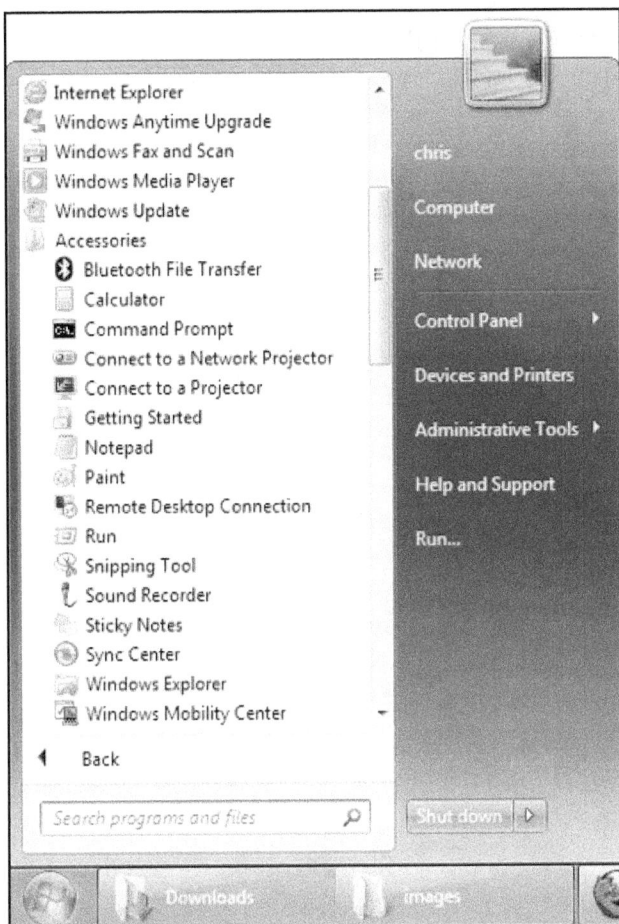

Calculator

In Standard mode, Calculator offers add, subtract, square root, invert, and other basic functions. Scientific mode (View > Scientific) adds trigonometric, power, logarithmic, and base functions. The View menu also offers Programmer and Statistics modes, as well as unit conversions, date arithmetic, and specialized worksheets. To operate Calculator, click its buttons with your mouse or press the corresponding keyboard keys. Help > View Help lists complete keyboard shortcuts.

Character Map

Character Map displays all characters and symbols for a particular font (page 158). Use it to copy and paste diacritical marks, currency symbols, copyright signs, and all the other characters that don't appear on your keyboard. To open Character Map, choose Start, type *character map* in the Search box, and then press Enter. To use Character Map, double-click characters to put them in the "Characters to copy" text box, and then click Copy. Now you can paste them into any document. Hover the pointer over a character for a pop-up tip showing the character's name and hexadecimal code. (If you're using Microsoft Word, the Insert > Symbol command is faster than using Character Map.)

Command Prompt

Command Prompt (formerly called DOS Prompt) lets you type commands rather than point and click. Rapid typists, Unix junkies, and people impatient with Windows safeguards love the command line, but new users find it cryptic and intimidating (experience teaches them to appreciate its efficiency).

```
Administrator: Command Prompt

C:\Users\chris>dir
 Volume in drive C is Windows
 Volume Serial Number is F45F-4BA2

 Directory of C:\Users\chris

01/12/2012  12:45 PM    <DIR>          .
01/12/2012  12:45 PM    <DIR>          ..
01/10/2012  09:49 PM    <DIR>          .kindle
01/10/2012  09:49 PM    <DIR>          Calibre Library
01/09/2012  08:48 PM    <DIR>          Desktop
12/31/2011  11:29 AM    <DIR>          Documents
01/12/2012  12:49 PM    <DIR>          Downloads
12/26/2011  11:34 AM    <DIR>          Links
11/09/2011  07:37 PM    <DIR>          Music
01/12/2012  09:47 AM    <DIR>          My Dropbox
01/12/2012  12:45 PM    <DIR>          Pictures
01/12/2012  12:45 PM    <DIR>          Searches
01/12/2012  12:45 PM    <DIR>          Videos
               0 File(s)              0 bytes
              13 Dir(s)  139,348,402,176 bytes free

C:\Users\chris>_
```

To open Command Prompt, choose Start > All Programs > Accessories > Command Prompt. To open Command Prompt quickly, choose Start, type *cmd* in the Search box, and then press Enter. To open a command window for a particular folder, in Windows Explorer, hold down Shift, right-click the folder in the file list or Navigation pane, and then choose "Open command window here" (alternatively, type *cmd* in the Address bar of the target folder window and then press Enter). To quit Command Prompt, click the Close button ![X], or type *exit* and then press Enter.

You can also run Command Prompt as an administrator (page 8) if you don't want to be pestered repeatedly by security prompts.

- The slow way: choose Start > All Programs > Accessories, right-click Command Prompt, and then click "Run as administrator".

- The fast way: choose Start, type *cmd* in the Search box, and then press Ctrl+Shift+Enter.

Either way, you'll get a Command Prompt window that contains Administrator in its title bar.

Command Prompt is handy for many routine tasks, but it shines when using a graphical interface is impractical. (Network administrators don't add 1000 user accounts by pointing and clicking, for example.) You can also use Command Prompt to (try to) run your old 16-bit DOS programs and games (page 244).

Scores of commands are available; search for *command prompt* and *command-line reference* in Help and Support (page 71). The basic commands are cd (or chdir), cls, copy, del, dir, exit, md (or mkdir), more, move, path, rename, rmdir, set, tree, type, and xcopy. Command Prompt remembers the commands you've typed. Press the up- and down-arrow keys to review your command history.

To customize Command Prompt, right-click its title bar and then choose Properties. A few recommendations: on the Options tab, select QuickEdit Mode, which lets you drag over text and then press Enter to copy it to the clipboard. Font tab: Switch the font to Consolas, 14-point. Layout tab: Set Window Size to 80 × 40 and Screen Buffer Size to 80 × 1000 (so you can scroll a large results history). Colors tab: Choose black text on a white background.

A quick way to run a single command—usually to open a program or file—without opening a command window is to use the Run dialog box. Press Windows logo key+R, type the command, and then press Enter. Or instead of typing a command, press F4 for a list of your recent commands, use the arrow keys to choose one, and then press Enter.

For advanced users, an alternative to Command Prompt is **PowerShell**, a command-line interface (shell) that provides a modern scripting language (in addition to all the Command Prompt commands) for automating Windows tasks. If you've been using VBScript or batch files to manage your computer or network, you may want to try PowerShell, which gives you access to the file system, the registry, and other parts of Windows. PowerShell is built on top of Microsoft's .NET Framework and accepts and returns .NET objects. To get started, go to *microsoft.com/powershell*. To open PowerShell, choose Start > All Programs > Accessories > Windows PowerShell.

Connect to a Network Projector

This utility (available in high-end Windows editions) lets you give a presentation over a network from any computer (desktop or laptop). The Connect to a Network Projector wizard connects to any available network projector over a wireless or a wired network. You can make a choice from a list of available projectors or enter a projector's network address. If the projector's icon has a small lock, you must enter a password to connect to it. The wizard also lets you choose whether all or part of your desktop appears on the projected image.

After the wizard completes, the Network Presentation dialog box opens. Use it to configure more settings and then minimize it to the taskbar when you give your presentation.

Connect to a Projector

This utility shows a pop-up list of options for using an external display, if one is connected. Keyboard shortcut: Windows logo key+P. You can show your desktop on only the computer's screen, only the external display, both at the same time (mirroring or duplicating), or on both with a continuous desktop (extending).

Games

The Start > Games window offers world-class productivity killers Solitaire, FreeCell, and Minesweeper, plus others. The Games folder is the central location for games on your computer. Newly installed games can place their icons in this window or create their own separate entries in the All Programs menu. In the Games folder, click Options (on the toolbar) to set up game updates and options.

Internet Explorer

Use Internet Explorer to browse the web. IE has features common to most browsers, as well as a few Microsoft touches:

- Tabbed browsing

- Bookmark management

- Pop-up blocking

- History and bookmark search

- Text search

- CSS support

- RSS subscriptions

- Thumbnail array of frequently visited sites

- HTML5, CSS3, VP8, and H.264 technologies

- InPrivate (protected) browsing mode

- Third-party add-ons

- Hardware acceleration for text, graphics, and video

- Websites can be pinned to the taskbar

- Jump lists and thumbnail preview controls for pinned sites

- Tear-off tabs

- Reopen accidentally closed tabs

- Isolation and automatic recovery of crashed tabs

- Tab recovery for timed-out webpages

- Combined search and Address bar

- Visual search suggestions shown as you type

- Accelerators for quick access to web services without leaving the page

- Compatibility mode to view websites designed for older browsers

- Protection from scripting, phishing, and social-engineering attacks

- Domain name highlighting in the Address bar

Notepad

Notepad, a bare-bones text editor, is one of the most useful tools in Windows. Use it to open, create, or edit text files, which contain only printable characters—no fonts, formatting, colors, graphics, or any of the clutter usually associated with a word processor. Notepad is the default program for .txt and .log files, but you can use it to view or edit .html files (saved webpages), .ini files (program initialization settings), or any other text-based file types.

Notepad offers a few handy features: press F5 to insert a time stamp (useful for keeping logs); choose Format > Font to set the screen and print font; or choose File > Page Setup to set headers and footers for printouts.

That said, Notepad is too austere and limiting for serious work. A web search for *windows text editor* turns up scores of free and paid alternatives.

Paint

Paint is a no-frills image editor with a few drawing, color, and manipulation tools. Use it to create your own works of art or to view or touch up photos or graphics that you imported, scanned, or downloaded. Paint supports bitmap (.bmp), JPEG, GIF, TIFF, and PNG file formats.

Snipping Tool

Snipping Tool lets you capture, annotate, save, and share screen images (also called screenshots).

For simple screenshots, use your keyboard instead of Snipping Tool: press the Print Screen (PrntScrn) key to capture the entire screen or press Alt+Print Screen to grab only the active window. The screen image is now stored on the clipboard (page 67), ready for pasting into a document, email message, or graphics program.

Sound Recorder

If your computer is has a sound card, speakers, and a microphone, you can use Sound Recorder to record sounds. To do so, choose Start > All Programs > Accessories > Sound Recorder. Click Start Recording, talk or make a sound, and then immediately click Stop Recording. Type a name for the sound file in the "File name" box, choose a folder for it, and then click Save. The sound is saved in a .wma file, a standard type of Windows sound file.

When you double-click a .wma file, the file opens in Windows Media Player and plays back immediately. (Press Esc to halt playback.) You can email sound files, posting them on websites, transfer them over a network, and so on.

Sticky Notes

Use Sticky Notes to post virtual notes on your screen, similar to the reminders that you stick to the edge of your physical display.

Windows Media Center

Windows Media Center is a home-entertainment hub that handles a variety of multimedia content. It's designed to be viewed on a big screen from a distance of up to 10 feet and controlled by a remote control. Media Center can do many of the same things as Windows Media Player, plus:

- Watch live or recorded TV

- Capture HDTV from cable or satellite TV broadcasts

- Play on-demand games

- Listen to FM radio stations

- Play digital media anywhere in your home (by using an extender or an XBox 360)

Windows Media Player

Use Windows Media Player to organize and play audio and video files.

- Import and play music and audio files

- Play music CDs

- Show audio visualizations

- Download song (track) and album information from the internet

- Rip (copy) music CDs to your hard drive

- Create playlists

- Burn (create) custom music CDs

- Play and listen to music across the internet

- Share music on a network

- Sync music or video with portable players (but not iPods)

- Buy music or movies from online stores

- Listen to internet radio

- Play video files

- Play DVD movies

- Play home videos

- Display personal photos

Windows Live Mail

Use Windows Live Mail to send, receive, and manage email. You must download Mail as part of the Windows Live Essentials software suite (page 259).

- Multiple-account support

- HTML or plain-text message composition

- Junk-mail (spam) filtering

- RSS feeds

- Multi-line message lists

- Search-indexed messages

- Message rules

- Emoticons (smileys)

- In-line spell checking

- Contacts management

- Calendar (appointment) management

- Conversations (grouping of related messages)

- Newsgroups

- Signatures

- Message-priority flags

- Support for WebDAV HTTP-based protocol

Windows Live Messenger

Use Windows Live Messenger for instant text messaging and file exchange. You must download Messenger as part of the Windows Live Essentials software suite (page 259).

- Text chat, audio chat (microphone required), and video chat (webcam required)

- Emoticons (smileys), winks, and formatted text

- Transfer files

- Send and receive email

- Send text messages to a cellphone

- Create and search contact (buddy) lists

- Save timestamped chat histories

- Trigger audible alerts

- Share games and activities

- Make free internet telephone calls

Windows Live Movie Maker and DVD Maker

Use Windows Live Movie Maker to edit video and create movies. You must download Movie Maker (but not DVD Maker) as part of the Windows Live Essentials software suite (page 259).

- Import video clips or photos from a phone or camera

- Record video or photos with a webcam

- Use a storyboard to create and edit durations, transitions, pan and zoom, and visual effects

- Add and edit audio

- Add text title pages, captions, and credits

- Apply professionally designed themes

- Save and export movies as .wmv files

- Post movies online

- Burn movies to a DVD (using DVD Maker)

DVD Maker is a wizard that helps you create DVDs with video, photos, audio, soundtracks, and navigation features, playable in a conventional DVD player. It comes installed on Windows, so you don't have to download it separately. Windows launches DVD Maker automatically when you tell Movie Maker (or Photo Gallery) to burn a DVD.

Windows Live Photo Gallery

Use Windows Live Photo Gallery to manage, organize, and touch up your photos. It can display video clips from your camera as well. You must download Photo Gallery as part of the Windows Live Essentials software suite (page 259).

- Import photos and video clips from a camera or memory card reader

- View photos and videos in a navigation tree

- Delete, duplicate, rate, and tag (page 183) photos

- Group and sort photos by custom criteria

- Find photos by filename, tag, or caption

- Zoom, crop, and rotate photos

- Fix red-eye and adjust exposure, sharpness, and color balance automatically

- Print photos or order high-quality prints online

- Email reduced-size photos

- Create slideshows or build a photo screen saver (page 125)

- Post photos to a Windows Live blog or in an online album (web gallery)

- Sync photo collections between two computers

Windows Live Writer

Use Windows Live Writer to compose blog entries and post them online. You must download Writer as part of the Windows Live Essentials software suite (page 259).

Blogs, or weblogs, are frequently updated online (public) journals. If you don't already have a blog, Writer lets you create one that's hosted by Microsoft for free. You can also use Writer if you already have a blog account, either on a Microsoft site (Windows Live Spaces or SharePoint) or elsewhere (Blogger, WordPress, TypePad, and so on). A blog post contains a title and body text, with optional pictures, links, tables, or videos. You can spell-check and preview the post before publishing it.

WordPad

WordPad is a simple, stripped-down word processor associated with .rtf (Rich Text Format) files. Like any word processor, WordPad lets you apply formatting (bold, italic, indents, justification, colors, fonts, and so on) to text. The Insert commands lets you embed images, sounds, movies, charts, spreadsheets, and other objects in your document. WordPad's native file format is RTF, but you can also open and save Word documents (.docx or .doc files) with some formatting restrictions. WordPad can also edit plain-text files.

6

Printing & Faxing

In Windows, the operating system—not individual programs—handles printing. When you print something in any program, you activate Windows' intermediary printing system, which accepts print jobs from programs and feeds them to the printer. This process, called **background printing**, lets you keep working in your program while your documents print.

Installing and configuring a printer is easy. After connecting and setting up your hardware, you can print individual documents with the default settings or override them for special printouts. If you have a fax modem, you can fax documents as easily as print them.

Installing a Printer

A **local printer** connects to your computer through a USB or FireWire port, an Ethernet jack, or a wireless signal (wi-fi or Bluetooth). Computers on a network can share a **network printer**.

When you connect a printer to your computer, Windows often recognizes it and searches its extensive collection of built-in drivers. A **printer driver** is software that lets programs send commands to a particular printer. If your printer isn't in Windows' library, you can use the driver on the CD that came with the printer or download the driver from the manufacturer's website. If you upgraded in-place from an earlier version of Windows, you inherited the existing printer driver and settings, and your printer will work fine.

Read the printer manual before installation. The manufacturer gives directions on how to attach or connect the printer, which Windows will install automatically. The printer also may include a CD to run before connection.

You can add a printer manually if Windows can't install it, or if you removed it and want to add it again.

To install a local printer:

1 Choose Start > Control Panel > Hardware and Sound > "Add a printer" (under Devices and Printers).

   or

   Choose Start > Devices and Printers > "Add a printer" (on the toolbar).

   The Add Printer wizard opens.

2 Click "Add a local printer". (When Windows says "Add printer", it means "Add printer driver".)

3 On the "Choose a printer port" page, make sure that "Use an existing port" and the recommended printer port are selected, and then click Next. In almost all cases, LPT1 (the default) is the correct port.

4 On the "Install the printer driver" page, select the manufacturer and model of your printer, and then click Next. Clicking an entry in the Manufacturer list displays Windows' standard drivers for that manufacturer in the Printers list. The Windows Update button connects you to Microsoft's website for drivers that were added since Windows' last update.

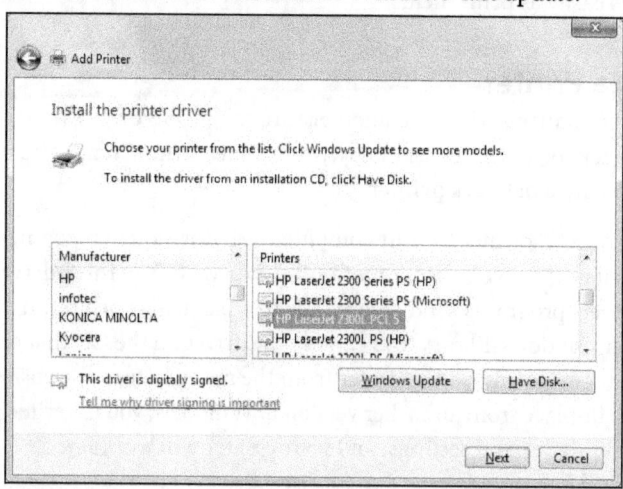

   or

If your printer model isn't listed and you have the printer installation disc, insert the disc, click Have Disk, and then browse to the driver software. (If Windows refuses your installation disc, download the current printer driver from the printer manufacturer's website.)

or

If your printer isn't listed and you don't have the printer installation disc, click Windows Update and then wait while Windows checks online for any available driver software packages. When a new list of manufacturers and printers is displayed, select the appropriate items in each list for your printer.

5   Complete the remaining steps in the wizard and then click Finish. Along the way, you can name the printer and print a test page. If you're sharing a printer, favor names that everyone on recognize. Indicate whether this printer is the one that you'll usually print with (the default printer).

After successful installation, the printer's icon appears in the Devices and Printers folder.

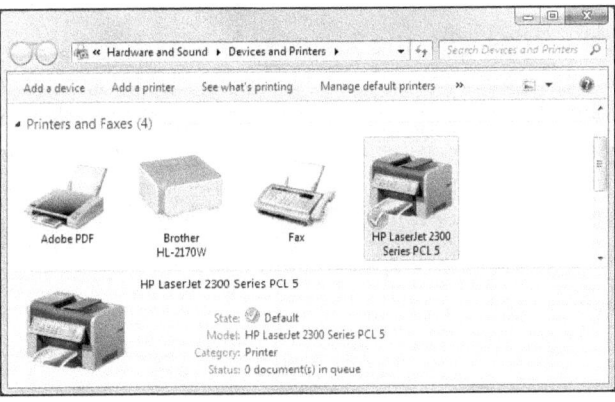

To install a network, wireless, or Bluetooth printer:

1   Make sure that your computer is connected to the network (or that your wireless or Bluetooth printer and adapter are turned on) and that you know the name of the printer that you want to add. If the name isn't posted on the printer itself, ask the printer owner or your network administrator.

2   Choose Start > Control Panel > Hardware and Sound > "Add a printer" (under Devices and Printers).

or

Choose Start > Devices and Printers > "Add a printer" (on the toolbar).

The Add Printer wizard opens.

3 Click "Add a network, wireless or Bluetooth printer".

4 In the list of available printers, select the one that you want to use and then click Next.

Available printers can include all printers on a network, such as Bluetooth and wireless printers, or printers that are plugged into another computer and shared on the network. If you're on a network domain (page 9), only printers for that domain are listed.

Your network administrator may have to grant you permission to use a printer before adding it to the computer.

5 Complete the remaining steps in the wizard and click Finish.

After successful installation, the printer's icon appears in the Devices and Printers folder or the Network folder.

Using Multiple Drivers for the Same Printer

You can install multiple drivers with different settings for the same physical printer and then switch among these "virtual" printers to suit what you're printing. If your printer has two paper trays, create Letterhead and Plain printers. To switch between printing high-resolution graphics and low-res text documents, create 1200 dpi (dots per inch) and 300 dpi printers. Separate Landscape and Portrait printers are popular too.

To create another printer:

1 Install the printer a second time, but under a different name that indicates its purpose.

2 After installation, right-click the printer in the Devices and Printers folder, choose "Printing preferences", and then select the settings appropriate to the printer's role.

3 In the Devices and Printers folder, right-click the printer that you use most of the time and then choose "Set as default printer".

From now on, you can choose the appropriate printer in any program's Print dialog box. See "Printing Documents" on page 280.

Finding Printer Drivers

For installation and troubleshooting information, go to the printer manufacturer's website or right-click the printer in the Devices and Printers folder and then choose Troubleshoot.

If the manufacturer provides no current driver for your printer, try the Windows XP driver. If no XP driver exists, try the Windows 2000 driver. No luck? Try the most recent driver for a different printer from the same manufacturer—but keep it in the family. Inkjet printers can't use laser-printer drivers, for example.

Still no luck? Try **printer emulation**. Check the manual to see whether your printer can mimic a different printer, and use that printer's driver. Many non–Hewlett-Packard laser printers can work with HP LaserJet drivers, for example.

The manufacturer's website will have printer-driver installation instructions, but you can also update a driver manually: right-click a printer in the Devices and Printers folder and then choose Properties > Hardware tab > Properties > Driver tab.

XPS Documents

In the Devices and Printers folder, you'll find a preinstalled icon for Microsoft XPS Document Writer. **XPS** (XML Paper Specification) is a Microsoft-developed file format supported in Windows and Microsoft Office 2007 and later. XPS competes with Adobe's Portable Document Format (PDF) as a standard file format for digital documents. Like PDF, XPS renders complex documents faithfully on any platform that supports it without font, layout, viewing, or printing problems.

Windows has a built-in XPS viewer that opens when you double-click an XPS (.xps) file.

To save a document in XPS format, choose File > Print, and then choose Microsoft XPS Document Writer in the list of printers. If XPS becomes popular, more programs will let you save to XPS directly in the Save dialog box.

To encourage use of the format, Microsoft sent the XPS specification to an independent standards board and released XPS under a royalty-free "we-won't-sue-you" license that lets companies freely create XPS readers, writers, and renderers.

Printing Tips

- To place a shortcut to the Devices and Printers folder in the Start menu, right-click the Start button and then choose Properties > Start Menu tab > Customize > select Devices and Printers > OK.

- Right-click a printer icon to show common printer tasks (many of which are duplicated in the Devices and Printers toolbar). Tiles view (page 174) displays printer status information next to the icon. Status information also appears in the Details pane at the bottom of the window (in any view).

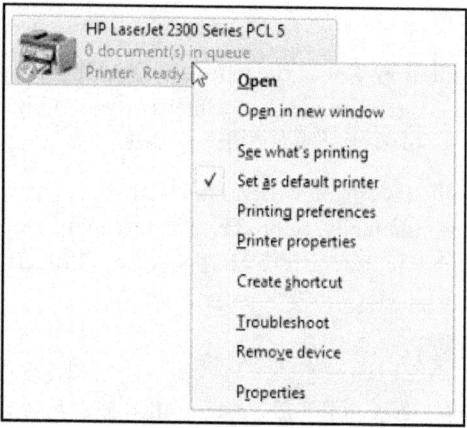

- To remove a printer that you no longer use, right-click it in Devices and Printers and then choose "Remove device". You can't remove a printer if you have items in the print queue (page 282). Either wait until the items print or cancel all the print jobs.

- A check mark appears on the default printer's icon. To change the default printer, right-click the desired printer in the Devices and Printers folder and then choose "Set as default printer".

- To rename a printer, right-click it in Devices and Printers and then choose "Printer properties" > General tab. The default name is usually the manufacturer name and printer model. For a shared printer, you may want to add a bit of text indicating the printer's location and capabilities (color, two-sided printing, and so on).

- A triangular warning symbol appears on the icon of a printer that has problems. Right-click the icon and then choose Troubleshoot.

- For information about installing fonts, see "Managing Fonts" on page 158.

Sharing a Network Printer

You can share a printer that's attached to your computer with anyone on the same network (page 307), as long as the printer is installed on your computer and attached directly with a USB or other type of printer cable. Whoever you choose to share the printer with will be able to use it to print, provided that they can locate your computer on the network.

Tip: A printer connected directly to a network—rather than attached to a computer— via a network port or wireless connection is available to anyone on the same network, without explicit sharing.

To share a printer that's attached to your computer:

1   Choose Start > Control Panel > Network and Internet > Network and Sharing Center > "Change advanced sharing settings" (on the left).

2   Click the arrow button ⊗ to expand the section for your current profile, click "Turn on file and printer sharing", and then click Save Changes.

Tip: To change a printer's sharing options quickly, right-click the printer in the Devices and Printers folder and then choose "Printer properties" > Sharing tab > select "Share this printer".

To use a shared printer:

1   Find out the name of the computer that has the shared printer attached to it.

You can ask someone who uses that computer, or go to the other computer yourself and look it up: choose Start > Control Panel > System and Security > System (or press Windows logo key+Break). The computer's name is listed under "Computer name, domain, and workgroup settings".

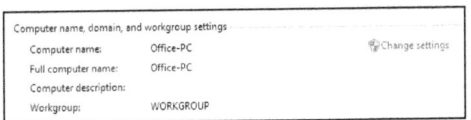

2   Choose Start, and in the Search box, type *computer_name*, where *computer_name* is the name of the other computer (for example, \\Office-PC), and then press Enter.

3   If Windows finds the computer on the network, a folder for the computer opens. Double-click Printers (or Devices and Printers) to show the shared printer.

(If you don't see the printer, ask a person who uses that computer whether the printer is connected, turned on, and shared with other users on the network.)

4   Double-click the printer icon.

Windows adds the printer to your computer automatically and installs the printer driver.

5   When the process completes, click Next and then follow the onscreen instructions.

When you finish, the shared printer appears in your Devices and Printers folder. You can select this printer in any program's Print dialog box to print a file. The printer's icon reflects its status: a shared local printer has a small Users badge.

Tip: When you share a printer connected to your computer, everybody's print jobs go through your copy of Windows, draining your system resources. Busy networks use a **print server** to arbitrate print requests. Stand-alone Ethernet or wireless print servers require no dedicated computer.

Setting Printer Properties

You can change a printer's default settings through its Properties dialog box. This dialog box varies by printer model because the manufacturer supplies the drivers whose features appear there. Options common to all printers include those in the General and Advanced tabs.

To change a printer's default settings:

1   Choose Start > Devices and Printers.

2   Right-click a printer and then choose "Printer properties".

3   On the following tabs, view or change the printer's default properties, and then click OK (or Apply).

General tab

Change the printer's name, location, or comments. To test the printer, click Print Test Page. If you're sharing a printer, add its location and a few helpful comments for other network users to see.

Sharing tab

See "Sharing a Network Printer" on page 277.

Ports tab

Review the printer's port assignment and configuration. You'll rarely want to change these settings.

Advanced tab

Change settings such as printer access hours and spooling (queuing) behavior. (Don't select "Print directly to the printer"; it turns off background printing.) Click Printing Defaults to view or change the default document properties for all users. Click Separator Page to add or change a separator page that prints between documents. With shared printers, separator pages make it easy to find your documents among others at the printer. You can create custom separator pages.

Device Settings tab

These options differ by printer model, depending on features, and affect such things as color, tray selection, fonts, printer memory, and duplex printing.

About tab

Review the printer's make and model, driver version numbers, and configuration date and status. You can compare the versions of the driver files with those of the latest drivers on the printer manufacturer's website.

Security tab

Review or set the printer's security settings. You can fine-tune these settings for groups or individual users.

Tip: For advanced printer management, choose Start > All Programs > Administrative Tools > Print Management.

Printing Documents

After your printer is up and running, printing a document is simple.

To print a document:

1 Open the document that you want to print.

2 Choose File > Print, press Ctrl+P, or click the Print button on the toolbar or ribbon.

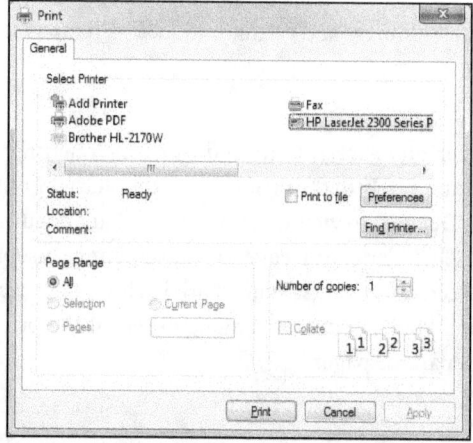

3 In the Print dialog box, select the printer and print options, and then click Print or OK (or press Enter). This dialog box varies by printer model and program, but the basic settings are:

Printer

Choose a local or network printer from the drop-down list or scrolling panel. If you've created several icons for different modes of the same printer, choose among them here.

Preferences/Properties

Click this button to open the Preferences or Properties dialog box. This dialog box, which varies by printer, lets you specify paper size (for multi-tray printers), orientation (landscape or portrait), print quality (dots per inch), and so on. These settings apply to the current printout, not to the printer in general.

Page Range
Specify which pages of the document to print. The Selection option isn't available if you didn't highlight any text before you opened the Print dialog box.

Copies
Specify the number of copies to print. You'll usually want to turn on collation for multiple copies.

Program-specific settings
Any program can add extra features to the Print dialog box.

Printer Troubleshooting

When you're having printer troubles, you want to determine whether the problem lies with the printer, Windows, or a particular program. Here are some things to check:

- Make sure that the printer is plugged in and turned on. Check for snug cable connections on the printer and computer ports.

- Make sure that the paper-tray slider is adjusted so that the paper fits snugly in the tray.

- Remove the paper tray, pop the printer's lid, and check for a jammed paper path.

- Streaks of white or gray in printouts mean you're low on toner (ink).

- Turn the printer off and on to clear its memory.

- Create a text file in Notepad (page 265), and then print it from the command prompt (page 262). Choose Start > All Programs > Accessories > Command Prompt; type *print filename.txt* and then press Enter. (Replace *filename.txt* with the name of your homemade text file.) If the file prints, you have a software problem; otherwise, you have a hardware problem.

- Consult the printer's manual, and then print a test page. (If the page prints, delete and reinstall the printer driver.)

- Try Windows' own troubleshooter: right-click the printer in the Start > Devices and Printers folder and then choose Troubleshoot.

- You may have a malfunctioning printer port (unlikely and somewhat complex).

Printer Tips

- During printing, a status icon appears in the taskbar's notification area. Point to this icon (without clicking) to see how many print jobs are pending. Right-click it to open the Devices and Printers folder. Double-click it for the print queue. (You may have to click the Show Hidden Icons button 🔼 to see this icon.)

- To bypass the Print dialog box and use the default printer and settings to print, click the Print button 🖨 on the toolbar or ribbon.

- If a document isn't open or visible onscreen, you can print it directly from a folder window or the desktop. Right-click the document's icon and then choose Print. Or drag a document's icon to a print spooler window (page 282).

- Most programs have additional print commands in the File menu, toolbar, or ribbon. Page Setup sets margins, orientation, and other layout options. Print Preview shows how a document will look when you print it.

- If you have a color printer, read about color management in "Configuring the Display" on page 128.

- If you're on a network domain (page 9), the Print dialog box has a Find Printer button that lets you search the network for a particular printer.

Controlling Printouts

When you print a document, it's intercepted by an intermediary program, called the **print spooler**, on its way to the printer. The print spooler holds your documents (on a drive or in memory) until your printer can accept them. The delay is short for text files but can be substantial for large graphics files. The spooler puts each document in a **print queue**, where it waits its turn to be printed. You can change the order of queued documents, pause or resume printing, or cancel specific print jobs. Spooling occurs in the background, so you can keep working in your program—or even quit the program—and documents still print.

To manage the print queue:

1   Choose Start > Devices and Printers, right-click a printer, and then choose "See what's printing". Or double-click the printer icon in the taskbar's notification area.

The print-spooler window opens, listing the documents waiting to print.

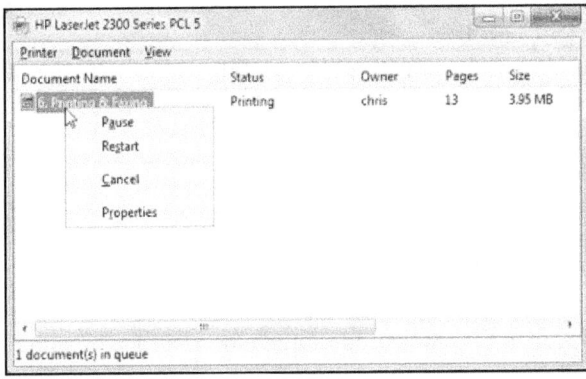

2 In the print-spooler window, do any of the following:

To cancel printing a document, right-click the target document name and then choose Cancel.

To cancel printing all documents, choose Printer menu > Cancel All Documents.

To pause (or resume) printing a document, right-click the target document name and then choose Pause (or Resume).

To pause (or resume) printing all documents, choose Printer menu > Pause Printing. (Choose it again to resume printing.)

To add another document to the queue, drag the document's icon from Windows Explorer or the desktop into the print-spooler window.

To rearrange the printing order, right-click a document name, choose Properties > General tab, and then drag the Priority slider. Higher-priority documents print before lower-priority ones. (You can't reorder the documents by dragging them.)

Tip: If you're on a network, by default you can pause, resume, restart, or cancel your own documents but not those of other users.

Unjamming Print Queues

If a long document stops partway through printing and canceling it in the print queue does nothing, try this:

1   Choose Start > All Programs > Accessories, right-click Command Prompt, and then select "Run as administrator".

2   Type *net stop spooler* and then press Enter. (This command halts the Print Spooler service.)

3   Leave the Command Prompt window open for a few seconds until the print queue clears.

4   Type *net start spooler* and then press Enter. Close the Command Prompt window after the service restarts.

Buying Ink

Printer manufacturers make money on replacement ink (toner) cartridges like razor manufacturers make money on blades, so be skeptical of your printer's "low ink" warnings, especially with inkjet printers; some multicolor cartridges shut down if even only one color runs out. For laser printers, remove the cartridge and shake it for some extra life.

A few money-saving tips:

- Buy low-priced third-party inkjet and laser cartridges locally or online. Search the web for *printer ink, printer cartridges,* or *ink refills* to find scores of discount ink stores.

- Don't throw out or return empty laser cartridges; look for a local computer-supplies store that will refill them (or ask an online store).

- When you buy a printer, be wary of printer-makers that use lockout codes to prevent cartridge refills.

Scanning and Faxing

Windows Fax and Scan lets you send and receive faxes, fax or email scanned documents, and forward faxes as email attachments from your computer without an actual fax machine. You'll need a phone line and almost any dial-up modem. Even an old 33.6 Kbps modem can send a multipage fax in a minute or two. Computer-based faxing conserves paper, saves money on ink and paper, and generates cleaner, more-legible faxes than ones sent via fax machine. You fax documents by using the File > Print command. (If you want to fax printed material, you must first scan it.) You can read incoming faxes onscreen, print them, or manage them as you would any other documents: move, copy, rename, email, archive, or delete them.

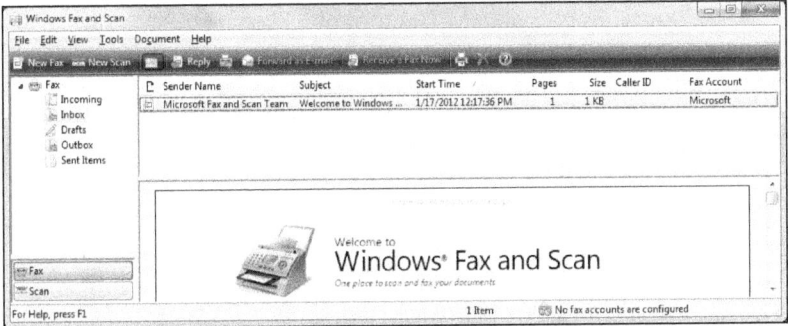

Install the modem (an internal, USB, or Bluetooth dial-up modem, not a DSL or cable broadband modem) before you start the setup process. Make sure that the modem is connected to a phone line and that the phone line is connected to a working jack. Some laptops have built-in modems; for desktops, you may have to install one. When you install a modem, Windows usually finds it and installs its drivers automatically. To install a modem manually, choose Start > Control Panel, switch to icon view, and then choose Phone and Modem > Modems tab > Add. You can also use the Modems tab to remove modems or view or change their properties.

Tip: If you don't want to buy a modem or tie up your phone line, search the web for *web-based fax service.*

Setting Up a Scanner

To fax documents that aren't computer files, you'll need a scanner. You can connect a local scanner directly to your computer, or you can connect to a network scanner shared over a network. In either case, you may need to install a driver or programs for using the scanner on your computer.

To install a local scanner:

1 Follow the instructions that came with the scanner.

If the scanner has a USB connector (most scanners do), you usually can plug it into your computer, and Windows will install its driver automatically. Some scanners make you install software before plugging in the USB connector; others make you turn on the scanner before or during installation.

To install a network scanner:

1 Make sure that your computer is connected to the network and that you know the name of the scanner that you want to add. If the name isn't posted on the scanner itself, ask the scanner owner or your network administrator.

2 In Windows Explorer, click the Network folder in the Navigation pane.

3 Locate the scanner, right-click it, and then choose Install.

4 Follow the onscreen instructions.

Scanning a Document

You can scan a document by using the software that came with your scanner or by using Fax and Scan.

To scan by using Fax and Scan:

1 Make sure that your scanner is connected to your computer and turned on.

2 Place a document on the scanner or the scanner's document feeder.

3 Choose Start > All Programs > Windows Fax and Scan.

4 Click Scan (at the bottom of the left pane) > New Scan (on the toolbar) > Profile list > Documents.

5 Change the default settings for scanning a document if desired.

6 Click Preview to see how a document will appear when scanned.

7 Change your scan settings if desired. You can drag the cropping handles to resize the image.

8 Click Scan to scan the document. When the scan completes, Fax and Scan displays the document to view and manage.

Image Formats

Scanning software usually lets you choose an image format for your scan. If you save an image in the wrong format, you can open it in Paint and then save it in another format by choosing Paint tab > Save As. To open Paint, choose Start > All Programs > Accessories > Paint. Common formats include:

Bitmap

Windows bitmap (.bmp) images tend to be large because this format can't be compressed. BMP is almost always the wrong choice for scanned documents and photos.

JPEG

Joint Photographic Experts Group (.jpg/.jpeg) files are highly compressed and an excellent choice for scanning photos, particularly if you're going to post them on the web. But the JPEG process sacrifices image detail permanently during compression. In most cases, the loss is invisible for onscreen viewing.

PNG

Portable Network Graphics (.png) files, which all modern browsers support, is patent free and license free, and it retains all detail during compression (unlike JPEG).

TIFF

Tagged Image File Format (.tif) files are compatible with most image-editing programs, even ancient ones. TIFF is a good choice for scanning text documents and grayscale images. TIFF's compression, like PNG's, preserves detail but results in larger files than JPEG. You can scan multiple pages into a single TIFF file; Windows Fax and Scan uses TIFF to send and receive faxes.

Organizing Scanned Documents

Scanned documents are stored in your My Documents folder in Scanned Documents, where you can move or copy them like any other files.

To organize your scanned documents in Fax and Scan, you can create new folders in Scan view. In the left pane, right-click a folder name and then choose New Folder. To move a scanned document to a folder, right-click the document, choose Move to Folder, and then select the target folder.

If you use Windows Explorer to create, delete, move, or rename folders and documents in the Scanned Documents folder, the changes won't appear in Fax and Scan until you close and reopen the program, or collapse and expand the folder tree in the left pane in Scan view.

Scanning Tips

- To remove a local scanner, unplug it from your computer at any time, or choose Start > Devices and Printers, right-click the scanner, and then choose "Remove device".

- If Windows doesn't recognize your scanner, use the Scanner and Camera Installation wizard to install its drivers. Make sure that your scanner is connected and turned on, and then choose Start > Control Panel, type *scanner* in the Search box, and then click "View scanners and cameras" in the results list. Click Refresh if your scanner isn't in the list. If it still isn't listed, click Add Device and then follow the onscreen instructions.

- To configure scanner routing and settings, use the commands in the Tools menu of Fax and Scan.

- If you're scanning a page with more than one picture, you can save each picture as a separate file: select "Preview or scan images as separate files".

- To forward scanned documents automatically to an email address or a network folder, choose Tools menu > Scan Routing.

- Faxes are sent in black and white at a default resolution of 150 × 150 dpi.

Setting Up Faxing

Before you can send or receive faxes, you must connect to a fax modem (or a fax server on your network) and configure Fax and Scan.

To connect to a fax device for the first time:

1 Choose Start > All Programs > Windows Fax and Scan.

2 Click Fax (at the bottom of the left pane).

3 Click New Fax (on the toolbar).

4 Follow the onscreen instructions.

To set up your computer to only *send* faxes, click "I'll choose later; I want to create a fax now".

To configure Fax and Scan:

1 Choose Start > All Programs > Windows Fax and Scan.

2 Click Fax (at the bottom of the left pane).

3 Choose Tools menu > Fax Settings.

4 On the General tab, select your fax modem; set it to send, receive, or both; and then specify whether you'll answer incoming faxes manually or automatically.

5 Click More Options.

6 Set TSID (Transmitting Subscriber Identification) and CSID (Called Subscriber Identification) to your business name and fax number, and then choose whether you want to print or save backup copies of incoming faxes in addition to the ones that Fax and Scan saves automatically in its Inbox.

The TSID is mandatory in some cases. This identification information usually appears in the header area of a received fax and serves to identify the sending fax machine. Some fax-routing software depends on TSIDs to determine where to direct incoming faxes. The CSID is displayed on the sending fax machine.

7 Click OK to return to the Fax Settings dialog box.

8 On the Tracking tab, specify when and how you want to be notified about the progress of a fax. Click Sound Options if you want audio indicators as well as visual ones.

9 On the Advanced tab, set the fax-transmission behavior, including where to store incoming and outgoing faxes, whether to include a cover sheet with outgoing faxes, automatic redialing attempts (for when a fax doesn't go through the first time), and times of day for discount calling.

10 On the Security tab, review or set the security settings for faxing and fax setup.

11 Click OK (or Apply).

12 (Optional) To set additional options, choose Tools menu > Options.

Fax Cover Pages

Cover pages help when you fax to big institutions where the fax might be misrouted. Fax and Scan has a few built-in cover pages that work fine, but you can design your own: choose Tools menu > Cover Pages. To set the information that cover pages display, choose Tools menu > Sender Information. The fields all are optional, but include enough for the recipient to contact you if a fax doesn't go through completely.

When you send a fax, the Cover Page drop-down list shows the built-in cover pages and any custom pages that you've created.

Sending a Fax

You can fax a document from Fax and Scan or another program.

To send a fax from Fax and Scan:

1   Choose Start > All Programs > Windows Fax and Scan.

2   Click Fax (at the bottom of the left pane).

3   Click New Fax (on the toolbar).

4   Create a new fax by using the options in the New Fax window, and then click Send. The New Fax window offers a complete set of editing, formatting, and other options. Use the toolbar options to attach a file or insert text and pictures from other files to send with your fax.

     The Fax Status Monitor automatically displays the progress of the fax. Click View Details to see the detailed status of each outgoing fax; click Hide Details if you prefer Windows to do its faxing less conspicuously. A pop-up message appears in the taskbar's notification area when a fax is sent successfully (or fails).

To send a fax from another program:

1   Open the file that you want to send as a fax.

2   Choose File > Print, press Ctrl+P, or click the Print button on the toolbar or ribbon.

3   In the Print dialog box, click the Fax icon or choose Fax from the printer list, and then click Print or OK, or press Enter. Fax and Scan opens a new fax with your file attached.

4   Specify the recipient fax numbers, cover page, and other options in the New Fax window, and then click Send.

Receiving a Fax

To receive a fax, you must have chosen to receive them in the Fax Setup wizard or selected "Allow the device to receive fax calls" in the Fax Settings dialog box (page 288). Faxes received in Automatic answer mode (best for dedicated fax lines) appear in the Fax and Scan Inbox. Use Manual answer mode if your computer and telephone share a line that you use mostly for talking.

To receive a fax manually:

1   When the phone rings, click the pop-up message in the taskbar's notification area.

    Fax Monitor opens and downloads the fax. If you're expecting a person to call, just pick up the phone, and the pop-up message disappears. If you miss this notification, quickly open Fax and Scan before the phone stops ringing, and in Fax view, click Receive a Fax Now (on the toolbar)

2   To view the received fax, look in Fax and Scan's Inbox (described next).

To manage and view faxes:

1   Choose Start > All Programs > Windows Fax and Scan.

2   Click Fax (at the bottom of the left pane).

3   In the left pane, expand the Fax folder if necessary. Fax contains the following subfolders:

    Incoming contains faxes that you're receiving now.

    Inbox contains faxes that you've received.

    Drafts contains faxes that you're still working on and aren't ready to send.

    Outbox contains faxes that Fax will send later or that failed to go through.

    Sent Items contains faxes that you've sent successfully.

4   Click the folder that you want.

5   In the right pane, click a fax and then choose a toolbar command, or right-click it and then choose a shortcut-menu command.

Faxing Tips

- To send a fax to more than one person, type the recipients' fax numbers in the To box, separated by semicolons (;). To choose recipients from your Contacts folder, click To and then double-click each contact in the list. Make sure that you've saved your recipients' fax numbers in the contact information.

- If the Dialing Rule drop-down list is set to (None), type the recipient's fax number as it should be dialed. (Parentheses, commas, and hyphens are ignored.) To use a Dialing Rule, choose one from the list or choose New Rule to create one. You can also create dialing rules by choosing Start > Control Panel > Hardware and Sound > Phone and Modem Options > Dialing Rules tab.

- To attach a document or picture to a fax, drag the file to the New Fax window. Attachments are converted to TIFF images (.tif files, page 287) so that they can be received by any fax device. (The original file isn't changed.)

- If your recipient uses a stand-alone fax machine (one not connected to a computer), each page of your fax—including any attachments—will be printed in order when the fax is received. If the recipient uses Windows Fax and Scan or a similar fax program, your fax will be received as a TIFF (.tif) file that can be viewed onscreen and treated like any other file.

- To fax or email a scanned file in Fax and Scan, click Scan (at the bottom of the left pane), and then click the file in the list of scanned files. On the toolbar, click Forward as Fax or Forward as E-mail. To scan a document and attach it to a fax, choose File > New > Fax from Scanner.

- The Fax printer appears by default in the Start > Devices and Printers folder. This icon appears in every program's Print dialog box because the Devices and Printers folder contains a generic fax driver. You can double-click the Fax icon to open Fax and Scan, but there's not much more to do with it than view its properties.

- The Preview pane (below the list of faxes in the right pane) shows the first page of the selected fax. To open the fax, double-click it. Use the scroll and zoom controls to view it.

7 Hardware & Drivers

Hardware is your computer and whatever connects to it (in the broadest sense, if you can touch it, it's hardware—everything else is software). A **device**, also called a **peripheral**, is any part of a computer other than the processor (CPU), motherboard, memory (RAM and ROM), and case. Your display, mouse, keyboard, trackpad, drives, scanner, and printer are devices, as are digital cameras, smartphones, MP3 players, iPods, ebook readers, backup drives, video recorders, speakers, microphones, USB flash drives, and synchronization cradles.

Windows treats any gadget connected to your computer as a device. The software that controls it is called its **device driver** or simply **driver**. A driver mediates communications between a device and Windows.

Connecting Devices to Your Computer

When you install a new device for your computer, you'll either connect it to a port on the computer's outside panels or insert it into a slot inside the computer case (laptop computers have only ports, not slots). The port or slot provides the channel that the computer and device use to exchange data.

New-computer manuals usually contain diagrams labeling the computer's internal slots and back-panel connectors. Look in the manual for the **motherboard**, also called the **mainboard** or **desktop board**.

Hardware needed for some common tasks:

Rip or burn a disc
    For ripping: a CD or DVD drive. For burning: a CD or DVD recorder.

Scan documents

A scanner or an all-in-one printer/scanner/fax. See "Scanning and Faxing" on page 285.

Send or receive faxes

A dial-up modem. See "Scanning and Faxing" on page 285.

Transfer photos to your computer

A digital camera and USB cable or a memory-card reader.

Transfer video to your computer

A digital video camera and a USB or IEEE 1394 (FireWire) cable, or a memory-card reader.

Use the internet

For a dial-up connection: a dial-up modem (preferably 56K). For a broadband connection: a DSL or cable modem. Add a router for security. See "Online Connections" on page 325.

Set up a network

For a wired connection: a network adapter, Ethernet cables, and a switch or hub. For a wireless connection: an 802.11 wireless adapter and an access point. See "Networks & Sharing" on page 307.

Videoconference

A webcam. (Some digital cameras have webcam mode.)

Listen to audio

A sound card or integrated audio, and speakers or headphones. See "Configuring Sound and Audio Devices" on page 134.

Listen to radio

A radio tuner card.

Watch TV

A TV tuner card.

Input with handwriting

A stylus and graphics tablet or a multitouch surface.

External Devices

External devices plug into **ports** on the computer's panels. If your computer doesn't have a particular port for your gadget, you must install an expansion card or connect an adapter to get it. If you set up your own computer, then you're familiar with ports because the display, keyboard, mouse, and printer all have cables or adapters that connect to ports (unless you use all wireless devices). Different shapes for different port types make it hard to plug a cable into the wrong port, but examine the plug and port, and don't force a connection.

Common ports and connections include:

USB (Universal Serial Bus)
A small, thin, rectangular port that accepts almost all Plug and Play devices: mice, USB flash drives, external drives, scanners, digital cameras, smartphones, MP3 players, iPods, keyboards, printers, Bluetooth adapters, and so on. Most computers have at least two USB ports, but you can buy an internal or external USB **hub** if you need extra ports. USB ports are **hot-pluggable**, allowing you to connect and disconnect devices without shutting down your computer; Windows automatically loads or unloads the drivers as needed. USB ports can provide power as well as data to the devices they connect. The USB version indicates the data-transfer speed: USB 3.0 connections are an order of magnitude faster than USB 2.0 connections. Old, slow USB 1.1 connections are rare now.

Serial ATA (SATA or eSATA)
A rectangular high-speed port used mainly for connecting external hard drives and CD/DVD drives. SATA is Plug and Play-compliant and hot-pluggable and can provide power to devices. An internal or external SATA hub (port multiplier) will add SATA ports.

IEEE 1394 (FireWire)
A small, rectangular, very fast port with a slightly tapered plug. These ports are ideal for video, external drives, multiplayer gaming, and network devices. IEEE 1394 is Plug and Play-compliant and hot-pluggable and can provide power to devices. You can buy an internal or external hub to add IEEE 1394 ports to your computer. Some hubs have both USB and IEEE 1394 ports.

Video
External displays, projectors, and TVs connect to a **VGA port** (an older rectangular port with 15 holes along 3 rows), a **DVI port**, or an **HDMI port**.

Ethernet (RJ-45)
A jack (which looks like a wide telephone jack) for Ethernet and network connections. If your computer doesn't have an RJ-45 jack, buy a network interface card (NIC) to add one.

Modem (RJ-11)

An ordinary telephone jack that lets you run a telephone line from the wall to your computer for faxing or dial-up internet connections. Some laptops have built-in RJ-11 jacks. If you need one, buy a 56K modem card or USB modem.

Sound

A row of small circular holes for connecting external speakers, headphones, microphones, and audio sources. Most computers also have built-in sound ports, but adding a good sound card gives you high-quality surround sound.

Obsolete Ports

The port graveyard contains specialized ports that have been replaced by USB ports.

- *Parallel (LPT)* ports for connecting old printers and tape drives

- *Serial (COM)* ports for connecting old serial devices (mice, external modems, serial printers, and so on)

- *PS/2* ports for connecting old mice and keyboards

- *Game* ports for connecting game controllers, joysticks, and steering wheels

- *S-Video* ports for analog video connections to projectors, TVs, and VCRs

- *Infrared (IrDA)* ports for line-of-sight data transfer through small lenses

Removing Hardware Safely

A small icon ![icon] appears in the taskbar's notification area when a USB, SATA, IEEE 1394, or other hot-pluggable removable-storage device is plugged into your computer. If no data are being transferred between the device and the computer, you can unplug the device at will. Usually, a light on the device or an onscreen warning signals whether data transfer is active. For example, many USB flash drives have an activity light that blinks during read–write operations.

If you want to be extra safe when you remove a device (make sure that an external drive's disks have stopped spinning, for example), you can stop the device before unplugging it. Right-click the notification area icon and then eject the device.

Internal Devices

Internal devices are connected inside your computer's case. Storage devices such as CD, DVD, floppy, tape, backup, and hard drives are mounted on stacked shelves, called **bays**, at the front of the case. Printed circuit boards with edge connectors—such as sound cards, video adapters, graphics accelerators, internal modems, Ethernet (network) adapters, and USB hubs—are called **expansion boards** or **cards**. These cards plug into expansion slots (or simply slots) on the main circuit board (**motherboard**).

Each type of slot has a different shape and color, so you're unlikely to insert a card into the wrong slot. Inserting a card into a slot takes a little courage and practice. You must seat the card firmly and accurately by using neither too much force nor too little.

Common slots include:

PCI

A white-cased socket about 3.25 inches (8.25 cm) long, with a white crossbar about three-quarters of the way down the slot. PCI (Peripheral Component Interconnect) slots, developed by Intel but supported by all manufacturers, are the most common type.

PCIe

PCI Express is based on PCI but is much faster (a PCIe card won't fit in a PCI slot). Windows supports PCIe software and hardware. PCIe has mostly replaced PCI and AGP on new equipment. PCIe slots vary in length and are labeled x1, x2, x4, x8, x16, or x32 (higher numbers indicating faster transfer rates).

Memory card

A small slot that takes a memory card from a digital camera, tablet, ebook reader, or other portable gadget.

PCMCIA (PC Card)

A slot on the side or back of a laptop computer that accepts a metal PC Card about the size of a credit card. A PC Card adds a particular feature to a laptop: a modem, Ethernet port, wireless antenna, or extra memory, for example. PC Cards are Plug and Play-compliant and hot-pluggable and can provide power to devices.

ExpressCard

The faster, smaller, lighter successor to PC Card and found on post-2005 laptops. ExpressCard slots are either 34 mm wide (laptops) or 54 mm wide (larger systems).

Obsolete slots

AGP and ISA slots have been phased out in favor of PCIe.

To install an internal expansion card:

1   Shut down Windows, turn off the computer, and then unplug the power cord.

2   Remove the computer's cover.

3   Remove the cover plate of an empty slot (to let the card's ports protrude from the computer case).

Before touching the motherboard or handling a card outside its protective packaging, touch a grounded metal surface (such as the computer case or a pipe) to discharge static electricity.

4   Seat the card in the slot firmly, according to the manufacturer's instructions.

5   Replace the screw that held on the cover plate, tightening it through the hole in the bracket on the back of the card.

6   Replace the cover, reconnect the power cord, and then turn on the computer. Windows will detect the new card after it starts.

Plugging a card into an expansion slot connects it to the **bus**—the shared collection of hardware conductors that allows computer components to exchange data.

Installing a New Device

Almost all devices made since 1995 are **Plug and Play** (PnP) devices, which means that you can install (plug in) and use (play with) them immediately—no configuration needed. To work properly, Plug and Play requires:

• A Plug and Play-compliant operating system, which Windows is.

• A device that identifies itself to Windows and that lets Windows configure it and install its drivers, which almost all devices do.

• A Plug and Play-compatible system startup chip on the motherboard (called the **BIOS**). Any computer that can run Windows has PnP BIOS.

The port or slot that a device plugs indicates its compatibility:

- All USB, SATA, IEEE 1394 (FireWire), Bluetooth, PCIe, ExpressCard, and PCMCIA (PC Card) devices are Plug and Play.

- All but the oldest PCI and parallel devices are Plug and Play.

- No ISA or serial devices are Plug and Play. Most such devices are quite old. If their manufacturers still exist, check their websites for a somewhat recent driver. If there's no such driver, you may be out of luck.

Windows stores thousands of drivers on your hard drive and gets more regularly via Windows Update (page 341), so Windows usually detects your device when you connect it and installs the proper driver automatically. If Windows doesn't have the right driver, you can install it from either the CD that came with the device or a driver file that you downloaded from the manufacturer's website. The following installation instructions are generic; you should always favor the instructions that came with your device.

To install a new device:

1 Run the device's setup program (if any). Some new devices come with a Setup CD that includes driver files. Run this program *before* you connect the device so that Windows can copy the drivers to your hard drive and have them handy for later in the installation.

2 Check the device's installation instructions to determine whether it should be turned on before, during, or after connection and installation.

3 Connect the device to your computer (see "Connecting Devices to Your Computer" on page 293).

   If Windows can install the device driver automatically, you'll be notified that the device is ready to use. Look for pop-up progress messages in the taskbar's notification area, ending with a "success" message. You're done.

   or

   If Windows can't find the right driver, then you can use the Devices and Printers wizard to solve the problem. Windows lets you know when it can't install your device. Click the pop-up "failure" message in the notification area to see the reason—typically, "No driver found". To find a driver or fix the problem, choose Start > Devices and Printers, right-click the problem device, choose Troubleshoot, and then follow the onscreen instructions.

Bluetooth Devices

Bluetooth (*bluetooth.com*) is a wireless technology that provides short-range (about 30 feet/9 meters) radio links among desktops, laptops, smartphones, iPods, printers, cameras, mice, keyboards, and other Bluetooth-equipped devices. It eliminates cable clutter while simplifying communications, sharing, and data synchronization between computers and devices. Bluetooth doesn't need a line-of-sight connection, so you can, say, listen to MP3 music from the laptop in your briefcase on a hands-free headset.

To set up a Bluetooth device, choose Start > Devices and Printers, click "Add a device" (on the toolbar), and then follow the onscreen instructions.

A **passkey** (or **passcode**) is a number that associates your computer with a Bluetooth device. For security, Bluetooth devices (except mice and a few other exceptions) make you use a passkey to ensure that your computer is connecting to your device and not someone else's nearby.

Passkey exchange (or **pairing**) gets Windows to positively identify the device that you want to connect to. With some devices, you do this by running the Add a Device wizard and then typing your passkey when prompted. Other devices use a different method; check the device's instructions.

If a passkey is listed in the device's documentation, use that one. If not, the Add a Device wizard can generate a passkey for you or let you create your own (up to 16 characters—longer is more secure).

Unsigned Drivers

A **signed driver** is one that has a digital signature to certify that it works properly and hasn't been tampered with since its creation. Driver signing combats the sloppily written, system-destabilizing, third-party drivers that plagued early Windows versions. The most stable systems run only signed drivers. When you try to install an **unsigned driver**, Windows displays one of the following messages:

Windows can't verify the publisher of this driver software
> This driver either lacks a digital signature or has an unverified one. Install this driver only if you trust the source.

This driver software has been altered
> This driver might contain a virus or malicious software. Don't install it unless it came straight from the manufacturer's CD or website.

Windows cannot install this driver software

Windows maintains its own list of drivers that it refuses to install because they are known to cause stability problems. Go to the manufacturer's website, and look for an updated driver.

Driver Information (.inf) Files

When Windows searches for a driver, it's actually looking for an information (.inf) file, which lists the driver files to use and registry entries (page 357) to make. Windows veterans may recognize that .inf files and initialization (.ini) files are quite similar. But .inf settings are subtler than .ini settings. Never edit an .inf file to try to solve your driver problems.

Hardware-setup packages can include an .inf file; a .sys file (the actual driver); and subordinate library (.dll), help (.hlp), Control Panel (.cpl), and webpage (.html) files. Some device drivers are only .inf files. A display, for example, may be set up by a single .inf file listing the valid resolutions, refresh rates, and other display settings.

Installation Tips

- To add a wireless, Bluetooth, or network device, choose Start > Devices and Printers, click "Add a device" (on the toolbar), and then follow the onscreen instructions.

- Windows stores drivers in \Windows\System32\DriverStore\FileRepository.

- A downloaded driver usually comes as a self-extracting executable (.exe) file or a compressed zip (.zip) file that you must decompress before installation. Look for setup instructions on the webpage or, after unzipping, in a read-me file.

- You can inspect, manage, and troubleshoot your devices by using the Devices and Printers folder (choose Start > Devices and Printers). Right-click or double-click a device to see device-dependent commands and windows. For low-level device management, use Device Manager (page 302).

- If, when you plug in a device, AutoPlay opens a program that you don't want to use, choose Start > Control Panel > Hardware and Sound > AutoPlay. If you never want to see the AutoPlay dialog box, choose "Take no action" next to the device. To choose an action each time you plug in a device, choose "Ask me every time". To have a program open automatically each time, choose the program.

Managing Device Drivers

Device Manager is a powerful tool that lets you inspect, manage, and trouble-shoot drivers for the hardware installed on your computer. It lists every device in or attached to your system in an Explorer-like tree.

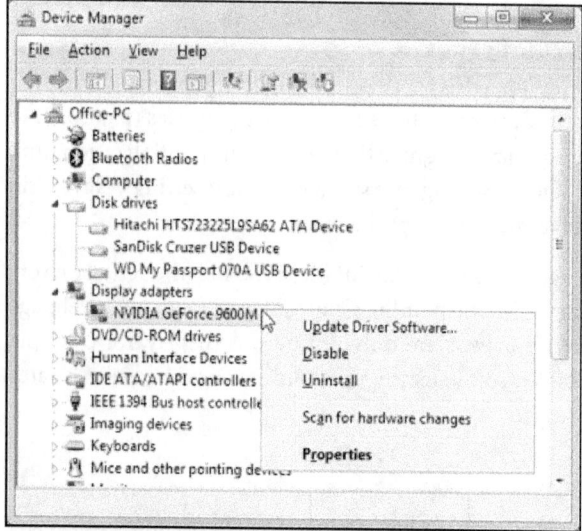

To open Device Manager:

- Choose Start > Control Panel > System and Security > System > Device Manager (on the left).

  or

  Press Windows logo key+Break and then click Device Manager (on the left).

  or

  Choose Start, type *device manager* in the Search box, and then press Enter.

  or

  Press Windows logo key+R, type *devmgmt.msc*, and then press Enter.

In Device Manager, click an arrow (▷ or ◢) to expand or collapse a category branch. Each branch lists all installed devices that fit into that category. Right-click a particular device for a shortcut menu, or double-click it to show its Properties dialog box. To expand all branches of the Device Manager tree, select the top-level (root) entry and then press * (on the numeric keypad). To show legacy (non-Plug and Play) devices, choose View menu > "Show hidden devices".

Like any other file, a device driver has properties that determine its behavior.

To show a device's properties:

- In Device Manager, right-click the device and then choose Properties.

  or

  Double-click the device's name.

The tabs of the Properties dialog box vary by device. The standard ones are:

General tab
Shows the name, type, physical location, and working status of the device.

Driver tab
Shows the currently installed driver's provider (which, unhelpfully, is its distributor, not its manufacturer), its date and version, and whether it's signed (page 300). The buttons let you manage the driver.

Advanced tab and *Details tab* (if they appear)
Contain device-specific properties.

Resources tab
Lists the system hardware resources (such as interrupts and memory range) that the device uses.

Tip: Some devices install their own Control Panel extensions, which let you view or change additional properties.

You can use Device Manager to install a driver that's newer than the current one. But newer doesn't always mean better or more stable. If a driver isn't broken, don't update it unless updating improves things.

To update a device driver:

1   In Device Manager, right-click the device whose driver you want to update and then choose Update Driver Software.

2   Follow the onscreen instructions. You can locate the new driver manually or let the Update Driver Software wizard look for it on your computer and on the internet.

Tip: Some devices have proprietary update programs that don't support the Update Driver Software wizard.

If a fresh driver causes more problems than it solves (not uncommon for unsigned drivers and prerelease drivers), the driver rollback feature lets you uninstall and replace it with the previous one. Rollback is available only if the driver has been updated since Windows was installed.

To roll back a device driver:

•   In Device Manager, right-click the device whose driver you want to roll back and then choose Properties > Driver tab > Roll Back Driver.

You can remove a driver permanently and erase all the configuration settings for its device. Generally, you uninstall a driver to reclaim system resources after you've removed hardware from your computer. But you can remove a troublesome driver completely, to scrap it or to reinstall it from scratch.

To uninstall a device driver:

•   In Device Manager, right-click the device whose driver you want to un-install and then choose Uninstall.

You can uninstall a Plug and Play device's driver only if the device is plugged in; otherwise, the driver isn't in memory. To reinstall the driver without unplugging, in Device Manager, choose Action menu > "Scan for hardware changes".

If you want to turn off a device without the hassle of removing it, you can disable it. Windows ignores a disabled device's existence and releases the system resources that it uses. You can also disable and enable devices to resolve device conflicts. If two devices are competing for the same resource, disable one of them, restart, and then see whether the other one starts working.

To disable a device driver:

- In Device Manager, right-click the device that you want to disable and then choose Disable. A down-arrow appears on the disabled device's icon.

   To enable a disabled device, repeat the procedure. (The Disable command becomes the Enable command.)

Troubleshooting Hardware

If you install and uninstall enough hardware on your system, you're going to have to deal with error messages and system conflicts. When trouble comes, the first step is to use the Devices and Printers wizard: choose Start > Devices and Printers, right-click the problem device, choose Troubleshoot, and then follow the onscreen instructions.

No luck? Use Device Manager: double-click a device to show its Properties dialog box and then click the General tab. If the device isn't working, the "Device status" box shows an error message and code. Search for an explanation of the problem at the Microsoft Support website (page 71).

8

Networks & Sharing

You create a **network** when you connect two or more computers to exchange data or share equipment. Setup is easy, thanks to Windows' built-in tools (but the hassle of buying and installing network hardware remains). You can add computers running earlier versions of Windows and Mac OS X to your network too. Networks let you share files (you can designate drives, folders, and files as shared network resources); share printers, scanners, backup drives, and other devices; and share an internet connection (page 325).

This chapter covers small, local workgroup networks (page 9), common in homes and small businesses with ten or fewer computers. A geographically limited network that spans a small area (typically, a building or two) is called a **local area network** (LAN).

Types of Networks

Before you can set up Windows' network software, you must install and configure network hardware. Your choice of network depends on your budget, the proximity of the computers to be networked, and your inclination to lay cable.

Ethernet (IEEE 802.3)

Ethernet is cheap, fast, and reliable, and it imposes few limits on where the networked computers are placed. To create an Ethernet network, you'll need the following components along with your computers:

Network adapter

Each computer must have a **network adapter** that provides a physical connection to the network. An adapter has an **RJ-45 jack** that you connect an Ethernet cable to. If you have an old computer that has no built-in

Ethernet jack, buy a **network interface card** (NIC) or a USB plug-in network adapter. To check your adapter, choose Start > Control Panel > Network and Internet > Network and Sharing Center > "Change adapter settings" (on the left).

Ethernet cables

The cables used in Ethernet networks are a little thicker than telephone cables, and the **RJ-45 connectors** at each end are wider than ordinary phone (RJ-11) connectors. You can buy Ethernet cables—called 10BaseT, 100BaseT, CAT5, CAT5e, CAT6, or twisted-pair cables—of common lengths with attached connectors. For custom lengths, you (or someone at the store) can cut the cable off a spool and attach connectors. Or you can join two lengths by using an RJ-45 female/female coupler. A connection's length shouldn't exceed 100 meters (328 feet). If you're drilling through walls to lay cable, consider hiring an installer (or using a wireless network).

Hub/Router

On an Ethernet network, you connect each cable from a computer's network adapter to a central connection point called a **hub**—a small box with a row of five to eight or more jacks (called **ports**) that accept RJ-45 connectors. Small green lights on the hub glow or flicker to signal an active connection. Computers communicate through the hub, so there's no direct connection between any two machines. One port (an **uplink** port) connects to a router, broadband modem, or another hub to expand the network. The other ports are numbered, but it doesn't matter which port you plug which cable into. You can also connect shared devices, such as printers, to the hub. If you have an internet connection, use a **router** instead of an ordinary hub to share the connection.

Wireless (IEEE 802.11)

Wireless networks are versatile and don't require cables. The wireless standard is called **wi-fi** or 802.11 (say *eight-oh-two-eleven*).

Each computer on a wireless network needs a wireless network adapter. Every laptop has a built-in wireless adapter. For a desktop computer, you may need to install a wireless adapter card. Wireless networks transmit and receive radio waves over a range of about 45 meters (150 feet), through walls. To share a broadband internet connection, you need a **base station** or **access point**. To check your adapter, choose Start > Control Panel > Network and Internet > Network and Sharing Center > "Change adapter settings" (on the left).

To stop neighbors or passersby from stealing your internet bandwidth and eavesdropping, turn on the password or encryption option—usually labeled WPA or WPA2. (Don't use WEP, an older and easily broken protocol.) Also, change the default router password. Other security methods—hiding or changing the SSID, disabling DHCP, and filtering MAC addresses—are less effective.

Wireless equipment comes in these flavors: 802.11a, 802.11b, 802.11g, and 802.11n. These protocols vary by compatibility, band, range, and speed. To make a long story short, buy only g or n equipment (n being the latest standard). Note that faster wireless equipment doesn't make your internet connection faster; the modem is the bottleneck.

Telephone Lines (HomePNA)

Network equipment certified by the Home Phoneline Networking Alliance, or HomePNA, uses your existing phone wires to connect computers. HomePNA networks don't interfere with other wire communications. You can use standard telephones, dial-up modems, DSL or cable modems, faxes, and answering machines simultaneously with HomePNA, because even though the devices use the same telephone wires, they occupy different frequency bands. These networks don't require a hub; instead, you plug your HomePNA network adapter into the nearest phone jack. For more information, go to *homepna.org*.

Electrical Outlets (Powerline)

Network equipment certified by the HomePlug Powerline Alliance uses the existing electrical wiring in your home to connect computers. Unlike phone jacks, power outlets are available in almost every room, ready to pull double duty as power sources and network ports. A Powerline network is easy to set up; you simply plug your Powerline network adapter into the nearest power outlet. The network range is about 305 meters (1000 feet), including the length that the wires travel in your walls. For more information, see *homeplug.org*.

IEEE 1394 (FireWire)

You can form a simple "IP over FireWire" network if your computers all have FireWire (IEEE 1394) jacks, which usually are used to capture digital video from camcorders. (You can buy a 1394 adapter to get these jacks.) Just hook together the computers with 6-pin-to-6-pin IEEE 1394 cables. There's no need to buy a hub or router. FireWire networks usually have only two computers, but you can chain more than two if each has two free FireWire ports. The computers have to be close; 1394 cables can't be more than 4.5 meters (15 feet) long. And you can't use this arrangement to share a printer or DSL/cable modem.

Crossover Cable

If your network has only two computers that are close together, you can connect them with a **crossover cable**, which runs directly between the two computers' Ethernet jacks. This no-hassle network saves you the cost of a hub and works exactly like a "real" Ethernet network. (If you expand the network to three computers, you must buy a hub.)

Network Speed

Network speed is measured in **megabits per second (Mbps)**. 10 Mbps, called *10BaseT* or *Ethernet*, is adequate for most homes and small businesses. Modern hubs and adapters handle both 10BaseT and *100BaseT* or *Fast Ethernet* (100 Mbps) on the same network; look for the label *10/100* or *dual speed*. Pricier *Gigabit Ethernet* (1000 Mbps) equipment also is available. (Network speed doesn't affect internet-connection speed; DSL and cable modems are 10 to 20 times slower than 10BaseT.)

Sharing an Internet Connection

To share one internet connection with every computer on a network, you have two options:

Install a router

> A **router** is a small box with one jack that connects to a hub and another jack that connects to a DSL, cable, or dial-up modem. A **router/hub** doubles as a hub, sharing the modem's bandwidth among multiple Ethernet ports that the network computers connect to. A slightly more expensive **router/switch** is faster than a router/hub and should be used when you're passing lots of data around the network (when playing network games or sharing music, for example).
>
> You're better off using a router than dealing with the limits of ICS (described next). A router is easy to install and configure, uses little power, lets any computer go online at any time, and has a built-in firewall (page 339). To the outside world, a router appears to be a computer, but one without programs and hard drives to attack or infect.

Use Internet Connection Sharing (ICS)

ICS is a built-in Windows feature that acts like a software router. It's free but limited compared to a hardware router. You must designate one computer as the **host**, or **gateway**, computer through which all internet traffic passes. For broadband connections, the host computer must have two Ethernet adapters: one that connects to the DSL or cable modem and one that connects to a hub. If the host computer is turned off, the other computers—called **clients**—can't go online. Like a router, ICS works best with a high-speed internet connection, but a dial-up modem works acceptably.

Setting Up Internet Connection Sharing

Some setup tips for ICS:

- Make sure that the host computer can go online before you enable ICS.

- The client computers can be running earlier Windows versions (except Windows 95/3.x).

- Turn on the host computer before turning on the client computers. Turning off the host kills all client internet connections.

- To enable ICS on the host, choose Start > Control Panel > Network and Internet > Network and Sharing Center > "Change adapter settings" (on the left). Right-click the connection that you want to share and then choose Properties > Sharing tab > select "Allow other network users to connect through this computer's Internet connection". Set the other options, as desired. (The Sharing tab isn't available if you have only one network connection.)

- When you enable ICS, your LAN connection gets a new static IP address. For instructions on reestablishing the TCP/IP connections between the host and clients, click "Using ICS (Internet Connection Sharing)" on the Sharing tab.

Setting Up a Network

After you've decided what type of network you want and bought the necessary hardware, you're ready to set up the network.

To set up a network:

1   Install network adapters in any computers that need them, according to the manufacturer's instructions (see "Types of Networks" on page 307).

2   (Optional) Set up an internet connection (page 325). A network doesn't need an internet connection, but most networks have one. To share an existing internet connection on the network, see "Sharing an Internet Connection" on page 310.

3   Connect the computers. The connections depend on the type of network adapters, modem, internet connection, and internet sharing.

4   Turn on all computers and devices (such as printers) that you want to be part of your network. If your network is wired (Ethernet or Powerline, for example), Windows will set it up automatically, and it should be ready to use.

or

If your network is wireless, choose Start > Control Panel > Network and Internet > Network and Sharing Center > "Set up a new connection or network" > "Set up a new network". Run the Set Up a Network wizard on the computer attached to the router. The wizard walks you through the process of adding other computers and devices to the network.

5   Test your network to make sure that all the computers and devices are connected and working properly. On each network computer, open the Network folder in the Navigation pane of any folder window, or choose Start > Network. (On network computers running old versions of Windows, choose Start > My Network Places.) You should be able to see icons for the computer you are on and for all the other computers and devices that you have added to the network.

The Network Folder

The **Network** folder (Start > Network) behaves like any other folder window. Double-click items to open or explore them, just as though you were working in the Computer folder (page 163) or a Windows Explorer window (page 170). You can see the contents of other people's shared drives, folders, and files (see "Sharing Files" on page 320). You can move and copy items between network computers or rename, delete, select, sort, group, tag, search for, view properties of, and manipulate them just as you would items on your local drive. Beware: If you delete a shared item on another computer, the item bypasses the Recycle Bin. For a high-level view of the network, expand the Network branch of the tree in the Navigation pane. Computers that are turned off, sleeping, or hibernating won't appear in the Navigation pane.

Workgroup Names

When you set up a network, Windows creates a workgroup and gives it a name automatically. You can join an existing workgroup on a network or create a new one. You can also change the name of the computer.

To rename a computer, join an existing workgroup, or create a new workgroup:

1   Choose Start > Control Panel > System and Security > System > "Advanced system settings" (on the left).

2   Click the Computer Name tab, and then click Change.

3   Type a new name for the computer, if desired. The name of each computer appears in the Network folder and in other network tools and windows.

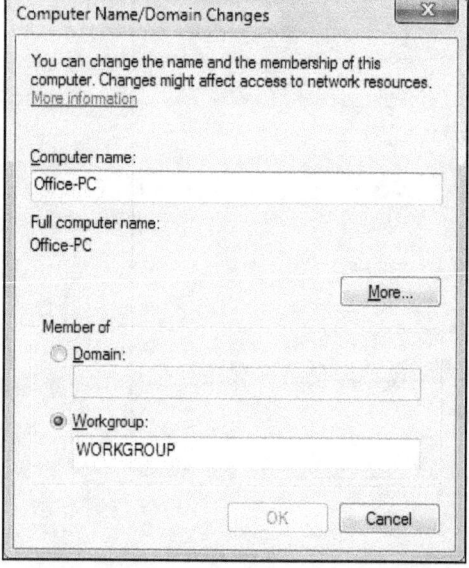

4   In the "Member of" section, select Workgroup.

5   Type the name of an existing workgroup that you want to join, or type the name of the new workgroup that you want to create. If you change the name of a workgroup on any computer, you also have to change the workgroup name (to match the new name) on each networked computer that you want to include in the new workgroup.

6   Click OK in each open dialog box.

Finding Missing Computers on a Network

If computers on the network are missing from the Network folder, try these solutions to common problems:

- On each computer, click the Network icon (🖳 or ⏹ⅢⅡ) in the taskbar's notification area (or choose Start > Connect To in some earlier Windows versions) and then connect to the network.

- On each computer, choose Start > Control Panel > Network and Internet > Network and Sharing Center > "Change advanced sharing settings" (on the left). If network discovery is turned off for the current profile, turn it on and then click Save Changes.

- Right-click the Network icon in the taskbar's notification area and then choose "Troubleshoot problems" (or "Diagnose and repair" in some earlier Windows versions).

- Make sure that all the computers are turned on and connected.

- Make sure that your hub, switch, or router is plugged in and turned on, and that all network adapters are firmly seated and cables are firmly connected to their jacks and ports. Use Device Manager (page 302) to make sure that each network adapter is working properly.

- Choose Start > Control Panel > Network and Internet > Network and Sharing Center > "Troubleshoot problems".

UNC Names

The **Uniform Naming Convention** (UNC) is a system of naming network files, folders, and other shared resources so that an item's address identifies it uniquely on the network. UNC uses the format:

*server**resource_path*

where *server* is a computer name or an IP address, and *resource_path* is a standard path (page 178). Some example UNCs for a folder, file, and printer are:

\\mars\budget\2012\qtr2

\\mercury\books\mynovel\chap01.docx

\\saturn\HPcolor

To view a shared item quickly, type its UNC name in an address bar (page 177) or in the Run dialog box (press Windows logo key+R).

Mapping Network Drives

You can **map** (assign) a shared drive or folder to a drive letter (page 165) so that you can access the item via the Computer folder (page 163) or the Open or Save dialog boxes. In a folder window, choose Tools > "Map network drive" (tap Alt if the Tools menu isn't visible), select a drive letter, browse for an item or type its UNC name, select "Reconnect at logon" (if desired), and then click Finish. The new "drive" appears in the Navigation pane. To kill the mapping, choose Tools > "Disconnect network drive".

Ad Hoc Networks

You can also set up a wireless **ad hoc** network, which is a temporary connection between computers and devices used to, say, share files, play multiplayer games, or share an internet connection. Choose Start > Control Panel > Network and Internet > Network and Sharing Center > "Set up a new connection or network" > "Set up a wireless ad hoc (computer-to-computer) network". Click Next and then follow the onscreen instructions.

Networking Tips

- In applications, shared files are available via the standard Open and Save dialog boxes. Choosing File > Save saves a file in its original network location; to save a copy on your local drive, choose File > Save As.

- To connect a laptop to an Ethernet network, plug one end of an Ethernet cable into the laptop and the other end into the hub or router. To connect to a wireless network, click the Network icon in the taskbar's notification area and then select the network in the list. If the network is secured, type the password.

- You can use command-line tools to get network information. The most useful are *hostname, ipconfig, net, netstat, ping,* and *tracert.* For usage and syntax, open Command Prompt (page 262) and then type a command following by a space and /?.

Managing a Network

Network and Sharing Center is a dashboard for managing your network and viewing its status in real time (useful when you're having setup or connection problems). You can use it to see whether your computer is connected to a network or the internet, choose the type of connection, and change your network settings. It also has links to Windows' other networking tools and wizards.

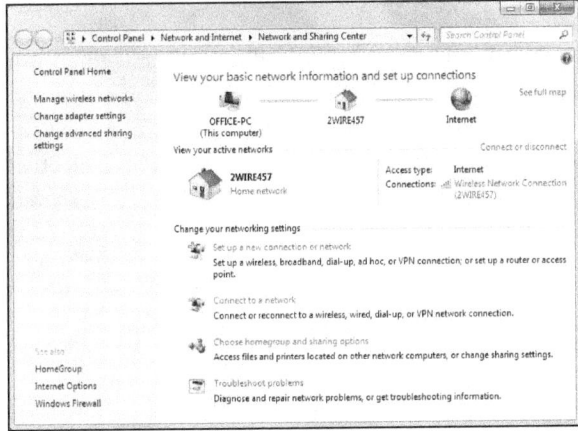

To open Network and Sharing Center:

- Choose Start > Control Panel > Network and Internet > Network and Sharing Center.

  or

  Right-click the Network icon (or) in the taskbar's notification area and then choose Open Network and Sharing Center.

Tip: If the Network icon is hidden, right-click an empty area of the taskbar and then choose Properties > Taskbar tab > Customize > "Turn system icons on or off" > Network > On.

Network Connection Status

To see the current status of a network connection, in Network and Sharing Center, click the link next to "Connections" (under "Connect or disconnect"). The Status dialog box shows the dead-or-alive state of the network and statistics on maximum speed, connection duration, and bytes uploaded and downloaded. Click Details for the IP address or Properties for more-advanced settings.

Network Locations

You choose a network location the first time that you connect to a network, letting Windows know which firewall and security settings to use when you connect:

Home network or Work network

Windows assumes that you trust the people and devices on the network, so it turns on network discovery, which lets you see other computers and devices on a network, and allows other network users to see your computer. You can also access shared files and devices on other computers, and other people can access files and devices on your computer that you've shared.

Public network

Windows keeps your computer invisible to the other computers around you (at a café, for example) by turning off network discovery.

Domain network

Your computer is joined to a network domain (page 9). In general, this location is controlled by your network administrator and can't be selected or changed.

If you're a traveling laptop user who connects to networks at home, school, work, airports, and coffee shops, you can change the network location based on where you are.

To change the network location, in Network and Sharing Center, click the "network" link (under "View your active networks"), and then click your location: Home, Work, Public, or Domain. (For details on which security settings prevail for each network location, click the "Help me choose" link.)

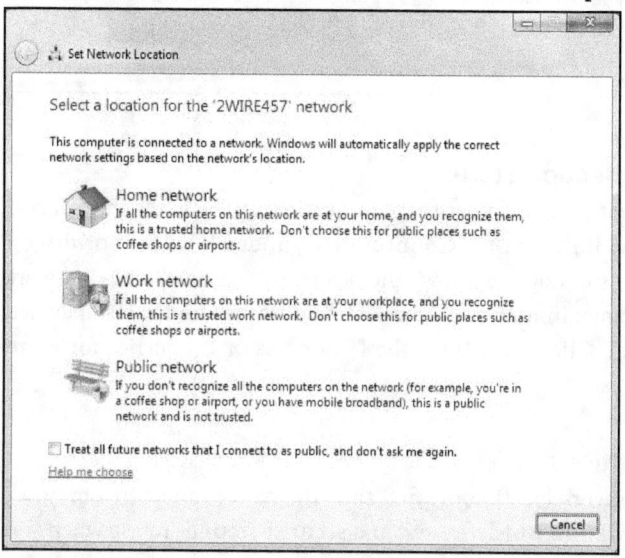

Changing Network Settings

You can control how your computer is seen and shared on the network. To configure the network connection settings, in Network and Sharing Center, click "Change advanced sharing settings" (on the left), turn on or off the settings for a location or profile, and then click Save Changes.

To expand or collapse a section, click its arrow button ⌄. Each section contains an explanation of the setting; the setting's options; and in some cases, links to change related settings and to display Help topics that explain the consequences of the change.

Most of the network settings are covered elsewhere in this book. Network discovery is described in "Network Locations" on page 317. File sharing and Public folder sharing are covered in "Sharing Files" on page 320. For printer sharing, see "Sharing a Network Printer" on page 277.

Network Maps

The network map at the top of Network and Sharing Center is live and interactive.

- Click your computer to open the Computer folder (page 163).

- Click another computer on the network to show its shared devices and folders.

- Click a network icon to show the Network folder (page 313).

- Click Internet to open a web browser.

- Click "See full map" to see a detailed map, with icons for all the computers on the network, connections, router, and so on.

- A superimposed × denotes a lost connection. Click the × to have Windows try to diagnose and solve the problem, or look for an unplugged cable or switched-off modem or router.

Disconnecting from a Network

If you don't want your computer to be on a network, you can disconnect it without unplugging cables.

To disconnect from a network:

1   In Network and Sharing Center, click "Change adapter settings" (on the left).

2   In the Network Connections folder, right-click the connection that you want to disconnect from and then choose Disconnect or Disable.

Tip: If you disable a LAN (local area) connection, the network adapter is disabled until you reconnect.

Sharing Files

Windows gives you two ways to share drives, folders, libraries, and files: Public folder sharing and any-folder sharing. Either method lets you share with someone using your computer or another computer on the same network.

The Public Folder

The easiest way to share files and folders is to put them in the **Public** folder. Everyone with a user account and password on your computer can access the Public folder, but you decide whether people on the network can access it. You can't choose who on the network can access it. You must grant access either to everyone on the network or to no one. You can set the permission level, however, by choosing whether those who have network access can only open files or also change and create them.

Use the Public folder if you want to able to see everything you've shared by looking in only one place, separate from your personal folders (My Documents, My Music, My Pictures, and so on), or if you want to set sharing permissions for everyone on your network rather than individual users.

To open the Public folder, choose Start > Computer (Windows logo key+E), double-click the Windows drive (the drive with the Windows logo ⊞ —typically the C drive), and then navigate to Users > Public.

You can copy or move whichever files you want to share to the Public folder or one of its subfolders, which help you organize shared files by content type. You have to place the files themselves; shortcuts won't work.

To control network access to the Public folder, in Network and Sharing Center, click "Change advanced sharing settings" (on the left). To control the level of access to the Public folder, use the "Public folder sharing" option. To control who can access the Public folder, set the "Password protected sharing" option.

Password-protected sharing doesn't work if you're a domain member (page 9). This type of sharing limits access to the Public folder to only those people with password-protected accounts on your local computer.

Any-Folder Sharing

Using the Public folder can be inefficient. If you're sharing hundreds of photos, for example, it's wasteful to store copies in both your (unshared) My Pictures folder and the Public folder. If you create or update files frequently, it's cumbersome to keep copying them to the Public folder.

Use any-folder sharing to share files, libraries (page 224), and folders directly from the location where they're stored (typically, in your personal folder, page 167). You can set sharing permissions for individual users rather than for everyone on your network, giving some people more or less access (or no access), whether you're on a workgroup or domain (page 9).

To share files from any folder on your computer:

1   In a folder window, locate the folder that contains the files you want to share.

2   Select one or more files, libraries, or folders that you want to share and then click "Share with" > "Specific people" on the toolbar (or right-click and then choose the same command).

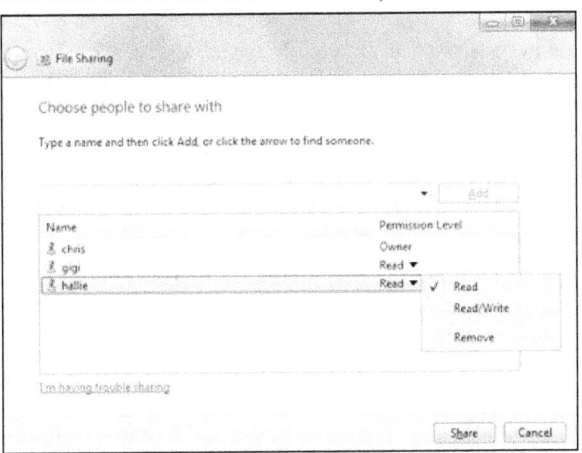

or

> To stop sharing a shared item, choose "Share with" > Nobody and then skip the remaining steps.

3   In the File Sharing dialog box, type or paste the name of the person or group that you want to share files with (or click the down-arrow to find someone) and then click Add. The name is added to the sharing list.

4   In the Permission Level column, click the arrow for a person or group and then choose Read to restrict the person or group to only viewing files in the shared folder, or choose Read/Write to let the person or group view, change, add, and delete files in the shared folder.

5   Click Share.

6   After you receive confirmation that your folder is shared, you can notify the people that you're sharing with and send them a link to access the files. To open your email program with a new email message containing a link to your shared files, click Email. To paste the link into an email message manually, click Copy (or right-click the shared item in the list and then choose Copy Link). If you don't want to send an email message, click Done.

Homegroups

If all the computers that you want to share with are running Windows 7 or later, you have another, easier way to share files on a home network: homegroups. A **homegroup** is a collection of computers that can share pictures, music, videos, documents, and printers. A homegroup is protected by a (changeable) password, which you type only once: when you join the homegroup.

Windows creates a homegroup automatically when you create a Home network. If you see the word *Joined* next to HomeGroup in Network and Sharing Center, then you belong to a homegroup. To create, configure, join, leave, or troubleshoot a homegroup, click the link next to HomeGroup and follow the onscreen instructions.

If you belong to a homegroup, the "Share with" menu provides Read and Read/Write options that apply to all the members of your homegroup. You can also choose your homegroup from the Add drop-down list in the File Sharing dialog box.

To access shared items on other homegroup computers, choose Start and then click your user name. In the Navigation pane, under Homegroup, click the user account of the person whose files you want to access. In the file list, double-click the library that you want to access and then double-click the item you want.

Homegroups are available in all Windows editions. In low-end editions, however, you can only join a homegroup, not create one. Computers that belong to a domain (page 9) can join a homegroup but can't share files; they can only access files shared by others.

Sharing Tips

- Make sure that the file-sharing options are turned on in Network and Sharing Center > "Change advanced sharing settings" (on the left).

- To see your computer's network-shared devices and folders, click "Show me all the network shares on this computer" in the File Sharing confirmation dialog box.

- A **share name** makes it easy for someone to find a shared folder on your computer. Right-click a folder that you've already shared and then choose Properties > Sharing tab. Click the Share button to start sharing, stop sharing, or change the existing sharing permissions. Or click Advanced Sharing for more-complex administrator-level sharing options.

- To share an entire drive, choose Start > Computer, right-click the drive, and then choose Properties > Sharing tab > Advanced Sharing.

- You can't share encrypted files and folders (page 347).

- The "Share with" menu won't appear for network or other unsupported locations.

9

Online Connections

You can connect to the internet or a network via broadband, wireless, dial-up, or virtual private network (VPN). Windows also includes tools for working remotely, online or offline.

The Network Connections Window

Before you create a connection, look in the Network Connections window for a list of your existing internet and network connections.

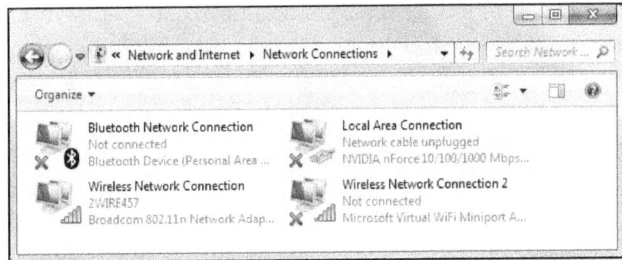

To open Network Connections:

- Choose Start > Control Panel > Network and Internet > Network and Sharing Center > "Change adapter settings" (on the left).

  or

  Choose Start, type *network connections* in the Search box, and then select "View network connections".

Network Connections Tips

- Network Connections works best in Tiles or Details view (click 🔲 ▾ on the toolbar).

- If you upgraded in-place (page 5) from an earlier version of Windows, your existing connections were preserved and should work fine.

- Every newly created connection appears as an icon in the Network Connections window. The newest connection becomes the default. To change the default, right-click the desired connection and then choose "Set as default connection". A check mark appears on the default's icon.

- To activate a dial-up or VPN connect manually, double-click its icon.

- Double-click an active connection to see its status, including how long you've been connected, how much you've downloaded or uploaded, and (click Details) the IP address.

- Right-click a connection to view its properties, create a shortcut, diagnose problems, or to enable, disable, delete, rename, or copy it.

Broadband Connections

Broadband (DSL, cable, or office-network) connections are fast, always on, and easy to set up. Most broadband connections autoconfigure by using **DHCP** (Dynamic Host Configuration Protocol), so require no setup from you beyond plugging in an Ethernet cable or choosing a wireless network. For **PPPoE** (Point-to-Point Protocol over Ethernet) connections, your internet service provider (ISP) or network administrator will give you a user name and password.

An **IP address** identifies your computer uniquely on the internet. Most PPPoE connections use dynamic IP addresses, which change each time that you connect. You can also connect by using a static (fixed) IP address, if you have one.

To connect to the internet via broadband (PPPoE):

1. Choose Start > Control Panel > Network and Internet > Network and Sharing Center > "Set up a new connection or network" > "Connect to the Internet" > Next.

2. Click Broadband (PPPoE).

   or

If a connection already exists and you want to set up another one, click "Set up a new connection anyway" and then click Broadband (PPPoE).

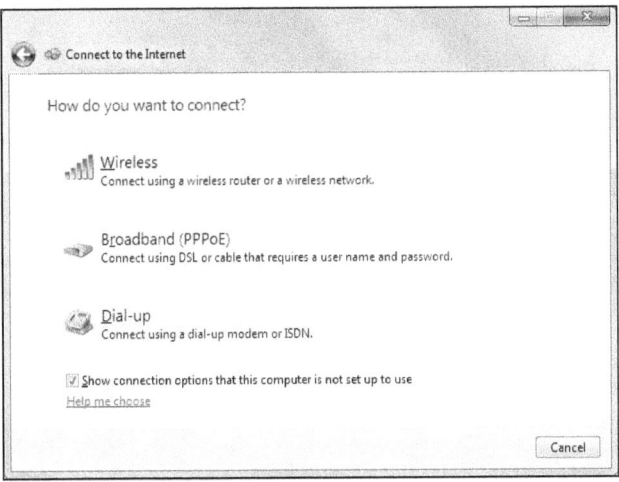

3 Follow the onscreen instructions.

Enter the user name and password that your ISP or network administrator gave you. Type a descriptive connection name—this name appears as an icon label in the Network Connections window (page 325).

4 To let all logged-on users use this connection, select "Allow other people to use this connection"; clear it if you don't want to share the connection.

5 On the last page of the wizard, click Connect to test the connection. If the wizard can't connect, it gives you a chance to retry connecting, diagnose the problem, or create the connection anyway.

Static IP Connections

A static (or fixed) IP address stays the same every time you connect. In a PPPoE connection, the IP address changes each time. Most connections are PPPoE. ISPs usually make groups of static IP addresses available only to business customers at extra cost, if at all.

To set up a static IP connection:

1 Choose Start > Control Panel > Network and Internet > Network and Sharing Center > "Change adapter settings" (on the left).

2 Right-click the Local Area Connection icon and then choose Properties.

3   On the Networking tab, double-click "Internet Protocol Version 4 (TCP/IPv4)" in the connections list. (If you're using IPv6, double-click "Internet Protocol Version 6 (TCP/IPv6)" instead.)

TCP/IP is the standard protocol for computer communications over the internet.

4   On the General tab, select "Use the following IP address", select "Use the following DNS server addresses", and then type your IP addresses.

5   Click OK in each open dialog box.

Tip: If you have a static IP connection, and Windows ever prompts you to connect, choose Start > Control Panel > Network and Internet > Internet Options > Connections tab > select "Never dial a connection".

Connection Tips

•   Network and Sharing Center (page 316) is the main hub for network and internet connections and activities. Choose Start > Control Panel > Network and Internet > Network and Sharing Center.

•   Hover the pointer over the Network icon (🖳 or ⚫) in the taskbar's notification area for a quick look at your current connections. Clicking the icon shows all available connections in a pop-up window. Right-click the icon for a few more commands. You can also right-click individual connections in the pop-up window. (If the Network icon doesn't appear, right-click an empty area of the taskbar and then choose Properties > Taskbar tab > Customize > "Turn system icons on or off" > Network > On.)

Wireless Connections

Wireless isn't really a connection type but a network type—a way to use an existing broadband connection. For a wireless connection, you need a wireless router or wireless network (page 308). Or you can connect through a hotspot—a public place (such as a café, airport, hotel, library, or possibly an entire town) with a wireless network. Many workplaces have secured hotspots throughout the floor or building. If you're at a friend's house, you can connect through his wireless network, provided that he gives you the password.

When you try to go online, Windows looks for a wired or wireless connection. It favors wired (because it's faster and more secure), but if lacking an Ethernet cable, Windows jumps automatically onto a wireless network, if possible. This is usually how you want a laptop to behave.

To connect or disconnect, click the Network icon  in the taskbar's notification area and then click a wireless network in the pop-up window. If the network is secured, type the password (security key). Depending on where you are, you may see ten or more in-range wireless networks in the list. Each list entry tells you whether the network is secured and gives its signal strength. You can move for a better signal. To update the list manually, click Refresh ↻.

Tip: If the Network icon  doesn't appear, right-click an empty area of the taskbar and then choose Properties > Taskbar tab > Customize > "Turn system icons on or off" > Network > On.

Dial-Up Connections

Each time that you connect to the internet or a remote network via **dial-up**, your analog modem dials your ISP or network over a standard phone line. (If you have only one line, callers can't reach you while you're online.) Dial-up connections are slow compared with broadband, but they're a good choice for frequent travelers, because big ISPs provide local access numbers over large geographic areas. In some areas, dial-up is your only choice.

You need an analog modem for a dial-up connection. If your computer didn't come with a built-in modem, buy a 56 Kbps internal or external (USB) model. To configure your modem, choose Start > Control Panel, switch to icon view, and then click Phone and Modem. A plug-in USB modem is easiest to install and configure. If you install an internal modem expansion card, plug the telephone cable from your wall jack into the modem's Line (not Phone) jack. If you have to run your modem and a phone off the same line at the same jack, run a second cable from the modem's Phone jack to the telephone's Line jack.

To set up a dial-up connection:

1   Choose Start > Control Panel > Network and Internet > Network and Sharing Center > "Set up a new connection or network".

2   Select "Connect to a workplace" and then click Next.

3   If you have an existing dial-up connection, select "No, create a new connection" and then click Next; otherwise, skip this step.

4   Click "Dial directly" and then follow the onscreen instructions. Along the way, you're asked for the phone number, destination name (for the icon label), user name, password, and (optional) domain. You can get this information from your network administrator.

5   To connect or disconnect, click the Network icon (🖳 or �) in the taskbar's notification area and then click the dial-up connection in the pop-up window.

If you're disconnected and you use a program that requires an internet connection (a web browser, for example), Windows displays a Connect dialog box to let you connect. To connect, click Connect. To connect automatically (suppressing the Connect dialog box in the future), click Properties, click the Options tab, and then clear "Prompt for name and password, certificate, etc." To control autoconnect, choose Start > Control Panel > Network and Internet > Internet Options > Connections tab, and then select a dialing option.

To add alternative numbers to a dial-up connection (as fallbacks if the primary number is busy), right-click the connection icon in the Network Connections window (page 325) and then choose Properties > General tab > Alternates.

When you close your browser or other internet program, a dial-up connection doesn't hang up automatically; it ties up your phone line until disconnected. By default, Windows disconnects automatically after 20 minutes of inactivity. To change this period, right-click the dial-up connection in the Network Connections window (page 325), choose Properties > Options tab, and then select a time limit from the "Idle time before hanging up" list.

VPN Connections

A virtual private network (VPN) lets you connect from your computer to a network securely and privately by using the internet as a conduit. VPNs overcome dial-up's twin evils: slow speeds and high costs.

To set up a VPN connection:

1   Choose Start > Control Panel > Network and Internet > Network and Sharing Center > "Set up a new connection or network".

2   Select "Connect to a workplace" and then click Next.

3   If you have an existing VPN connection, select "No, create a new connection" and then click Next; otherwise, skip this step.

4   Click "Use my Internet connection (VPN)" and then follow the onscreen instructions. Along the way, you're asked for the internet address, destination name (for the icon label), user name, password, and (optional) domain. You can get this information from your network administrator.

5   To connect or disconnect, click the Network icon (🖥 or 📶) in the taskbar's notification area and then click the VPN connection in the pop-up window.

Troubleshooting Connections

Windows includes a few tools that let you inspect and troubleshoot your internet and network connections.

* Right-click the Network icon (🖥 or 📶) in the taskbar's notification area and then choose "Troubleshoot problems".

* Use command-line tools to get connection information. The most useful are *ipconfig, netsh, netstat, pathping, ping,* and *tracert.* For usage and syntax, open Command Prompt (page 262) and then type a command following by a space and /?.

* To determine your actual internet connection speed (as opposed to what your ISP tells you), use a speed-test service like *speedtest.net* or *speakeasy. net/speedtest.*

Working Remotely

Windows offers specialized tools for telecommuters, travelers, and laptop users.

Remote Desktop

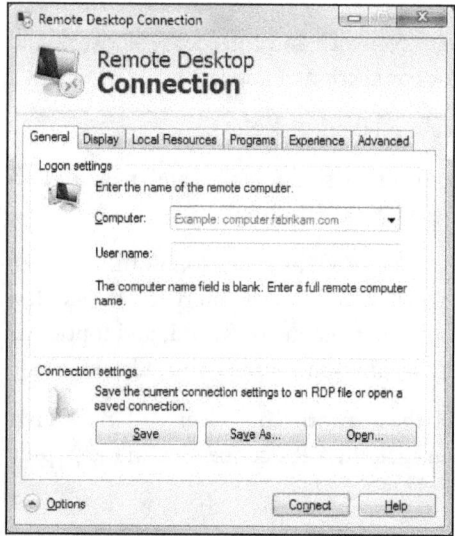

Remote Desktop lets you connect to a remote computer and use it as though you were sitting in front of it. You can control the remote computer's full desktop, with its Start menu, taskbar, icons, documents, and programs. Programs run on the remote computer, and only the keyboard input, mouse input, and display output are transmitted over the connection. The **remote computer** is the computer that you want to control from afar. The **local**, or **client**, **computer** is the one that you'll be sitting at, driving the remote computer.

You can access a remote computer running Windows from a local computer running Windows if they're both connected to the same network or to the internet. The remote computer must be turned on and Remote Desktop must be enabled.

To set up a remote computer, choose Start > Control Panel > System and Security > System > Remote Settings. Select one of the "Allow" options under Remote Desktop. If you're enabling Remote Desktop for just yourself, your user name is added to the list of remote users automatically; otherwise, click Select Users to add other users. When you're done, the remote computer listens for incoming Remote Desktop connection requests.

To connect to a remote desktop from a local computer, choose Start > All Programs > Accessories > Remote Desktop Connection. If you want to change the connection settings before you connect, click Options. To connect, click Connect, type your credentials for the remote computer, and then click OK. Your screen goes black momentarily, and then the remote computer's desktop fills the screen, hiding your desktop and taskbar.

You can operate the distant computer as though you were sitting in front of it. All your actions—running programs, printing, sending email, installing drivers, whatever—happen on the remote computer. Anyone looking at the remote computer in person sees a Welcome screen or an Unlock Computer screen; that person can't see what you're doing.

A full-screen remote desktop shows a retractable title bar (which can be pinned in place) at the screen's top edge, letting you switch between your local desktop and the remote desktop. You can use the standard cut, copy, and paste commands to transfer text, graphics, and files between the two computers. If both desktops are visible, you can drag between local and remote windows. To log off, shut down, sleep, restart, or lock the remote computer, choose Start > Windows Security on the remote computer's desktop.

If the Remote Desktop window is maximized, the standard Windows keyboard shortcuts apply to the *remote* computer. Alt+Tab, for example, switches between programs on the distant computer, not your local one. But if the Remote Desktop window is active and floating on your desktop, those same shortcuts apply to the *local* computer. (Alt+Tab will switch between locally running programs.) Fortunately, you can use two sets of keyboard shortcuts to perform the equivalent actions on the local desktop and an active, floating Remote Desktop window:

To	Press
Switch among programs	Alt+Tab (local) or Alt+Page Up (remote)
Switch among programs in reverse order	Shift+Alt+Tab (local) or Alt+Page Down (remote)
Cycle through programs in the order in which they were started	Alt+Esc (local) or Alt+Insert (remote)
Open the Start menu	Ctrl+Esc (local) or Alt+Home (remote)

To	Press
Display Task Manager or, for domains, the Windows Security dialog box	Ctrl+Alt+Delete (local) or Ctrl+Alt+End (remote)
Switch the remote desktop between a window and full screen	Ctrl+Alt+Break (remote)
Display the active window's control menu	Alt+Delete (remote)

Offline Files

Offline Files is designed for travelers who work with a laptop computer that's often disconnected from the network (while flying, for example). When you make a file or folder available offline, Windows makes a temporary copy of it on your laptop; you can work with this copy as you would the original. When you reconnect to the network, Windows **synchronizes** your laptop documents with the network originals so that you have up-to-date versions in both places. Offline Files is available in only high-end Windows editions.

To turn on offline files, choose Start > All Programs > Accessories > Sync Center > "Manage offline files (on the left)" > General tab > "Enable offline files" > OK. If you work with offline files in many different folders, click "View your offline files" to see them all without opening each folder individually. You can use the other tabs to limit drive space for offline files, encrypt offline files, or work offline automatically if your network connection is slow.

To make a file or folder available offline, while connected to a network (on your laptop), locate the network file or folder that you want to make available offline (under Network in the Navigation pane of a folder window). Right-click the file or folder and then choose "Always available offline". The next time that you try to access the file or folder, you'll be able to open it even if the network copy is unavailable. You open offline files as though you were working with them online. A small "sync" badge on the icon reminds you that you're working offline.

You *must* log off or shut down to effect synchronization. If you simply disconnect from the network, Windows won't have time to sync files.

Windows Mobility Center

The **Windows Mobility Center** window lets you adjust your laptop settings in a central location. It has controls that let you adjust the speaker volume (page 134), check the status of your wireless network connection (page 328), change the power plan (page 152), and more. To open Mobility Center (on laptops only), choose Start > Control Panel > Hardware and Sound > Windows Mobility Center, or press Windows logo key+X. You can also right-click the Power icon ⌷ in the taskbar's notification area and then choose Windows Mobility Center.

Stylus and Touch Features

Windows has an extensive collection of features and gestures for use with tablet computers (styluses) and touchscreen displays (fingers). Choose Start > Help and Support and then search for *touch* or *tablet pc*. You'll find multitouch gestures, flicks, pen features, digital ink, handwriting recognition, Windows Journal, Input Panel, and more.

10

Security & Privacy

Windows's security and privacy features include tools like Action Center, Windows Firewall, Windows Update, Microsoft Security Essentials, Parental Controls, and encryption.

You can also use secure logon (page 22), secure-empty the Recycle Bin (page 206), and use InPrivate mode in Internet Explorer (page 264). When you try to do something potentially dangerous (like run a program downloaded from the internet), User Account Control (page 19) will warn you and prompt you for an administrator password (page 8).

Tip: A good source of information about web privacy and security is the Electronic Frontier Foundation (*eff.org*).

Action Center

Action Center is a one-stop program for checking the status of your firewall, automatic updates, antimalware programs, and other security essentials on your computer. When something is amiss, an Action Center warning message appears in the taskbar's notification area. This message and icon appear (or sometimes only the icon does) if Action Center thinks that your computer has insufficient protection, or if it doesn't recognize the firewall and antivirus program that you're using.

Tip: If you're on a network domain (page 9), you may not be able to use Action Center if your network administrator manages your security settings.

To open Action Center:

- Click the Action Center icon 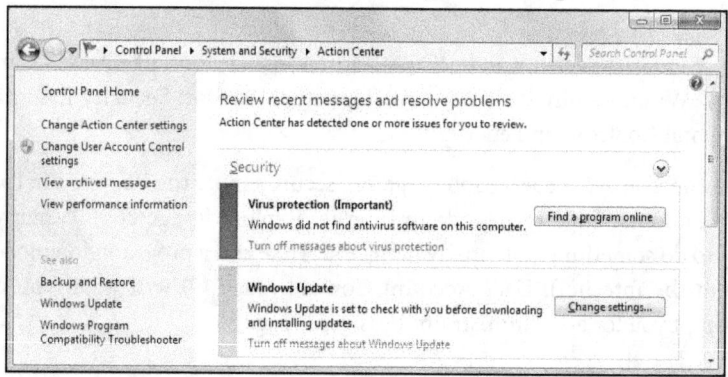 or pop-up message, if it appears.

  or

  Choose Start > Control Panel > System and Security > Action Center.

  or

  Choose Start, type *action center* in the Search box, and then press Enter.

  or

  Press Windows logo key+R, type *wscui.cpl*, and then press Enter.

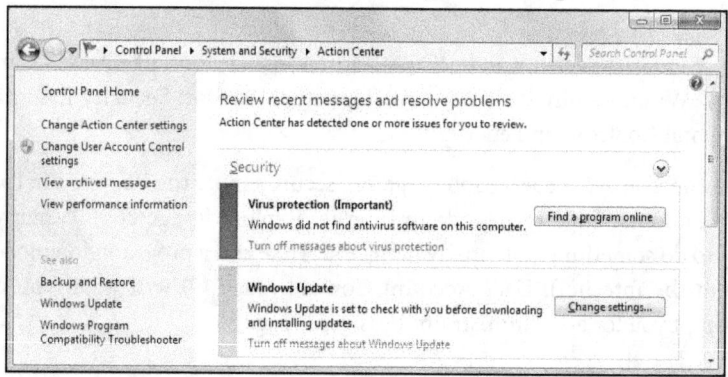

Action Center is a dashboard of warnings, buttons, and indicator "lights" for your computer's firewall, updates, antimalware, and other components. For each item, a yellow or red bar indicates the severity of the warning. Click one of the links or buttons to learn what the problem is and what to do about it. Action Center offers a status report and provides links to the relevant settings, online resources, and Control Panel programs that you'll need to fix things.

If you don't want to be bothered with Action Center alerts, you can turn them on or off individually: in Action Center, click "Change Action Center settings" (on the left), turn the messages on or off, and then click OK.

Baseline Security Analyzer

Microsoft Baseline Security Analyzer is a little-known but excellent tool that scans your computer for security holes and suggests how to fix them. Download it for free at *technet.microsoft.com/en-us/security/cc184924*. Its diagnoses contain some technical language but make clear where the problems lie.

Windows Firewall

A **firewall** is a piece of software or hardware that helps screen out human enemies and viruses that try to reach your computer over the internet. It's the most important security component on your computer or network; if you don't have one, attackers can compromise your computer minutes after you go online. Windows provides Windows Firewall for free, but consider using a router too.

A **router** is a small box that distributes the signal from your modem (DSL, cable, or dial-up) to the computers on your network. A router has a built-in firewall and appears to the outside world to be a computer without programs and hard drives to attack or infect; it's the safest type of firewall, because it protects your entire network and is always on. Even if you're not on a network, you can put a router between your computer and your modem. If you're on a network, a router won't protect you from other computers on the network if one of them becomes infected because someone downloaded a virus. For that kind of protection, you need a software firewall on your individual computer. See also "Networks & Sharing" on page 307.

Windows Firewall is available in Control Panel and turned on by default with the safest settings chosen. In general, the only reason to switch off Windows Firewall is if you are troubleshooting a connection or have installed a third-party firewall, called a **personal firewall**. (Windows Firewall turns itself off automatically if you install a Windows-aware personal firewall.)

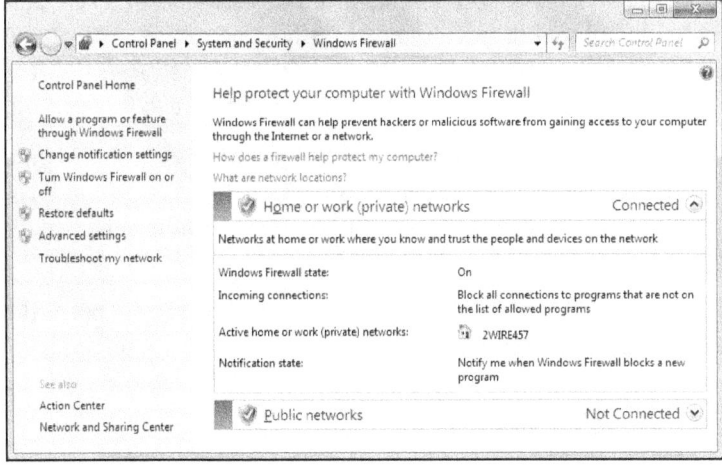

To turn on or off Windows Firewall:

1 Choose Start > Control Panel > System and Security > Windows Firewall.

   or

   Choose Start, type *windows firewall* in the Search box, and then select Windows Firewall in the results list.

   or

   Press Windows logo key+R, type *firewall.cpl*, and then press Enter.

2 Click "Turn Windows Firewall on or off" (on the left).

3 Turn on or off the firewall for your network location(s), and then click OK.

Tip: You can select "Block all incoming connections" to block all unsolicited incoming traffic, even traffic that normally would be permitted by an exception (described next). Use this extra-secure mode when you connect to a public wireless hotspot in a café, airport, or hotel, or when a virus is spreading over your network.

Opening and Closing Ports

Traffic flows in and out of your computer through **ports**—small, authorized doors in the firewall. (These ports aren't the same as the hardware ports that you connect devices to.) A port number identifies each port uniquely, and certain ports handle only a specific type of traffic. Port 80 is used for HTTP (web) traffic, for example. Other ports allow instant messages, printer sharing, and so on. (You can find others by searching the web for *well-known ports*.)

Windows Firewall leaves some ports open by default (File and Printer Sharing and your local network connections, for example) but blocks most of them to incoming traffic, so when a new program wants to get online, the firewall displays a dialog box asking you whether it's OK. Click:

- *Allow access* if you recognize the program name. The firewall opens the relevant listening port for this connection and future incoming connections. If a security prompt appears, type an administrator password or confirm the action.

- *Cancel* if you don't know which program the firewall is asking about, or if you know it but don't want it phoning home. The program might not work properly if it can't accept incoming traffic (desirable in some cases).

Common sense applies to opening ports: open one only when you really need it, don't unblock a program that you don't recognize, and close a port when you no longer need it. But sometimes you'll change your mind about a program or will be tricked into unblocking a hostile program named to fool you. Windows Firewall lets you create **exceptions** for programs and manage them manually.

To configure programs and ports:

1 Open Windows Firewall.

2 Click "Allow a program or feature through Windows Firewall" (on the left).

3 In the Allowed Programs window, click "Change settings", and then do any of the following:

To open or close ports for specific programs, select or clear the checkboxes.

To add a program, click "Allow another program", and then select it in the list or browse to it.

To remove a program, select it in the list, and then click Remove. (You can't remove the preconfigured programs.)

To specify which network location types to add a program to, select the program in the list and then choose Details > "Network location types" (if it appears).

4 Click OK.

Adding a program is preferable to opening a specific port because it's easier to do, you don't need to know which port number to use, and the firewall is open only while the program is waiting to receive the connection.

To protect or unprotect individual internet and network connections, or to restore the firewall's default settings, click "Advanced settings" or "Restore defaults" in the Windows Firewall window.

Windows Update

Microsoft regularly releases free updates and bug fixes for Windows and its component programs. Some changes are minor additions to the Windows feature set, whereas others plug security holes, fix stability problems, and update drivers. Critical fixes are designated **important updates**, which plug security holes or fix stability problems. Mundane fixes are designated **recommended updates**. Periodically, Microsoft combines new fixes and previously released ones into a package called a **Service Pack** (SP). Never wait for an SP to install updates, particularly important updates.

Windows Update lets you choose how and when updates are installed on your computer. By default, Windows Update is set to the most secure option: Automatic, which checks Microsoft's website regularly for important fixes and, if they're available, downloads and installs them automatically. Action Center (page 337) objects to any other setting and alerts you with a "Change Windows Update settings" message if you choose something weaker than Automatic.

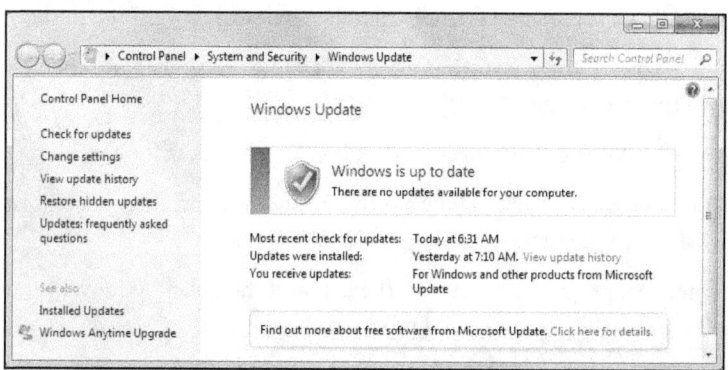

Microsoft releases security patches via Windows Update on the second Tuesday of each month, called **Patch Tuesday**. Critical flaws cause Microsoft to issue fixes more frequently than the second-Tuesday cycle. You can read about each update at Microsoft Security Bulletins (*technet.microsoft.com/en-us/security/bulletin*). You should update Windows as soon as a patch is released. Malware writers tend to quickly release new attacks that they have reverse-engineered from patches.

To set up Windows Update:

1   Choose Start > Control Panel > System and Security > Windows Update.

or

In Action Center (page 337), click the Windows Update link (on the left).

or

Choose Start, type *windows update* in the Search box, and then press Enter.

2   Do any of the following:

To check for updates now, click "Check for updates" (on the left).

To review the updates installed to date, click "View update history".

To see or install updates that you previously declined to install, click "Restore hidden updates" (on the left).

To change when and how updates are applied, click "Change settings" (on the left), choose among the following options, select or clear the checkboxes to fine-tune the update method, and then click OK.

Install updates automatically (recommended)
This set-it-and-forget-it option downloads and installs all updates automatically, according to the schedule you choose. This option is appropriate if you have an always-on internet connection (DSL or cable). If you miss an update because you're offline, it'll catch up with you when you go back on.

Download updates but let me choose whether to install them
The download happens in the background, silently and without interfering with anything that you might be downloading yourself. After download, Windows alerts you to get your permission to install the update. This option lets you research the patch before you install it to see whether it's giving people trouble.

Check for updates but let me choose whether to download and install them
Windows alerts you when it detects an update on the Microsoft website. With your permission, it downloads and installs it in separate steps. This option is a good choice for on-the-go laptop users.

Never check for updates (not recommended)
No updates occur. Choose this option if you want to update Windows manually (by clicking "Check for updates") or if you're on a network domain (page 9) and you update from a network server rather than from Microsoft directly.

Update Tips

- To troubleshoot Windows Update, choose Start > Control Panel, switch to icon view, and then choose Troubleshooting > System and Security > Windows Update.

- If you ignore Windows Update when it's ready to install an update and try to shut down, a shield appears on the Power button ▣ Shut down in the Start menu. Clicking this button ends your session, installs the updates, and then shuts down your computer.

- You can *un*install an update if it's causing problems. Choose Start > Control Panel > Programs > Programs and Features > "View installed updates", select an update, and then click Uninstall (on the toolbar).

- Windows Update can provide new device drivers for your computer's hardware. Unlike the other types of updates, this one should be approached skeptically, because Windows Update has a history of recommending the wrong drivers for some hardware. In general, let Windows Update update drivers for only Microsoft-branded hardware. For third-party products, download drivers from the manufacturers' websites directly. If Windows Update installs a driver and then your device stops working, you can roll back; see "Managing Device Drivers" on page 302.

- See also "Installing Service Packs" on page 374.

Malware

Malicious software, or **malware**, includes viruses, spyware, adware, trojan horses, worms, keyloggers, and rootkits, whose attacks range from mild (slowing your machine) to irritating (spewing pop-up ads or crashing your system) to transforming (destroying your data or stealing your identity). Most malware conceals itself. If your computer is a malware-infected **zombie**, it secretly obeys a remote server, typically sending spam in the background by using your bandwidth and processor. (A collection of zombies is a **botnet**, which third parties can rent from the infector for spam campaigns, remote attacks, or click fraud.)

Malware commonly spreads via infected files, email attachments, networks, USB flash drives, rogue antimalware programs, and social engineering. Websites that push installable "add-ons" generally aren't to be trusted. Another risk is a **drive-by download**: malware that exploits browser security holes to secretly self-install when you simply visit a website.

The best way to avoid malware is to behave safely and develop a sense of what the real risks are and a feel for suspicious files and websites. Despite the propaganda, **antimalware programs** (also called **antivirus programs**) are unnecessary. Like a gated community, antimalware makes you no safer and may prompt you to take more risks through a false sense of security. Vigilant computer users are paranoids who don't use antimalware and yet rarely, if ever, get infected.

Antimalware programs tend to be bloated resource-suckers that increase startup and load times, and assert themselves throughout your workspace. Their frequent warnings, self-updates, and pop-up messages will interfere with your workflow, program installations, routine internet transactions, and peace of mind. If you use one, keep in mind that its barrage of cry-wolf warnings will eventually cause you to regard all warnings as false positives, and you'll blandly click "Yes" when a real threat finally comes along.

Also, antimalware publishers can't keep up with the enormous number of malware variants in the wild, and independent tests show low rates of malware recognition (even for malware hidden by rudimentary techniques). Still, if you notice suspicious disk, network, desktop, or browser activity, scan your machine for malware. If an infection or threat is recognized, it's deleted or quarantined; otherwise, you must wait for a fix, hire a techie, reinstall Windows, or live with the infection.

Microsoft Security Essentials

Microsoft Security Essentials is a free Microsoft-created antimalware program that protects you from viruses, spyware, rootkits, trojans, and other threats. Download and install MSE from *microsoft.com/security_essentials*. MSE includes real-time and on-demand malware protection, idle-time scanning, threat reports and cleanup, automatic updates from Microsoft's threat database, and a "green = good, red = bad" interface. After you install MSE, uninstall any third-party antimalware software (McAfee, Symantec, and so on); running multiple antimalware programs degrades performance.

Tip: Microsoft Security Essentials is superior to **Windows Defender**, which comes with Windows. Installing MSE disables Windows Defender.

Parental Controls

Parental Controls lets you manage how your children (or anyone) can use the computer. You can set limits on web access, logon hours, games played, and programs run. You can also log a user's activities for later review.

Before you start, set up a standard user account for each child, and log on yourself as an administrator. Parental Controls can be applied only to standard users, not administrators. To create accounts, see "User Accounts" on page 8.

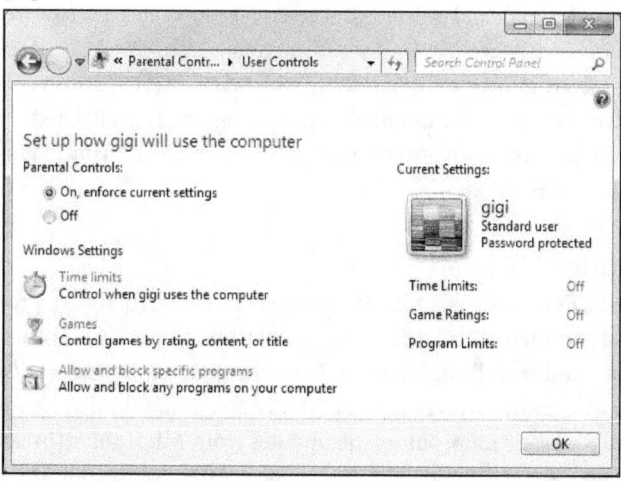

To set up Parental Controls:

1   Choose Start > Control Panel > User Accounts and Family Safety > Parental Controls.

2   (Optional) To use activity reports and web filtering to review and control the user's online comings and goings, enable them in the "Additional controls" section.

3   Click the standard user account to which you want to apply parental controls.

4   Under Parental Controls, select "On, enforce current settings".

5   Adjust the individual control settings, and then click OK.

Encrypting Data

Encryption, which scrambles and password-protects your data, is the strongest way to secure your documents and personal information. Windows offers:

- Encrypting File System, for encrypting specific files and folders

- BitLocker Drive Encryption, for encrypting whole drives

BitLocker is more secure than EFS because the latter lets administrators (page 8) use a Group Policy back door to recover your encrypted data.

Encrypting File System

Windows' **Encrypting File System** (EFS) scrambles files and data so that only you can read them, providing an extra measure of protection for user accounts. EFS is transparent: encrypted file and folder icons change color, but otherwise, you open, edit, and save them in the usual way.

The following restrictions apply to EFS:

- EFS is available in only high-end Windows editions.

- EFS works on only NTFS-formatted hard drives, not FAT or FAT32. To check a drive, choose Start > Computer, right-click a drive icon, and then choose Properties > General tab. The "File system" should be NTFS.

- NTFS-compressed files (page 207) can't be EFS-encrypted (but you can encrypt zip files).

- You can't encrypt system files (page 165), such as those in the Windows folder.

To encrypt a file or folder by using EFS:

1 In Windows Explorer, right-click the file or folder that you want to encrypt and then choose Properties > General tab > Advanced. (If the Advanced button is missing, then the selected file or folder isn't on an NTFS drive.)

2 Select "Encrypt contents to secure data". The Advanced Attributes dialog box won't let you choose both compression and encryption.

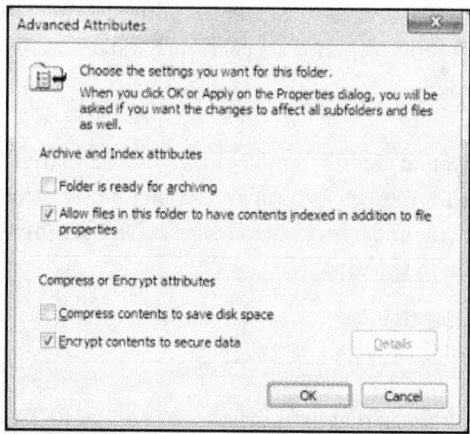

3 Click OK in each open dialog box.

EFS Tips

- If you encrypt only a folder, EFS won't encrypt any files currently in the folder, but it will encrypt any new files that you copy, move, or create within the folder.

- If you encrypt a file in an unencrypted folder, Windows displays an Encryption Warning dialog box that lets you choose whether to encrypt only the file or both the file and its parent folder.

- EFS encrypts any file or folder that you move into an encrypted folder but won't decrypt one that you drag out unless you decrypt it manually by clearing the Encrypt checkbox, drag it to a FAT or FAT32 drive, or share it via email or network. (Lesson: Don't keep encrypted material on shared network drives; other users can read it without your account password.)

- When you decrypt a folder, Windows asks whether you want all files and subfolders within the folder to be decrypted as well. If you choose to decrypt the folder only, the encrypted files and folders within the decrypted folder remain encrypted. But EFS won't encrypt new files and folders that you copy, move, or create within the decrypted folder.

- To display EFS-encrypted files and folders in a different color in Windows Explorer, choose Organize (on the toolbar) > "Folder and search options" > View tab > select "Show encrypted or compressed NTFS files in color" > OK. Consider *not* coloring encrypted files so that onlookers won't know that you're using EFS.

BitLocker Drive Encryption

BitLocker Drive Encryption automatically encrypts (scrambles) and password-protects everything on your hard drive, including Windows itself, or on a USB flash drive. After you set up BitLocker, it runs in the background. Everything works like before, with no noticeable performance hit, except now your data are secured against laptop thieves, hard-drive thieves, cops, and customs agents at border crossings.

To use BitLocker, you need:

- A high-end edition of Windows.

- A **Trusted Platform Module** (TPM) version 1.2 or later. A TPM is a special security chip on some newer computer motherboards.

  or

  An ordinary USB flash drive (an alternative to TPM).

- Two NTFS-formatted partitions (page 356): one that will be encrypted and one (to remain unencrypted) that Windows will use to boot the system. Only startup files, not the entire Windows folder, are copied to the unencrypted partition. This partition needs to be the active partition (where the system boots from)—that's unlikely, so for most people using BitLocker means repartitioning their drive and reinstalling Windows.

After you turn on BitLocker, you can turn it off at any time, either temporarily by disabling it or permanently by decrypting the drive.

To turn on BitLocker:

1 Choose Start > Control Panel > System and Security > BitLocker Drive Encryption.

2 Click "Turn on BitLocker" for the desired volume (**BitLocker to Go** encrypts USB flash drives), and then follow the onscreen instructions.

To turn off BitLocker:

1 Choose Start > Control Panel > Security > BitLocker Drive Encryption.

2 To decrypt the drive, click "Turn off BitLocker", and then click "Decrypt drive".

or

To temporarily disable BitLocker, click "Suspend protection".

BitLocker Tips

• For detailed instructions, search for *windows bitlocker drive encryption* at *technet.microsoft.com*.

• Adding files to a BitLocker-encrypted drive encrypts them automatically. Files copied to an unencrypted drive or computer are decrypted. If you share files with other users, such as over a network, these files are encrypted while stored on the encrypted drive, but they can be accessed normally by authorized users.

• Forgetting your BitLocker password means losing your data permanently.

• Microsoft insists that BitLocker has no "back door" for police or governments (*blogs.msdn.com/si_team/archive/2006/03/02/542590.aspx*).

Other Encryption Tools

If EFS's back door is too insecure or BitLocker's requirements are a hassle (or if you don't trust Microsoft), try TrueCrypt (*truecrypt.org*) or PGP Whole Disk Encryption (*symantec.com*). Read about whole-drive encryption vs. individual-file encryption in Bruce Schneier's article "How to Secure Your Computer, Disks, and Portable Drives" at *schneier.com/blog/archives/2007/12/how_to_secure_y_1.html*.

11

Maintenance & Troubleshooting

Windows provides tools to keep your system running smoothly, monitor the health of your hardware, and recover from crashes. (See also "Getting System Information" on page 76.)

Task Manager

Task Manager is one of the most useful tools in Windows. It displays running programs, background processes, performance statistics, network activity, and user information. It can also shut down misbehaving programs.

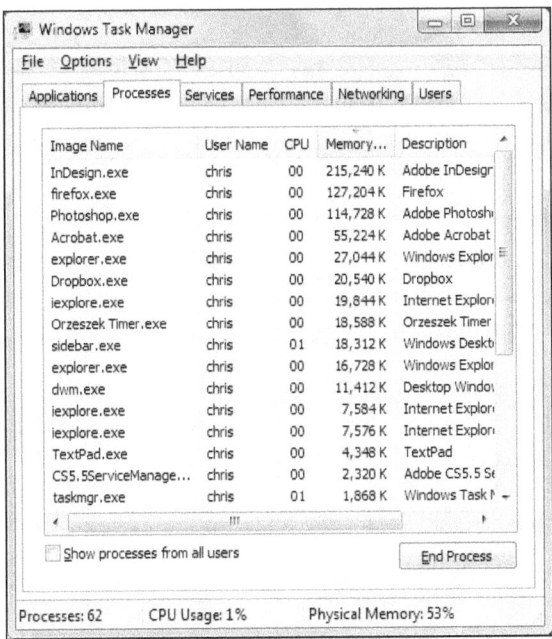

To start Task Manager, right-click an empty area of the taskbar and then choose Start Task Manager (or press Ctrl+Shift+Esc). Click any of the following tabs.

Applications
> Lists foreground applications and the status of each one. See also "Killing Unresponsive Programs" on page 248.

Processes
> Lists all programs running on your computer, including background programs and those shown on the Applications tab. Click a column header to sort by that column.

Services
> Lists programs that run in the background to support other programs.

Performance
> Shows real-time graphs and statistics of system performance, including the load on your processor(s) and memory.

Networking
> Shows real-time graphs and statistics of network traffic.

Users
> Lists logged-on user accounts and the status of each one.

To select preferences, use the Options and View menus (these menus' commands change depending on the selected tab). To make Task Manager float over all other windows, choose Options > Always On Top. You can right-click an entry in the Applications, Processes, Services, or Users tab for a shortcut menu.

Cleaning Up a Drive

Over time, your hard drive will accumulate temporary files, stale components, recycled junk, and space-wasters that you can remove safely. Use **Disk Cleanup** to reclaim space if you're running out of room.

To remove unneeded files:

1 Choose Start > All Programs > Accessories > System Tools > Disk Cleanup.

   or

   Choose Start > Computer, right-click a drive, and then choose Properties > General tab > Disk Cleanup.

   or

Press Windows logo key+R, type *cleanmgr*, and then press Enter.

2   Select a drive, if a Drive Selection dialog box appears.

3   In the Disk Cleanup dialog box, select the checkboxes of the files that you want to delete. The right column shows how much space you can make available. The text below the list box describes the selected option.

4   Click OK.

Tip: The Temporary Files option deletes only temporary files more than a week old, so the right column may show 0 KB even if your temporary folder contains many files. To clean out this folder manually, close all programs, press Windows logo key+R, type *%temp%*, press Enter, and then delete the files in the folder window that appears.

Defragmenting a Drive

When a file grows, it won't fit back into its original location and becomes physically fragmented into noncontiguous pieces on the drive. As more files become fragmented, Windows has to retrieve the chopped-up pieces and reassemble them, which impairs the drive's performance and reliability. **Disk Defragmenter** consolidates fragmented files, making both files and free space contiguous. Large blocks of available space make it less likely that new files will be fragmented. Disk Defragmenter runs on a schedule, but you can defragment manually.

To defragment a drive:

1   To prepare to defragment, save your work, exit all programs, turn off antimalware and other background programs, empty the Recycle Bin, and then run Disk Cleanup (page 352).

2   Choose Start > All Programs > Accessories > System Tools > Disk Defragmenter.

or

Choose Start > Computer, right-click a drive, and then choose Properties > Tools tab > Defragment Now.

or

Press Windows logo key+R, type *dfrgui*, and then press Enter.

3 To determine whether a drive needs to be defragmented, select it and then click "Analyze disk".

4 To defragment a drive, select it and then click "Defragment disk". You can use your computer during defragmentation or cancel at any time.

Defragmentation takes between a few minutes and a few hours to finish, depending on the size and degree of fragmentation of your drive. You can choose which drives (volumes) to defragment and change whether and when Disk Defragmenter runs automatically.

Checking for Drive Errors

Improper shutdowns—usually caused by power outages, mechanical problems, or system crashes—can create defects on drive surfaces. These errors can accumulate and cause such problems as random crashes, data corruption, or the inability to save or open files. **Check Disk** scans the drive surface for errors and fixes any that it finds.

To detect and repair drive errors:

1 Exit all programs.

2 Choose Start > Computer, right-click a drive, and then choose Properties > Tools tab > "Check now".

3 Select any of the following options:

Automatically fix file system errors. Select this option to make Windows repair any errors that it finds; if it's not selected, errors are merely reported, not fixed. If the drive is in use, or if you're checking the system drive (the one with Windows on it), then a "disk in use" message box opens; click "Schedule disk check" to defer the scan until the next time that you restart your computer.

Scan for and attempt recovery of bad sectors. Select this option to make Windows recover readable files and folders that it finds in the drive's defective sections and then move them elsewhere on the drive. This option fixes errors as well, even if the other option isn't selected. Unrepairable sections are locked out of available storage.

4 Click Start to begin the checking process. The progress bar indicates the phase that Check Disk is in. When all phases are complete, a dialog box tells you how things turned out.

Tip: The best protection against drive dings from power fluctuation is an Uninterruptible Power Supply (page 157).

Managing Drives

Disk Management lets you inspect and manage drives. On new hardware, you can initialize a drive and create or format partitions. You can also assess a drive's health, assign drive letters, format, and do related tasks.

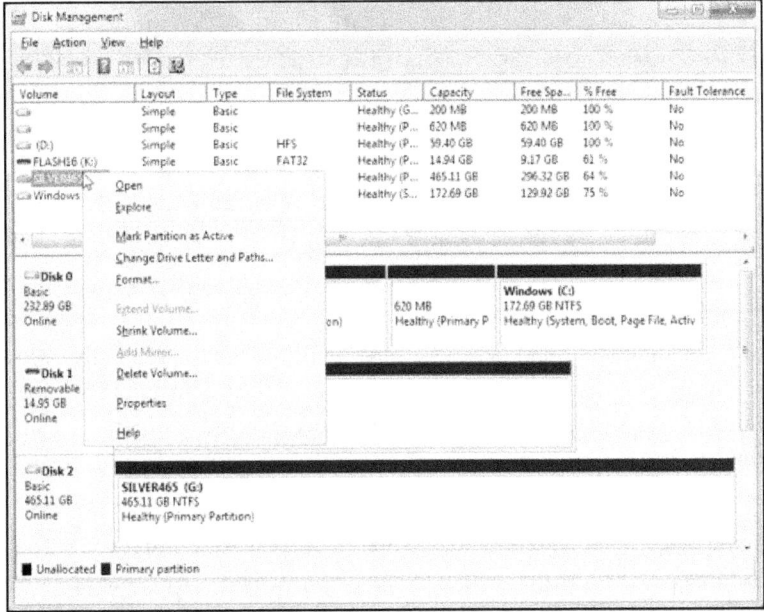

To open Disk Management:

1 Choose Start > Control Panel > System and Security > Administrative Tools > Computer Management, and then click Disk Management (on the left, under Storage).

   or

   In the Start menu, right-click Computer, choose Manage, and then click Disk Management (on the left, under Storage).

   or

   Press Windows logo key+R, type *diskmgmt.msc*, and then press Enter.

2   Right-click any drive or partition for a list of commands, or use the View menu to specify how drives are displayed.

Partitions

A **partition**, or **volume**, is a portion of a physical drive that functions as though it were a separate drive. After you create a partition, you must format it and assign it a drive letter before you can store data on it. Every drive has at least one partition. You you can create multiple partitions on a single drive, mainly to:

- Separate files and folders from the operating system, keeping your personal documents safe if an OS upgrade turns ugly

- Create dual-boot systems with multiple OSes (page 370)

Unfortunately, Disk Management erases a drive before partitioning it, which makes it suitable for only blank or new drives. Use a third-party tool to create or resize partitions without erasing: search the web for *windows partition tool*.

Scheduling Tasks

Periodic maintenance and backups aren't useful unless they actually occur periodically—and human memory often fails here. **Task Scheduler** schedules automated tasks that perform actions at a specific time or when a certain event occurs.

Task Scheduler can open programs, send email, and show pop-up messages. In some cases, it's adequate simply to open a program or remind yourself of something on schedule, but for true automation you should use command-line commands that run to completion without your intervention.

A **command name** is a program's filename as typed at a command prompt (page 262). For example, Disk Defragmenter's command name is *defrag*, and Backup's is *wbadmin*. **Command-line options**, or **switches**, are space-separated parameters—prefixed by the - or / character—that follow the command name and control that command's behavior.

Search Help and Support (page 71) for *command-line reference* and then click the link for the command-line reference to find commands, their switches, and examples.

You can place multiple command-line commands in a text file with a .bat extension and then run this **batch file** as a single task instead of running each command individually. Advanced users can run PowerShell scripts (*microsoft.com/powershell*).

To schedule a task:

1   Choose Start > All Programs > Accessories > System Tools > Task Scheduler.

2   In the right pane, below Actions, click Create Basic Task. Follow the steps in the Create Basic Task wizard. When you finish, the task will run according to schedule, even if somebody else (or nobody) is logged on.

Scheduling Tips

- Task Scheduler is fairly complex. For help, choose Help menu > Help Topics.

- The center pane in Task Scheduler lists tasks that have run (and whether they completed successfully) and have yet to run.

- Click the taskbar clock to confirm that your system date and time are accurate (page 140). Task Scheduler relies on this information.

- Command-prompt junkies can use the *at* command instead of Task Scheduler. Read the Microsoft article "How To Use the AT Command to Schedule Tasks" (*support.microsoft.com/kb/313565*).

Editing the Registry

Windows stores its configuration information in a large database called the **registry**, containing information about all hardware, software, and drivers. Windows references this information and updates it quietly and continually. Editing it incorrectly can damage your system severely. Lots of books, magazines, and websites, however, offer useful tips that involve registry changes. As long as you have precise instructions, editing the registry is easy.

To edit the registry:

1   Press Windows logo key+R, type *regedit*, and then press Enter. Registry Editor opens (to back up the registry before you edit it, choose File menu > Export).

2   In the left pane of Registry Editor, use the Explorer-like tree to navigate to the desired folder.

3   Double-click an entry (called a **key**) in the right pane, edit its value, and
then click OK.

Tip: To learn about the registry, read the Microsoft article "Windows registry information for advanced users" at *support.microsoft.com/?kbid=256986*.

Solving Problems

Windows has tools that help you identify and resolve hardware, software, and
networking problems.

Troubleshooting

Troubleshooting is a Control Panel tool that's a good place to start when
you have a problem (before you start searching the web for a solution).
To open it, type *troubleshooting* in the Search box of the Start menu or
Control Panel and then click Troubleshooting.

Reliability Monitor

Reliability Monitor measures hardware and software problems and other
changes to your computer. It provides a stability index that ranges from
1 (least stable) to 10 (most stable). You can use this index to evaluate the
reliability of your computer over time. Any change that you make to your
computer or problem that occurs on your computer changes the stability
index. To open Reliability Monitor, choose Start > Control Panel > System
and Security > Action Center > Maintenance > "View reliability history".

Problem Steps Recorder

Problem Steps Recorder is a simple screen-capture tool records a series of
actions. To open it, type problem steps recorder in the Search box of the
Start menu or Control Panel and then click "Record steps to reproduce
a problem". After you click Start Record, the recorder tracks your mouse
and keyboard, and captures screen shots with any comments that you
add. After you stop recording, it saves the whole thing to a zip file (page
209)—containing an HTML-based slideshow of the steps—that you can
send to a friend or techie to help solve your problem.

See also "Getting Help" on page 71, "Getting System Information" on page
76, and "Running Older Programs" on page 244.

Boosting Memory

ReadyBoost can use storage space on USB flash drives and other flash-memory devices to speed your computer. ReadyBoost uses only fast flash memory. (If your device contains both slow and fast memory, only the fast is used.)

Set ReadyBoost memory to one to three times the amount of physical memory (RAM) installed in your computer. If your computer has 2 GB of RAM and you plug in a 8 GB USB flash drive, set aside between 2 GB and 6 GB of that drive for the best performance boost. To see how much physical memory you have, press Ctrl+Shift+Esc to open Task Manager and then click the Performance tab.

To use flash memory to speed your computer:

1   Insert a USB flash drive or other flash-memory device.

2   When the AutoPlay dialog box appears, click "Speed up my system".

   If the AutoPlay dialog box doesn't appear, use the ReadyBoost tab in the device's Properties dialog box: choose Start > Computer, right-click the device, and then choose Properties. Or you can turn on AutoPlay: choose Start > Control Panel > Hardware and Sound > AutoPlay.

3   Select "Use this device" and then choose how much memory to use for system speed. Use the slider to choose an amount one to three times the amount of your physical memory.

4   Click OK.

Nothing bad happens if you remove the flash drive prematurely. All data on the flash drive are also on the hard drive. All drive-resident data are encrypted.

Restoring Your System

If your system becomes persistently unstable—thanks to an incompatible program, faulty driver, or bad system setting, or for no apparent reason—use **System Restore** to return Windows to its previous working state without risk to your personal files.

System Restore uses a feature called **System Protection** to create and save **restore points** regularly on your computer. These restore points contain snapshots of the system files (page 165), registry (page 357), and settings that Windows needs to work properly. You can also create restore points manually. Note that System Restore protects only Windows *system* files; use Backup and Restore (page 362) to protect your personal files.

To configure System Restore:

1 Choose Start > Control Panel > System and Security > System (or press Windows logo key+Break).

2 Click "Advanced system settings" (on the left) > System Protection tab.

Restore points are created every day automatically and just before significant system events, such as the installation of a program or driver.

3 In the Protection Settings section, select each drive, click Configure, set its System Protection options, and then click OK. (Typically, you protect only the Windows system drive and unprotect the others.)

4 To create a restore point now for the protected drives, click Create, type a description for the restore point (something like Before video driver update), and then click Create.

5 Click OK (or Apply).

When your computer behaves badly, you can return Windows to one of the restore points that System Restore, or you, created. But do so only as a last resort. Remember, if a driver upgrade doesn't work out, you can roll back (page 302) just the driver rather than your entire system. Similarly, you can uninstall a suspect program (page 239).

To restore system files and settings:

1 Exit all programs.

2 Choose Start > All Programs > Accessories > System Tools > System Restore.

or

Click System Restore in the System Protection tab of the System Properties dialog box.

(If no restore points exist, you'll see a page explaining how to create them and configure System Restore.)

3 Click Next.

4 Select the restore point that you want to use and then click Next. All restore points are time-stamped. Pick the one just before things went bad. You always can roll back further if that one doesn't work.

5   Click Finish. Your computer restarts in its previous state. Check the system
    to see whether it's running correctly.

Restore Tips

- If restoring the system didn't fix your problem (or made it worse), you can
  repeat the process and choose a restore point further back in the past. Or
  you can undo the restoration: open System Restore, click "Undo system
  restore", click Next, review your choices, and then click Finish.

- System Restore requires at least 300 MB of free space and uses up to 15
  percent of the drive. (Older restore points are deleted to make room for
  new ones.) When a drive runs low on space, System Restore turns itself
  off silently, losing that drive's restore points. It turns itself back on when
  you free enough space.

- You can't rely on System Restore to protect you from malware (page 344).
  By the time you discover the infection, it may have spread to other files
  that System Restore doesn't touch, in which case rolling back does you
  no good. Use an antimalware program instead.

- If you dual-boot (page 370) to Windows XP, then XP deletes all your
  restore points.

Restoring Documents

Shadow Copy protects your personal files like System Restore protects Windows' system files. It lets you recover a document in an earlier, unedited (or
undamaged) condition.

Shadow Copy runs invisibly and automatically while System Restore is turned
on. It copies only files that have changed since the last restore point was created, and only once a day.

To recover an old version of a file or folder, right-click it, choose Restore Previous Version, select the desired version in the File Versions list, and then click:

- *Open* (safe) to open the old version onscreen and inspect it.

- *Copy* (safe) to create a copy of the old version without destroying the
  current one.

- *Restore* (dangerous) to reinstate the old version, destroying the most recent
  version in the process.

Shadow Copy isn't a substitute for normal backups (page 362) because it (usually) stores all copies on the same drive. If your drive dies, you'll have nothing. Also, you can't recover old versions of deleted files.

If you dual-boot (page 370) to Windows XP, then XP deletes all your shadow copies.

Backing Up Your Files

Your hard drive will eventually betray you and fail catastrophically, taking your data with it. Make backup copies of your work. Copies protect you against misbehaving hardware and software, accidental deletions, and malware attacks. They also let you archive finished projects for remote storage.

You'll worry less if you schedule regular, automatic backups. How often you back up—daily, weekly, or monthly—should depend on how often you update or create files and on the pain involved in re-creating them. You can also back up manually between automatic backups.

You *can* back up to:

- Hard drives (internal and external)

- Other removable drives

- Network locations (high-end Windows editions only)

- Writeable CDs and DVDs

- USB flash drives

You *can't* back up to:

- Windows system or boot drives

- Non-NTFS, -FAT, or -UDF drives

- The same drive that you're backing up (you can't back up drive C to drive C, for example)

- Tape drives

Never back up to a different partition (page 356) on the same physical hard drive, because if the drive fails, all partitions go with it. If your drive fails and you have no backup, try to recover by using a third-party data-recovery tool such as SpinRite (*grc.com*). You can also hire a data recovery service (quite expensive).

Backup and Restore can back up an entire hard drive (system image) or specified files and folders periodically. Wizards walk you through the process of backing up your files or restoring backed-up files when disaster strikes.

To back up files:

1   Choose Start > Control Panel > System and Security > Backup and Restore.

2   Click "Back up now" (or "Set up backup") and then follow the onscreen instructions.

Only *saved* files are backed up, so any files that are open and being edited during backup will need to be backed up the next time. The following files aren't included in backups:

• System files (page 165)

• Program files

• Files in the Recycle Bin (page 203)

• Files on FAT-formatted drives

• Temporary files

• Web-based email not on a hard drive

• EFS-encrypted files (page 347)

• User profile settings (page 17)

Tip: On high-end Windows editions, you can click "Create a system image" to create a backup copy of your entire system (a snapshot of your programs, system settings, and files), which you can restore if your computer dies. Create a system image when you first set up your computer and update it every six months.

To restore backed-up files:

1   Choose Start > Control Panel > System and Security > Backup and Restore.

2   Click "Restore my files" (or one of the other links in the Restore section) and then follow the onscreen instructions.

Recovering After a Crash

If a faulty driver or program keeps Windows from booting—perhaps greeting you with a black screen, a blue screen, or a frozen logo—you can use a boot option to recover.

To choose a boot option:

1   Remove all CDs, DVDs, USB flash drives, and floppies, and then restart your computer.

2   When the computer startup messages finish (and before the Windows logo appears), tap the F8 key repeatedly until the Advanced Options menu appears. If you have a dual-boot system (page 370), use the arrow keys to select the OS that you need, and then press F8.

3   Use the arrow keys to select a boot option, and then press Enter. The commonly used boot options are:

Safe Mode

Starts Windows with only its fundamental files, drivers, and components. Only your mouse, keyboard, display, and drives will work. A generic video driver makes everything appear in jaggy 640 × 480 screen resolution. Safe mode lets you run most essential configuration and troubleshooting tools, including Device Manager (page 302), System Restore (page 359), Registry Editor (page 357), Backup (page 362), Services, and Help and Support (page 71). You can uninstall (page 239) a program or driver that you suspect is causing the problems.

Safe Mode with Networking

Offers the same functions as safe mode, plus access to your network connections. Use this mode if you need files or drivers from another computer on the network. This mode won't work for laptops that connect via a PC Card network adapter; PC Card drivers are disabled in safe mode.

Safe Mode with Command Prompt

Loads the same set of services as safe mode but displays only the command prompt (page 262) instead of the Windows graphical interface. This mode is for command-line geeks only.

Enable Boot Logging

Creates a file, ntbtlog.txt, that lists all drivers installed during startup.

Enable low-resolution video (640 × 480)
> Starts the computer with the safe-mode VGA driver but doesn't invoke any other part of safe mode. Use this option to boot past a bogus video driver.

Last Known Good Configuration (advanced)
> Starts the computer by using the registry information and drivers that were in effect the last time your computer was working, effectively undoing the changes that caused the problems. (This is the old Windows 2000 system rollback option; System Restore (page 359) is preferable, because it restores OS system files too.)

Disable automatic restart on system failure
> Stops Windows from restarting automatically when an error occurs. Choose this option if you're stuck in a loop where Windows fails, restarts, fails,....

Start Windows normally
> Starts Windows in the usual way.

12

Installing Windows

If your computer came with Windows installed, you may be able to use it for the life of the machine without reinstalling Windows. Otherwise, you must install Windows by doing an in-place upgrade or a clean install (page 5). If you've been using your current computer for a few years, consider doing a clean installation (instead of an in-place upgrade) to eradicate malware, partially uninstalled programs, and other accumulated crud.

For clean installs, a Windows upgrade DVD requires a copy of the earlier version of Windows installed on the target drive (a hassle for frequent reinstallers and hardware upgraders). If no Windows installation disc came with your computer, look for a **restore image** on a separate disc or on its own hard-drive partition (page 356). Running the image restores the computer to its factory configuration, erasing all existing programs, settings, and documents.

Microsoft's "Installing and reinstalling Windows 7" (*windows.microsoft.com/ en-US/windows7/Installing-and-reinstalling-Windows-7*) is a complete guide to installing Windows in most situations. The Windows installer is a wizardlike program that steps you through installation. If you see a compatibility report during installation, you can resolve any issues after installation completes.

Windows 7 runs on only the **NTFS file system**; you can't install to a FAT or FAT32 drive. You can't uninstall Windows 7 to revert to your previous operating system; to use your old OS again, you must reinstall it.

Before You Install Windows
Review this checklist before you install Windows:

Check system requirements
> Microsoft lists Windows system requirements (memory, processor speed, graphics horsepower, and so on) on the side of the Windows box and at "Windows 7 system requirements" (*windows.microsoft.com/en-US/ windows7/products/system-requirements*). These requirements are minimal—running Windows on a borderline system would probably be intolerable. You'll need a lot of RAM and processor power if you're going to edit digital video, do scientific calculations, or play 3D network games. If you're upgrading a computer, don't skimp on RAM. Lots of memory and a fast hard drive (7200+ RPM) can compensate for a slowish processor.

Check system compatibility
> **Upgrade Advisor** flags potential problems that your computer may have if you upgrade from an earlier version of Windows. Download Upgrade Advisor from "Windows 7 Upgrade Advisor" (*microsoft.com/download/en/ details.aspx?id=20*) and then install it on your current version of Windows. When you run it, Upgrade Advisor scans your system and generates an action list for you, telling you whether your computer can run the new version of Windows and what you need to do before you install.

Back up your files
> Back up your files just before installation by using your usual backup medium (such as an external hard drive, writable CD/DVD, USB flash drive, network location, second computer, or web-based backup service). See also "Transferring Existing Files and Settings" on page 373.

Turn off your antimalware program

If you're upgrading from an earlier version of Windows, update your antimalware (antivirus) program and then turn it off, lest it interpret the new version as a harmful infestation.

Connect to the internet

If you're upgrading from an earlier version of Windows, make sure that your internet connection is working so that you can get the latest security and driver updates that Microsoft has released since it published the Windows disc. The installer will download and apply these updates. If you don't update during installation, you can do it later via Windows Update (page 341).

If you're doing a clean install, you can use Windows Easy Transfer (page 373) to transfer your internet connection settings from old Windows to new. If you're worried, you can gather your connection settings beforehand and write them down. Your ISP's website will have information, such as access numbers for dial-up connections; customer service has a record of your account user name. While you're at it, you may want to write down or back up your user names and passwords for websites that you visit regularly. Consider using a password manager like Password Safe (*passwordsafe.sourceforge.net*).

Plug in and switch on devices

Make sure that devices, such as your mouse, keyboard, printer, or scanner, are attached to your computer and powered up so that Windows can detect them during installation.

Get network settings

You'll need your computer name if your computer is connected to a network: press Windows logo key+Break/Pause to open the System dialog box and then read the computer name. You'll also need the name of your workgroup or domain (page 9); your domain user name and password (if you're on a domain); and an IP address (if your network doesn't have a DHCP or WINS server).

Find your product key

Your Windows **product key** is a long alphanumeric string of characters that you must type during installation. Microsoft uses this key to validate your copy of Windows. The key's location depends on how you got your copy of Windows. It may be stuck on the side of your computer (for computers that come with Windows), on the installation disc holder inside the

Windows package (for retail DVD purchases), in a separate email message or text file (for downloaded purchases), or on a separate sheet of paper (for discount DVD purchases). You may not need to enter a product key if you're installing a volume-licensed copy of Windows.

Installation Types

The Windows installer eventually hits a branching point for doing one of the following installation types. Your choices may be limited depending on which version of Windows (if any) you're running now. If your target computer has a blank drive, your only choice is a clean install.

Clean install (also called a custom install)
> Installs a fresh copy of Windows on your hard drive, replacing any existing operating system and erasing all files on the drive. During a clean install, you reformat or repartition your hard drive, wiping out all its accumulated crud, including outdated drivers, fragmented files, incompatible programs, and stale registry entries. A clean install has a restorative effect on a computer that's grown sluggish over time.

Upgrade
> Only certain versions of Windows qualify for an upgrade (page 5); if yours doesn't qualify, you must do a clean install. Upgrading preserves your existing settings; installed programs; and data files, including your personal desktop elements, Favorites list, and everything in your personal folder (page 167). Windows also attempts to upgrade device drivers to compatible versions. Upgrading saves you from rebuilding or transferring your files and settings but doesn't invigorate your computer the way a clean install does. Before you upgrade, use Upgrade Advisor (page 368) to flag potential problems. Following the upgrade, you may find that Upgrade Advisor missed some problems. If a program runs poorly, try reinstalling it, or look for an update on the publisher's website.

Dual boot
> If you want to preserve your existing version of Windows and run the new one, you can set up your computer to maintain both of them side by side. Each time you turn on your computer, it asks you which operating system to run. Dual booting is useful if you have a critical piece of hardware or software that runs only on the older OS or if you're not sure whether you want to use the latest version of Windows as your everyday OS and want to be able to fall back on the older one.

You can't install both OSs on the same drive partition. Instead, you can buy a second drive to use for one of the two OSs, or, more commonly, partition your existing drive—that is, divide it so that each portion functions as though it were a separate drive, with its own icon and drive letter in the Computer folder (page 163). The Windows installer offers a tool that can create, extend, delete, and format partitions, but see "Partitions" on page 356 to find better third-party partitioning tools.

Windows Boot Manager appears when you turn on your computer and offers you a choice of operating systems. If you don't choose within 30 seconds, the computer chooses for you. To change the default OS, choose Start > Control Panel > System and Security > System > "Advanced system settings" (on the left) > Advanced tab > Settings (below Startup and Recovery) > "System startup" section.

Note: If you ever need to install Windows from an upgrade DVD (rather than a full-version DVD) on a clean drive, you must first install the old version of Windows and then install the new one on top of it (one reason to take care of your old Windows discs).

Running Windows on a Mac

If you have an Intel-based Apple Macintosh, you can use one of these programs to run Windows at native speed:

- Boot Camp (*apple.com/support/bootcamp*), part of Mac OS X 10.5 Leopard and later, partitions your hard drive for you to install Windows. Hold down the Option key whenever you start your Mac and choose to boot to OS X or Windows.

- Parallels Desktop (*parallels.com/desktop*) is virtual-machine software that lets you run Windows simultaneously with Mac OS X.

- VMware Fusion (*vmware.com/fusion*) is similar to, and competes with, Parallels Desktop.

See also Wikipedia's "Comparison of platform virtual machines" (*en.wikipedia.org/wiki/Comparison_of_platform_virtual_machines*).

Booting from a Windows Disc

If your computer doesn't give you the option to boot from a CD or DVD at startup, use BIOS to select the CD or DVD drive as the startup drive. BIOS (basic input/output system) is the set of low-level hardware routines that your computer invokes at startup. The procedure varies by computer, so check the manufacturer's instructions or website. Here's a typical way to change the startup drive:

1   Turn on your computer, insert the Windows installation disc, and then restart your computer.

2   Look for a startup (boot) menu and then choose BIOS Setup, BIOS Settings, or something similar.

3   When the BIOS menu appears, look for an option named Boot Order or something similar.

4   Select your CD or DVD drive as the first startup device.

5   Save your settings and then exit BIOS setup. Don't mess with any other BIOS settings unless you know what you're doing.

Activating Windows

Activating Windows prevents you from running the same copy on more than one computer. During installation, Windows examines your computer; computes a unique identifier by using the system time and data about key internal parts (drive, video card, motherboard, memory, and so on); and then sends this identifier, along with your 25-character product key, over the internet to Microsoft, thereby activating Windows.

If you selected "Automatically activate Windows when I'm online" during installation, Windows tries to contact Microsoft and self-activate for the first few days after installation. To check whether Windows is activated, choose Start > Control Panel > System and Security > System (or press Windows logo key+Break) > "Windows activation" section. If you skipped activation during installation, nagging reminders pop up occasionally in the taskbar's notification area. Click a reminder or the link to start the Windows Activation wizard. You have 30 days to activate; if you don't, Windows will stop working properly.

Later, if you install the same copy of Windows on another computer, Microsoft will discover your duplicity during activation and lock you out of Windows on the second computer. If you own a desktop and a laptop, you must buy

Windows twice. If you replace enough hardware in your computer over a four-month period, Windows will think that it's on a new machine and de-activate—contact Microsoft for a new activation key.

According to Microsoft, activation is anonymous and transfers no personal information to Microsoft or other parties. Bulk-purchased business, govern-ment, and education copies of Windows are often exempt from activation, and many new computers come with a preactivated copy.

Transferring Existing Files and Settings

Windows Easy Transfer is a step-by-step program for transferring files and settings (but not programs) from one copy of Windows to another. The Win-dows 7 DVD includes a version of Easy Transfer that runs directly from the DVD on Windows computers (Windows 7 or earlier). You have two choices:

If you have one computer
Run Easy Transfer from the Windows 7 DVD before you install Windows 7, and then save the files and settings to a second drive. Do a clean install of Windows 7 and then rerun Easy Transfer to import your saved files and settings.

If you have two computers
Run Easy Transfer on the old computer and then transfer the files and settings to the new computer via a network connection, external hard drive, flash drive, or direct cable connection.

If you opt for a cable connection, an **Easy Transfer cable** (available in electronics stores or online) connects two computers USB-to-USB. It's the easiest way to transfer files and settings and works with Microsoft Windows 2000 (files only), XP, Vista, and 7.

To save files and settings from your old copy of Windows:

1 Insert the Windows 7 installation disc into your computer's DVD drive. Run setup.exe on the DVD if the Install Windows page doesn't appear automatically.

2 Click "Transfer files and settings". Windows Easy Transfer opens.

3 Click Next and then follow the onscreen instructions. A progress page indicates when Easy Transfer has finished sending your files and settings to the location that you specified.

To import files and settings to your new copy of Windows 7:

1   Choose Start > All Programs > Accessories > System Tools > Windows Easy Transfer.

2   Click Next and then follow the onscreen instructions. At the branching point, choose "This is my new computer". Easy Transfer will ask you for the location of the files and settings that you saved. The location will be a path (page 178) to a local or network drive, or a connection to another computer running Easy Transfer.

3   Click Finish. Review the summary report that appears. You must manually change any settings that Easy Transfer couldn't restore.

You can choose what to transfer: files and folders, email, contacts, user accounts, internet favorites, music, photos, video, and so on. If you choose to transfer files and settings into existing user accounts (rather than to create new accounts), then the users' current files and settings are replaced. You can also use Easy Transfer to transfer files and settings from one copy of Windows 7 to another.

Installing Service Packs

Microsoft occasionally releases a large package of fixes, enhancements, and other patches to Windows. Each package, called a **Service Pack** (SP), contains new updates and accumulated earlier updates and SPs (if any).

You can install a service pack in the following ways:

Windows Update
    Windows Update (page 341) downloads and installs the SP. This method is faster than using a stand-alone installer because Windows Update downloads only the parts of the SP that your computer needs; it ignores the parts you installed in earlier updates. Most home and small-business users use this method.

Stand-alone installer
    You download the complete SP (and any prerequisites) from Microsoft in a single large file. System administrators and IT departments often use this method to roll out mass updates, but it's also useful for updating computers without internet access (or with only dial-up access).

Integrated DVD

If you bought your Windows DVD or computer after the SP was released, then your copy of Windows already has the Service Pack; no separate installation is necessary.

Before installing a Service Pack:

- Make sure that the SP hasn't already been installed: choose Start > Control Panel > System and Security > System > "Windows edition" section.

- Uninstall any beta, release candidate (RC), or other prerelease versions of the same SP, if necessary.

- Back up all users' personal files (page 362).

- If you're updating a laptop, plug it in.

- Exit all programs, including antimalware and other background programs.

- Log off everyone but yourself if you're using fast user switching (page 25).

Note: Windows creates a system restore point (page 359) automatically before it starts installing an SP. The restore point backs up your system files but not your personal ones.

Deleting Crapware

Crapware (or **shovelware**) is the bundle of third-party programs that computer manufacturers are paid to pre-install on new machines. Out of the box your brand-name computer will have non-Microsoft junk like antimalware trials, extended-service offers, online games, ISP sign-ups, instant messengers, toolbars, media players, and other come-ons. Crapware slows your system and clogs your drives with useless, redundant, bloated, uncertified, or panhandling programs. Here are a few things that you can do:

- When you buy, offer to pay extra for a crapless computer. Or complain creatively.

- Use a clean Windows DVD to reinstall Windows (don't use the manufacturer's restore image, which reinstalls crapware).

- Uninstall crapware the usual way (page 239). This usually takes hours, and it can be hard to identify each craplet. Some crapware may be useful (Adobe Reader and disc burners, for example).

- Ask a hobbyist to clean your computer, or pay a computer store to do it.

- Run msconfig.exe from the Start > Search box and then deselect the craplets in the Startup and Services tabs.

- Use free crapware tools: CCleaner (*piriform.com/ccleaner*), PC Decrapifier (*pcdecrapifier.com*), or, for techies, Autoruns (*technet.microsoft.com/en-us/sysinternals/bb963902*).

Index

www.ingramcontent.com/pod-product-compliance
Lightning Source LLC
Chambersburg PA
CBHW051623170526
45167CB00001B/34